ANNE MORROW LINDBERGH

FIRST LADY OF THE AIR

Kathleen C. Winters

palgrave
macmillan

ANNE MORROW LINDBERGH

First published in 2006 by
PALGRAVE MACMILLAN™
175 Fifth Avenue, New York, N.Y. 10010 and
Houndmills, Basingstoke, Hampshire, England RG21 6XS
Companies and representatives throughout the world.

PALGRAVE MACMILLAN is the global academic imprint of the Palgrave Macmillan division of St. Martin's Press, LLC and of Palgrave Macmillan Ltd. Macmillan® is a registered trademark in the United States, United Kingdom and other countries. Palgrave is a registered trademark in the European Union and other countries.

ISBN-13: 978–1–4039–6932–3
ISBN-10: 1–4039–6932–9

Library of Congress Cataloging-in-Publication Data

Winters, Kathleen C.
    Anne Morrow Lindbergh : first lady of the air / Kathleen C. Winters
        p. cm.
    Includes bibliographical references and index.
    ISBN-13: 978–1–4039–6932–3
    ISBN-10: 1–4039–6932–9
    1. Lindbergh, Anne Morrow, 1906–2001. 2. Women air pilots—United States—Biography. 3. Authors, American—20th century—Biography. 4. Lindbergh, Charles A. (Charles Augustus), 1902–1974—Family. I. Title. II. Title: First lady of the air.

TL540.L5W48 2006
629.13092—dc22   2006043290

A catalogue record for this book is available from the British Library.

Design by Newgen Imaging Systems (P) Ltd., Chennai, India.

First edition: November 2006

10 9 8 7 6 5 4 3 2 1

Printed in the United States of America.

ANNE
MORROW
LINDBERGH

In memory of my mother, Helene Hopkins Molloy

CONTENTS

LIST OF ILLUSTRATIONS

PERMISSIONS

ACKNOWLEDGMENTS

The spark for this book was an article I wrote about Anne Morrow Lindbergh in 2001. As a pilot whose passion for aviation started some years ago, I had hoped to uncover details of Anne's flying career. To my astonishment, I found that previously published biographies had paid scant attention to this very important aspect of her life. Another surprise awaited me when I was contacted by Eiluned Morgan, whose mother Constance Morrow Morgan was Anne Lindbergh's younger sister. Both she and Reeve Lindbergh, the youngest child of Anne and Charles Lindbergh, had read my article, and I was asked to speak at a forthcoming Lindbergh Symposium. A second spark was lit and this book's journey continued after my presentation in February 2002.

It has been my great pleasure to have benefited from the generosity and warmth of both Eiluned Morgan and Reeve Lindbergh. Their help was invaluable in countless ways. In particular, I am deeply indebted to Reeve Lindbergh for allowing me access to the restricted family papers at Yale University. Housed in the archives at Yale and the Missouri Historical Society are troves of information about the Lindberghs' flights: diaries, letters, logbooks, radio logs, and folders of aviation material, among other resources. Using this documentation I pieced together facts about Anne's solo flights and her many aerial jaunts with her husband. (Most pilots will say that their logbooks are a more accurate autobiography than other paper trails; they are certainly more colorful.)

Several institutions provided me with research assistance. I am grateful for the help I received from Judith Schiff and the staff of Manuscripts and Archives in Sterling Memorial Library at Yale University and the staffs of the Missouri Historical Society, the Minnesota Historical Society, and the Ninety-Nines Museum of Women Pilots. Kelley Welf and Marlene White of the Lindbergh Foundation were helpful also.

To historians and authors of books on the Lindberghs, I give my thanks for their works.

Many thanks as well to: Del Blomquist, Ev Cassagneres, Gary Fogel, Robley Greilick, Trudi Hahn, Harriet Hamilton, Patricia Hange, Lisa Hanson, David Harrison, Russ and Susie Hazelton for their hospitality in St. Louis, Michael Hoover, Harald Mallwitz, Patrick Molloy, Richard Mullen, Kathleen Peippo, Susan Perry, Bobbi Roe, Bertha Ryan, and Tammy Silk.

To those at Palgrave Macmillan, especially my editor, Airié Stuart, and her associate, Chris Chappell, I deeply appreciate your enthusiasm and guidance. I wish to thank my literary agent, Andrew Zack, whose perseverance for this project carried me forward.

Finally, I owe profound gratitude to my family. My husband, Jim Hard, and my daughter, Claire Winters, read drafts of the book and made helpful suggestions, and during this book's home stretch Jim pitched in even more. My heartfelt thanks.

Kathleen C. Winters
March 2006

PROLOGUE

THE MAGIC OF FLIGHT

The Lindberghs' fate lay in the winds and the light of the moon. On the night of December 5, 1933, high above the horizon over Bathurst, Gambia, a reddish moon would wane to a sliver only. Without moonlight they couldn't launch their Lockheed Sirius seaplane from the British outpost on the west coast of Africa, the start of a nonstop flight across the South Atlantic Ocean to Natal, Brazil—a distance of 1,875 miles. During the previous week the single-engine seaplane had floundered like a sated gull on its long runs along the muddy Gambia River. But now it was 200 pounds lighter: Charles had removed its excess weight, snipping out an extra fuel tank with tin cutters and throwing nonessentials overboard. Still, the heavy plane needed a headwind to help loosen its floats from the river's grip, and the winds had withered during the day.

As the dead-calm daylight hours came to a close at Bathurst, Anne walked alone to the pier, holding a rumpled handkerchief. Waiting and watching, she searched the sky for telltale signs, listening for the wind. Then a breeze rustled through the palms, blowing gently across the river. Out of breath, she rushed to tell her husband, "The wind has changed. There's enough to lift a handkerchief!"[1]

In the darkness, working by the dim light of swinging lanterns, Anne and Charles prepared the Sirius for takeoff. They packed the cabin, pumped water out of the pontoons, and preflighted, using written checklists. Their survival mandated careful scrutiny and precaution. Many pilots had gone down in the drink, after they became lost over the Atlantic or their machines failed them, never to be seen alive again.

Ready to board, Anne jumped onto a silver pontoon, then onto a wing before she climbed the fuselage into her rear cockpit—her "little room," as she called it.[2]

Once settled in her cushioned seat, she stowed sandwiches and then worked the flight controls, checking for free movement. She pushed on the rudder pedals and worked the stick sideways, forward, and aft, seeing that the aileron and elevator control wires were unobstructed. Her cockpit check complete, she put on goggles, fastened her cotton flying helmet, and cinched tight her seat belt. Looking out, she watched palms swaying in the rising wind, barely lit by the moon. Above in the tropical sky stars twinkled, like guideposts in the dark.

In the front cockpit, Charles flipped the master switch, started the engine, and watched the wingtip lights flicker—green on the starboard side, red on the port. He advanced the throttle, the engine growling, the gauges flickering. The plane plowed through the river on a downwind sweep while he searched for debris on the takeoff path. After he swung the nose into the wind, he turned to Anne: "All set?"

"Yes. All right."

He gunned the throttle, the 710-horsepower engine roaring as he eased back on the stick, the pontoons spanking the river, spray sluicing across the windshield and wings. Faster, faster . . . the airspeed inched higher and the pontoons skimmed above the water. Suddenly, the river released its grip and the Sirius leaped aloft over Bathurst. Charles pivoted the plane to a 224-degree true course toward Natal, an ocean away.

Anne slid back the rear canopy, shutting out the noise and wind, and put on her headphones. She was the sole radio operator on board, giving position reports to the outside world and obtaining weather conditions and landing information in Morse code. Across the Atlantic, up and down the South American coast, Pan American Airways's radio operators listened for KHCAL, the Sirius's call sign. For a week, they had been on alert around the clock, waiting for the Lindbergh launch.

Working by touch alone in her rear cockpit, Anne pressed coils into their sockets in the radio transmitter box, switched on the receiver, and released the antenna's brake. Springing loose with a whir, the copper antenna unwound through the floorboards to trail more than 100 feet below the plane. Anne tapped out the takeoff time—2:00 GMT, midnight at Bathurst—for her first transmission, the start of hourly reports to Pan Am. For two hours she sat hunched over the radio dials, trying to hear through the static in her headphones while she changed coils. At the third hour she reported light overcast skies at 2,000 feet, unlimited visibility, and a slight tailwind of 10 knots at 030 degrees. The Sirius, meantime, streaked through the air at 100 knots, only 1,200 feet above the seas.[3] An hour later the plane bounced in turbulence. They flew blind, in and out of pitch-black clouds and through thunderstorms, relying only on their instruments. Anne fought a rising trepidation but remembered that all transoceanic pilots had gone through this.

Six hours into the flight, the storms ended, a salmon-pink dawn draped the horizon, and the Sirius scooted under patches of pale-blue sky. A long message came in from a Pan Am operator at PVJ, the Rio de Janeiro station, explaining where to land at Natal. The transmission buoyed Anne's spirits—it was as if she had already linked the continents. A little later, via station WCC in Chatham, Massachusetts, nearly 4,000 miles away, the *Boston Herald* requested a radio interview. Astonished and annoyed, Anne tapped back that she was busy getting weather from PVJ.

A few hours later, beneath the dome of a slate-gray sky dappled with high cirrus clouds, whitecaps scuffed the great ocean's surface. Charles continued to fly, steering the craft by hand—strenuous work over long distances—while Anne maintained constant radio contact, her eyes closed, her body exhausted. She shook herself to stay awake, nibbled at a sandwich, daubed her face with water from a canteen. Her back ached from bending over the radio key, her ears hurt from the headphones' tight clamp, and her thumb and index finger were sore from pressing the key. But when Charles passed back a note asking her to fly while he took sights with the sextant, a surge of energy pulsed through her and she took over the controls.

A seasoned crew member with several years experience, Anne had served as a relief pilot on all the Lindberghs' expeditions. With her hand on the stick, she stretched her feet out to the rudder pedals. Her head was no longer buried in the cockpit but raised high, her eyes sweeping a horizon dotted with puffs of white cumulus clouds. Between peeks at the clouds, skimming the seas at 800 feet, she made sure to maintain a correct heading on the aperiodic compass in front of her.

Ten hours into the flight and back at the radio, Anne heard nothing but static through her headphones. Concerned about the lull in receiving stations, she added "Lindbergh plane" to her call sign and soon had a bite: a ship bound for Rio, the S.S. *Caparcona*. The plane scudded across the equator during the eleventh hour, and at 14:00 GMT a German catapult ship, the S.S. *Westfalen*, responded to Anne's call. A floating refueling base, the ship launched Deutsche Luft Hansa flying boats when they landed mid-ocean on their transatlantic mail runs. The *Westfalen* gave Anne radio bearings, and at 15:20 GMT the Sirius swooped down low, buzzing its deck. Anne looked down to see all hands waving their caps. She held up her arm and waved back, exhilarated by the face-to-face contact after the surreal and lonely world of code and static.

Fifteen hours after takeoff, Charles waggled the wings, alerting Anne to lift her head from the radio work and look out. Far ahead, she saw the green Brazilian coast emerging through a sultry blue haze. The Sirius closed the distance quickly. From the front cockpit Charles raised a hand, signaling five minutes to landing. While he throttled back and spiraled down to bleed off altitude, Anne quickly reeled in the antenna before it hit the water. She snapped on the antenna brake, turned off the radio switches, and unplugged her headphones.

At 17:55 GMT, five minutes shy of a sixteen-hour flight, the Lockheed Sirius settled gently on the calm waters of the Potengi River near the Pan Am barge at Natal. It was 3:00 P.M. local time on December 6, and the sun beat down brightly. On shore, Anne weaved unsteadily, trying to shake her sea legs—the result of hours of rocking motion aloft.

Two days later the flight continued, as the Lindberghs flew northwest to Belém, on the South American coast, and then moved inland, grazing the Amazon River to Manaos. Then, on December 19, after stops in Trinidad, Puerto Rico, Santo Domingo, Miami, and Charleston, the Sirius came upon Manhattan skyscrapers jutting from a winter haze. Within half an hour, it landed on Flushing Bay, Long Island, where it had launched five months and ten days earlier. Since taking off on July 9, the Lindberghs had flown 30,000 miles to four continents and twenty-one countries, and across the North and the South Atlantic Oceans, a 261-hour exploration flight charting potential air routes for Pan American, during which Anne had logged 202 hours as the radio operator and had acted as copilot and navigator.[4]

The long journey ended, Anne had become the first woman to fly across the South Atlantic, one of many "firsts" she earned during her flying career. In 1934 she became the first woman awarded the National Geographic Society's Hubbard Medal for her critical role crewing on a 10,000-mile survey to China in 1931 and the 1933 Atlantic survey. Today many Americans know of Anne only as a gifted writer and as the wife of the legendary aviator Charles Lindbergh. Her husband's fame has overshadowed her own contributions as a pilot and explorer, and her place in aviation history has faded with time. Yet in the first decade of her marriage she received enormous recognition for her life in the air, and journalists christened her "First Lady of the Air."[5] This shy and sensitive young woman, petite and dark-haired, earned the accolade not simply because she flew with her husband, but for her flying skills. Within two years of marrying Charles, Anne was licensed to fly airplanes and to operate an aircraft radio, and had become the first woman to earn a first-class glider pilot's license. Even before she herself became licensed, she went with her husband on aerial jaunts inaugurating Caribbean routes for Pan Am and domestic lines for Transcontinental Air Transport: 30,000 miles of air travel within the first year of her marriage. She was "crew," her husband boasted to his flying compatriots, while adding that she flew as well as he, and maybe even better.[6]

Anne and Charles Lindbergh flew during aviation's golden age, an explosive era when the air crackled with excitement, when men and women acted on their dreams for glory in the skies. With her husband Anne partnered to pioneer commercial aviation, scouting future airways and potential airport sites at a time when other brave souls perished doing the same. In the early 1930s Anne crewed while exploring the far corners of Earth, from the Canadian wilderness to the coast of Africa. Some routes the Lindberghs traversed had never seen the shadow of a plane. Though demanding, the trips enabled Anne to share in her husband's work and his vision to link the continents, and by doing so she helped foster the public's confidence in the future of aviation. The Lindberghs put aviation on the map, and a public hungry for heroes rewarded their derring-do by treating them as if they were royalty. Newspaper headlines proclaimed their deeds; thousands of people scrambled to catch sight of their idols at airfields. (Thrust into the limelight, stalked by reporters, they had to fly to be alone with one another.)

Even after Anne retired from crewing, flying never left her spirit. Whether crossing the Bering Sea toward Siberia or charting a course across Greenland's ice cap, she had gained insight into people and places around the world. By melding her literary talent with the adventures she had shared with her husband, she subsequently launched a successful writing career. Anne's thirteen critically acclaimed books included aerial travelogues, along with fiction, poetry, essays, and collections of diaries and letters. A poet and a romantic, she was one of the very few aviators whose writings captured the allure of flight. As she wrote in her first book, *North to the Orient*, "If flying, like a glass-bottomed bucket, can give you that vision, that seeing eye, which peers down to the still world below the choppy waves—it will always remain magic."[7]

1

A Walled Garden

Anne Spencer Morrow, born on June 22, 1906, in Englewood, New Jersey, grew up sheltered and wealthy, reared by parents whose work ethic and ambition had led to a meteoric rise from genteel poverty. During her youth, she seemed sequestered in what she called a "walled garden," removed from world events: "Freud, Marx, Henry Ford, and—I might add—Charles Lindbergh, had not yet cut their way through the brambled hedges that surrounded the sleeping princesses."[1] Even though she emphasized her isolation, she lived on a new frontier of scientific inquiry and social upheaval, in an era of incredible inventions and rapid change. Three years before her birth, the Wright brothers had made the world's first manned, powered flight over windswept dunes at Kitty Hawk, North Carolina. It was an event that would define her life: the growth of aviation led to her marriage, to her expeditions around the world, and to her career as a writer. Anne was a dreamy, quiet girl, however, and no one was more surprised than her parents at how her adventurous life took shape.

Fortune smiled on Anne, the second daughter and second child of Dwight Whitney Morrow and Elizabeth Reeve Cutter, both of whom were blessed with what Anne called a "super abundance of Puritan energy."[2] This trait, and the wealth they accumulated, led to their ascent in American society, and they would number among their friends educators, diplomats, and politicians. It was a good time to be an American, especially if one had money. The Morrows had begun to enjoy a lavish lifestyle during Anne's youth, at a time when upper-crust Americans freely flaunted their wealth. With no income taxes or death taxes imposed until after 1913, many of the rich lived like royalty, decorating their palatial houses with foreign art and furnishings that included Flemish tapestries, Greek classical statues, and Italian Renaissance paintings.

Yet both of Anne's parents had come from humble beginnings. Born in 1873 and reared in Allegheny, Pennsylvania, Dwight Whitney Morrow was the fourth of eight children of a mathematics professor, James Elmore Morrow, and a pious homemaker, Clara Johnson. Of Irish stock, the Morrows traced their lineage in America back to the early 1800s, nearly three generations before Charles Lindbergh's ancestors arrived in the United States. James Morrow's last three children died in infancy. Struggling to get by on a professor's salary, Clara lamented that the family had "far too many books; far too little money."[3] Learning, godliness, and cleanliness were the virtues stressed most by Pater and Mater, as their children called them. At mealtimes, Pater engaged in "dinner-table sport," his term for shooting rapid-fire questions at his children on any and all topics, but especially mathematics. (Later, Dwight would follow this same practice with his own children, which so upset Anne that throughout her life her mind would go blank if anyone asked her sudden arithmetic questions.) Religion dominated the Morrow household, with Sundays strictly kept and no visitors allowed, while during the week the family gathered for afternoon and evening worship.

At age seventeen Dwight took the examinations to enter West Point, where his older brother, Jay, was a student. Although he scored highest in his district, his congressman failed to appoint him, certain he would be criticized if two Morrows attended the academy at the same time. Bitterly disappointed, Dwight cast about for other schools. A family friend, a professor at Amherst College in Massachusetts, suggested he sit for the entrance tests

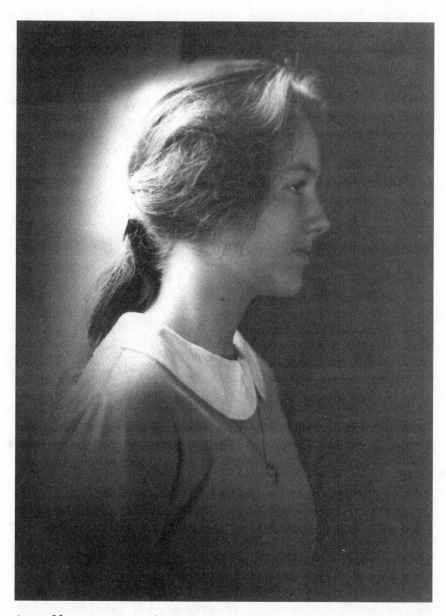

At age fifteen, Anne was a shy, introspective girl who turned to her diary to express her thoughts and feelings. Lindbergh Picture Collection, Manuscripts and Archives, Yale University Library. Reproduced with permission.

there. Though Dwight failed Greek and a few other subjects, Amherst allowed him to enter on probation and retest at the end of his freshman year.

While at Amherst he scraped by financially with tutoring jobs and with help from his family. He worked hard and did well there, won prizes in mathematics, speaking, and writing, and was elected to Phi Beta Kappa. What distinguished him most from his classmates, however, were his energy and intuitive grasp of people and social situations, attributes his fellow students recognized by voting him "most likely to succeed."[4] One student casting a vote was a terse and frugal New Englander named Calvin Coolidge, and he and Dwight would remain friends and political allies. Dwight earned his undergraduate degree in 1895; he would go on to graduate from Columbia Law School in 1899.

Aside from laying an intellectual foundation, Amherst set the stage for romance when, in his sophomore year, Dwight met his future bride at a nearby dance attended by Smith College students. Elizabeth "Betty" Reeve Cutter enchanted him, so much so that he told his sister he had found the girl he would marry. A short man whose head was disproportionately large compared to his body, Dwight could not be considered handsome. He also had a slightly crooked arm, ill set after he tumbled from an apple tree at age twelve. Miss Cutter, on the other hand, was a slight, becoming woman with high cheekbones and small features, the same age and height as Dwight. Certainly, her first impression of him didn't match his ardor. Even all his charm couldn't hide his physical features and his slightly disheveled appearance. Moreover, her own career goals and doubts about Dwight's future prospects precluded marriage; thus, a ten-year courtship ensued.

Betty Cutter, born in 1873 and brought up in Cleveland, Ohio, was one of five daughters of Charles Long Cutter, a lawyer, and Annie Spencer Cutter, a devout housewife. While socially a notch above the Morrows, the Cutters, too, had their share of financial woes and struggled to maintain their status. Charles, the stepson of a Yale-educated lawyer, had "no ability to make money," his granddaughter Constance would later write. He started in law and went on to banking yet "no profession or business occupation interested him"; he was instead a gentleman scholar who preferred to spend time with his books and family. A strong Presbyterian faith also grounded the Cutters, yet it was a more lenient variety than that of the Morrows': they were free to participate in dancing, card playing, and the arts—social outlets closed to young Dwight. And unlike Dwight, Betty had prosperous relatives with whom she traveled and who welcomed her at their stately homes in New Orleans and Houston.[5]

At nine years of age, Betty's twin sister, Mary, died from tuberculosis. The tragedy, according to her family, became the root of her constant over-achievement, spurring her to accomplish the work of two. As the oldest child, she felt responsible for easing her mother's burden of managing the household, a task made more difficult when another daughter was born severely retarded. After attending a girls' preparatory school, Betty's dream to go to college came to fruition when family members offered her financial help. With two new dresses, an old desk, and a painting to adorn her room, she headed to Smith College, an all-women's school located in Northampton, Massachusetts. She enjoyed great success at Smith, where she became a member of Alpha Society, an elite group, and editor of the Smith College *Monthly*. In 1896 she graduated with honors, her heart set on a literary career.

After returning home to Ohio, though, she found she couldn't earn a living writing, having published only one story and a few poems. She taught in a private school for a short time—long enough to conclude that she did not want a teaching career. "I must accomplish something . . . I must do something . . . I must be something," she confided to her diary. Yet education remained one of the few professions open to college-educated women, and she began a new career: "parlor-teaching." Intermittently for three years, she lectured to Cleveland ladies assembled in their elegant homes, work for which she was well paid but found demeaning.[6]

Just as the doors of opportunity seemed to shut around Betty, her family offered to send her and her sister, Annie, abroad to continue their education. The Cutters later rented out their house and joined them in Europe, where

Betty's father recuperated from a bout of despair brought on by the loss of his job. After studying in Paris and Florence, Betty returned to Cleveland in 1901 with her family, but there she again faced a bleak future.

At age twenty-eight, increasingly aware of society's limitations, Betty turned to the now attractive idea of marriage. She accepted Dwight Morrow's proposal, won over by his ambition and his position at a distinguished New York law firm. His incessant letters had also played a part in wooing her. Following a two-year engagement, on June 16, 1903, they married in a small ceremony ringed by college classmates and family at the Cutter home in Cleveland. Relatives said they were well matched, with the couple sharing high ambitions as well as their Presbyterian faith. After a honeymoon in the New England hills, the Morrows settled in Englewood, New Jersey. For their entire marriage, Dwight and his beloved "Betsy," as he named her, would remain deeply in love. Theirs was an equitable partnership, one that stood in contrast to their daughter Anne's later marriage to Charles Lindbergh, in which her husband often made unilateral decisions.

Nestled in the Palisades, a wooded area along the Hudson River's west bank, the newly incorporated city of Englewood offered a railroad depot, banks, churches, and shops within walking distance of most residences. An hour's commute by train or ferry linked it to Manhattan and the offices of Simpson, Thacher & Bartlett, where Dwight worked as a corporation lawyer, earning $3,000 annually. Englewood had begun to blossom with an influx of influential citizens, including the bankers Henry P. Davison and Thomas W. Lamont of J. P. Morgan & Company. Friendships blossomed, too: Lamont's wife, Florence, and Betty Morrow were former classmates at Smith College.

Both Betty and Dwight believed that the cornerstone of success was education and to this end, they considered a college degree essential. Indeed, their alma maters became lifelong passions: Dwight threw his talents into fundraising for Amherst and served as a trustee while Betty acted as the first woman chairman of the Board of Trustees at Smith. She also established a poetry library there and later served as interim president of the college.

Not surprisingly, however, the hub of the Morrows' social life came to be the Englewood Presbyterian Church, and from there the couple focused their energies on civic boards, charities, and education. By and large, Englewood offered a "simple and leisurely" style of life, remembered a family member, with neighborhood children frolicking under trees and parents congregating at the Shakespeare Club or gathering for bridge games.[7]

Within six years, three children filled the family's "little brown house," as they fondly named their large rental on Spring Lane, a two-minute walk from the railroad depot.[8] The firstborn, Elisabeth Reeve, inherited her father's wit and charm and became the family favorite. A vivacious blonde, academically and socially successful, she personified what her mother had wanted in her youth. Her pale beauty belied her fragile health, however: a childhood bout with rheumatic fever had caused severe and permanent damage to her heart, and she would struggle with poor health her entire life.

Anne, born two years later, lived in Elisabeth's shadow during her formative years. Indeed, following her sister's path would be a tough act for anyone, but it was doubly hard for Anne, an introspective child who only expressed her emotions in private diary entries far from the scrutiny of her family. In one such entry, she labeled herself "such a goose next to the swan, Elisabeth." Further compounding the sibling rivalry was Anne's self-consciousness about her looks. With wavy dark hair framing her face, stunning violet-colored eyes, and a diminutive stature, Anne was pretty, but not photogenic. Her slightly wide nose, exaggerated by photographs, caused her chronic consternation. Fully grown, she stood five feet two inches tall. With her small-boned frame, she appeared delicate and feminine, but she was healthy and strong willed— a "Tiny Titan," as her children later called her.[9]

In 1908 Dwight Jr. was born, the only Morrow boy and the child who would wrestle most with meeting his parents' exacting standards. The near-impossible task of following in his father's footsteps loomed larger as his father became more renowned, a stress that might have contributed to serious psychological problems during his youth. What caused his mental illness is unclear, but Dwight, who early on developed a stammer, couldn't help but feel he fell short of his parents' expectations. A handsome but unathletic boy, he would later confide in Anne—with whom he developed a close bond—his problems at Groton, his prep school. "It sounded like torture," she would write about his being bullied at the hands of his classmates.[10]

A year after Dwight Jr.'s birth, the Morrows purchased a sprawling house on Englewood's Palisade Avenue. The five-bedroom, multistoried house sat on a wooded acre of land that included lush gardens, a tulip tree, and a sweet gum tree. A partner in Simpson since 1905, Dwight now earned a salary of about $30,000, an amount ten times higher than when he had married. Mr. Simpson had authorized the partnership to prevent his most promising and hardest-working lawyer from accepting a faculty position at Columbia Law School. Although Dwight turned down the school's offer, he continued to harbor romantic illusions of another career: "Once we have made $100,000 we shall retire from the practice of law. I shall teach history, you will write poetry, the children will earn their own living," he told Betty.[11] In the early 1920s Dwight would decline an offer of the presidency of Yale University, a decision he sometimes regretted, remembered Anne.

During the summer of 1911, the entire family undertook a grand continental tour of Europe, their first vacation abroad. Although Dwight returned to work in midsummer, the children, their German governess Fraulein Matter, and Betty boarded at Villa Montana, in Bad Harzburg, Germany, before the family reunited in Englewood on October 2. It was young Anne's first glimpse of the wider world, a trip that perhaps planted a seed for her lifelong interest in exploring new places.

The third daughter and baby of the family, Constance Cutter, was born in the Palisade Avenue house in 1913. With a large age gap between her and her sisters, she avoided their rivalry and developed the most easygoing disposition of all the children. Like her father, she possessed an analytical mind and in another era might have been a lawyer, as one of her daughters pointed out.

And like her mother before her, she would serve many years as a trustee of Smith College. She and Anne would remain close throughout their lives.

✈

One evening Dwight awoke in a cold sweat from a nightmare, clutched his wife, and recounted a "so vivid, so ghastly" premonition: "I dreamt, Betsy, that we had become rich. But *enormously* rich." According to family lore, she retorted, "That's nothing to be scared about. You can trust me to set *that* right."[12] His nightmare became reality in December 1913, when his neighbor Thomas Lamont, a Morgan partner himself, asked Dwight to join J. P. Morgan & Company. What prompted the invitation was a speech Dwight had made in Englewood, which so impressed Morgan partner Henry Davison that he recommended the firm take him on. Thomas Lamont enthusiastically endorsed the plan.

From its three-story limestone building at the junction of Broad and Wall Streets, the banking firm of J. P. Morgan ruled capitalism worldwide. Though enormously flattered by the job offer, a position that would soon catapult him to multimillionaire status, Dwight vacillated, much to the chagrin of Lamont. He and Betty vacationed three weeks in Bermuda, where they mulled over the fantastic offer. While drafting his resignation letter to Mr. Simpson, Dwight turned to Betsy and said, "We [are] bankers after we mail this letter." She smiled and replied, "Well, I hope we'll be as happy as we've been as lawyers." Hired on in April, Dwight became partner in July 1914.[13]

Morrow soon developed expertise in foreign financial affairs and acquired a reputation as a skilled mediator. During his youth his peers and family had valued his understanding nature, even dubbing him an ambassador—talents well honed during his legal career. Working for J. P. Morgan, he also became a partner in the firm's Philadelphia, London, and Paris affiliates. After the Great War broke out in Europe, the Morgan partners' workload increased: the firm had been appointed purchasing agent for Great Britain in the United States. At home, Dwight talked with the Secretary of the Treasury about financing the war and worked to save the credit of the City of New York. After the war, Dwight played an important role in discussions on war debts and reparations, and he and Jean Monnet, a French political economist, worked together in reconstructing postwar Europe, then in economic chaos. Dwight also counseled the du Pont family and took charge of public offerings. One of his clients, the American copper baron Daniel Guggenheim, would form the Guggenheim Fund for the Promotion of Aeronautics in 1926 with an endowment of $2.5 million. Dwight would serve on its Board of Trustees, one of his many auxiliary involvements.

While Dwight's career soared to new heights, far beyond his dreams, his wife became active in civic affairs. The rarity of college-educated women did not stop her, or her colleagues, from making their voices heard. Women of privilege, they embraced social responsibility and committed to improvements through volunteer and charitable works. Surrounded by a coterie of like-minded women, Betty continued her philanthropy throughout her life. Years later, Reeve Lindbergh, Anne's daughter, would fondly label her grandmother a "committee" woman. It is interesting to note that, in addition to organizations like the Y.W.C.A. and the Community Chest, Betty Morrow also spent time working for Planned Parenthood. In part because of their new obligations, many educated women of the early twentieth century preferred smaller families to the bustling broods of the Victorian era. Discussions about contraceptive devices and birth control, once only whispered in parlors, became open. In 1916 Margaret Higgins Sanger, America's pioneer advocate of family planning, opened a birth control clinic in Brooklyn, New York, a radical move that earned her a thirty-day jail sentence. Betty Morrow began sponsoring Planned Parenthood meetings in her home in the 1930s, which Anne took note of but did not participate in.

As Betty and Dwight scaled society, their children became more and more hard-pressed to emulate them, as could be expected of any child of exemplary parents whose raw ambition had catapulted them to high achievements. "You and Daddy are brilliant and got all sorts of distinctions," a young Anne wrote her mother about her inability to meet her parents' successes at their schools. The Morrows created a competitive, structured, and disciplined environment at home, too. One family acquaintance compared the family to "high-strung thoroughbreds," and another said they were "nuts on education."[14]

Religion, too, had its place: there were morning prayers, and on Sunday evenings the children listened wide-eyed to sermons and bible stories at Betty Morrow's green sofa. "Whatever thy hand findeth to do, do it with thy might," she urged them one evening as tears welled in her eyes. Lessons continued at the dining table, with Dwight Morrow drilling his children in arithmetic, a practice taught to him by his father. And when visiting dignitaries—including Judge Learned Hand, Jean Monnet, and Dean Woodbridge—sat with them, a frequent occurrence, a hush descended over the children. "To be 'seen and not heard' was still the rule—or at least the habit—even up to the time I was married," Anne remembered. Discipline also extended to the children's European vacations: they trudged to literary shrines and historic sites their parents selected, trips that Anne described as "meticulously scheduled and documented." The ambitious couple who had set their own course in life allowed little deviation from the prescribed path they set for their children.[15]

However, Anne would later wonder, "With all this education and travel, how can one explain the haze of insulation which permeated our early years, our indefinable sense of isolation from the real world?"[16] As she grew into adulthood, profound changes swept across the "real world," revolutionizing how Americans lived. When Anne turned fourteen, in 1920, Congress ratified the Nineteenth Amendment, granting women the right to vote, a political victory hastened by their wartime labor and support. This same year saw the Prohibition Era usher in the Roaring Twenties, a decade of exuberance and excess. The "new women," dubbed flappers, wore short-sleeved, wispy dresses whose knee-length hems shocked their elders. They bobbed their hair, danced the Charleston in nightclubs, and saw Al Jolson in "The Jazz Singer," the first talking picture. And economic barriers eased as young women, formerly restricted to teaching, social work, nursing, and clerical work, took up new occupations.

Even so, Anne avoided any mention of these events in her first collection of published diaries and letters, which covered the years 1922–1928. It is true that Anne had no radio or television to follow the news, as she later wrote, yet newspapers were readily available. She appeared oblivious to the changes taking place and more so, it would seem, than some of her peers. By contrast, Corliss Lamont, a son of Thomas Lamont, and Anne's friend, would later write in his memoir that during his youth his family had "lively conversations" at the dinner table, in which politics were discussed in an "open forum."[17]

Anne was not entirely sequestered in Englewood, of course. She started elementary school by following Elisabeth to the Dwight School for Girls, which billed itself as a preparatory and finishing academy. (At this time, her future husband, Charles, in contrast, was drifting from one school to another.) At the Dwight School young Anne began to display talents in drama and in writing, acting in school productions and scripting plays, such as "The Enchanted Prince" and "The Goody-Witch." By the time she reached thirteen, she wrote in her diary every day, an activity she started because she was "shy and couldn't talk in front of people," she later explained.[18]

Shortly after the First World War ended, Anne's world expanded: Her father, whose workday began with 8:00 A.M. breakfast meetings and ended late at night, wanted a more convenient residence, so her parents purchased a palatial apartment overlooking Manhattan's Central Park. The apartment on the eleventh floor at 4 East 66th Street, a stone's throw from Fifth Avenue, boasted fifteen bedrooms, a ballroom, and a marble hall. They relegated the Englewood home to a weekend retreat.

Living in Manhattan proved to be a godsend for young Anne. In 1919, when she was thirteen, she entered Miss Chapin's School for Girls, a preparatory academy housed in two brownstones that provided an ideal environment for her. Free from Elisabeth's sway—she was boarding at Milton Academy in

Massachusetts—Anne treasured her independence at Miss Chapin's. In a 1923 diary entry, she reminisced about her first years there: "It was a relief and joy and heaven to be in school—on an equal with everyone else. There I was '*Anne Morrow*' not 'Elisabeth's little sister!' And they liked *me, me, me!* I simply expanded like an inflated balloon, I basked in content[ment] and beauty and excitement."[19]

At Miss Chapin's five years, she excelled in both academics and in athletics. She not only was the chief contributor to *The Wheel,* the school's newsletter, she flourished in extracurricular activities that included the Dramatic Club, Athletic Association, chorus, student council, and hockey and basketball teams. And she savored the companionship of her fellow classmates, girls from upper-class families with similar interests who, away from school, attended afternoon teas, the opera, and chaperoned dances. During her senior year, they elected Anne captain of the Gold Hockey Team and president of Self-Government, hard-earned honors.

In her junior year at Chapin's, her confidence blossoming, trying desperately to maintain her independence, Anne attempted to enlist Elisabeth's help in a defiant move against her mother. She did not want to go to Smith College, her mother's beloved alma mater—and the school where Elisabeth had enrolled. In a September 1922 letter, Anne pleaded to her sister, "I want to go to a different place from you and Mother and I want to bring back a different view of things to our family . . ." She wanted to attend Bryn Mawr, the school of choice of all her friends at Miss Chapin's. Earlier, she had spoken her desire to her mother, who was disappointed but not enough to "disinherit" her, as Anne put it. Even though she wanted a college where she had "nobody to 'emulate,' " her cry for autonomy fell flat. All the Morrow daughters attended Smith College, heeding their mother. Indeed, until Anne became engaged she would live obediently, according to her parents' wishes. She remained an introspective young woman and turned to her diary to express her true feelings.[20]

In late 1923, her diary entry portrayed a maturing young woman who, after a summer trip to Panama, questioned her good fortune: "I realized my opportunities, I realized my wonderful chances and advantages and blessings but I simply was frightfully sick of everything all the time. Social conditions, poverty, seemed so glaring. It frightened me. Why was *I* shielded? What was *I* doing? What right had *I* to these privileges? I hated to look at poor people and at crowds of workingmen; it made me feel so small and unworthy. And then I had the wanderlust and was dying to run away, far away, to go to sea. The sea was so peaceful and great and one had time to think and there was beauty and cleanliness and broad swoops of blue."[21] Although Anne pined for adventure, she could shake neither the influence of her family nor the restraints society imposed on girls of her social class. She could not travel unless chaperoned and lacked the confidence to truly assert herself. Besides, at the time, if young women wanted to pursue independence, they received incredulous stares from their parents.

At the graduation dinner at Miss Chapin's, she was asked her life's ambition. "I want to marry a hero," she responded.[22] Like many young women then, she concealed her dreams and believed marriage was her best option. On some level, Anne probably worried about leaving college with only a "spinster of art" degree. Society expected women to marry and rear a family, regardless of their educational level. Indeed, women's colleges were sensitive to charges of their graduates not marrying and hastened to prove otherwise, waving statistics to back up the numbers. But what prompted Anne to say she wanted to marry a hero? Perhaps it was an impulse—or perhaps she knew marrying a hero would bring her adventure and help free her from what society and her family mapped out for her.

In September 1924, a few months after her high school graduation, she arrived at Smith College, chaperoned by her mother. After her mother unpacked her trunks and arranged her room, both stopped off for tea with President Neilson and his wife. Homesick, with her carefree days at Chapin's behind her, Anne initially felt overwhelmed by Smith's heavy academic workload. Yet she persevered, made many friends, and graduated with honors. She majored in English literature and studied creative writing under Mina Kirstein Curtiss, a Smith alumna and accomplished author of books on Proust, Bizet, and Degas.

Anne was also an inveterate letter writer and corresponded with her sisters and mother frequently, sometimes writing daily. Writing her mother on March 4, 1925, still in her first year at Smith, she complained about her "awful slump" but said that it was nearing an end: "I'm beginning to pick up now." She also enclosed her grades from the last term, all above average except a C she earned in Greek, yet she called the results "awfully poor." Apparently, she felt that anything less than a B deserved censure. The letter ended describing the praise she had recently received from Mrs. Curtiss, whose comments left her "smothered with joy." About an essay of Anne's, Mrs. Curtiss had remarked, "Very nice, indeed, written with insight and taste and the rare ability to choose the right quotations."[23]

Mrs. Curtiss took Anne under her wing for the next few years, mentoring her and encouraging her literary career. She prompted Anne to submit her poems and stories to the Smith College *Monthly*, the school's literary magazine; later, she would encourage Anne to send her work to outside publications. Writing her mother on May 28, 1925, Anne exclaimed about her essay, "The Monthly took—'A A Milne vs. Robert Louis Stevenson'! But not any of the poems." Anne's contributions continued, and in 1927 she joined the *Monthly*'s board.[24]

A bookish and serious young woman, Anne showed a remarkable propensity for solitude and reading, more so than other girls her age. She later said, "Even in college I would go off alone and sit on a stump and think." When she sailed to Europe on a family vacation in 1926, she confided to her diary her delightful seclusion with books—"no deck tennis, no men." While touring a monastery in Grenoble, she recorded her joy at the monks' lives of "books" and "no interruptions." At the same time, however, she seldom read newspapers in college. About Charles Lindbergh's famous flight in May 1927, she later told an interviewer she "knew nothing" until she heard everyone in her dormitory "talking about Lindy. 'Who is this Lindy?' I asked to sounds of astonishment and girlish sighs. I was quickly enlightened, and chastised, I might add, for my ignorance."[25]

While a student at Smith, Anne summed up her concerns about her future: "I must say over and over to myself. *Make your world count . . ."* Though determined to provide their students with a sound classical and liberal arts education, the prestigious Seven Sisters schools expected their matriculants to contribute to society—not that this surprised Anne, who later wrote that her parents had been consumed with the idea of public service, or "bettering the world." In turn, years later she would say "one must make a contribution to your world."[26]

During Anne's young years, the Morrows wintered in Nassau and spent summers in roomy beach rentals on Cape Cod, where frequent family reunions enlivened the brood. Anne declared celebrations were "not complete without the larger family circle of aunts, uncles, and cousins." Before long, summer vacation venues shifted, with North Haven Island in Penobscot Bay, Maine, replacing rented Cape Cod cottages. Later, in 1928, the Morrows would build a summer residence there. North Haven had its drawbacks, Anne noted during her teenage years, because it was "such a people-y place. People dropped in and you had to see them. You were with them all the time. There were picnics and Sunday afternoon roughhouses and Sunday singings and golf and races and the Lamonts' yacht picnics."[27]

Dwight Morrow rose to national prominence in the fall of 1925, the start of Anne's sophomore year at Smith. On Sunday, September 13, he opened his newspaper and saw his picture and those of eight other prominent men, and went on to read that President Calvin Coolidge had ordered them to Washington to form the Aircraft Inquiry Board, its mission to report on the best means of "developing and applying aircraft in national defense."[28] They had no chance to refuse and would receive no compensation for what would become an eight-week task. It was a plum assignment for Dwight. Although disappointed that Coolidge had not earlier appointed him to a cabinet position, he had refrained from voicing his feelings. On the other hand, perhaps the president used the Inquiry Board appointment as a spring-board to launch Dwight into politics, as some people suggested. Certainly, it would pave the way for an entry and make him known outside financial circles. In fact, Dwight's colleagues elected him chairman of what was soon called the "Morrow Board," which further propelled his name into the spotlight.

Coolidge had commissioned the board in response to a vociferous and public critic of the country's armed services: Brigadier General William "Billy" Mitchell. Mitchell had called for a strong independent air force, warned of the vulnerability of battleships to attack from the air, and forecast that the next war would begin in the Pacific. The president, in turn, had no choice but to order the secretary of war to court-martial Mitchell for his insubordination. But the Morrow Board did not want "panic legislation" and recommended against a separate air arm, Mitchell's concept. With aviation in its infancy, the board members did not grasp the future role of aircraft. They wore blinders when it came to aerial weaponry, concluding, "The next war may well start in the air but in all probability will wind up, as the last one did, in the mud."[29] In time, however, Mitchell's suggestions and neglected prophecies would come to pass.

Misplaced tradition aside, the Morrow Board rightfully earned praise from pilots and aviation journalists alike for its recommendations, which in 1926 led to the Air Commerce Act. This federal legislation created a Bureau of Aeronautics in the Department of Commerce, which would regulate America's civil aviation: licensing mechanics, planes, and pilots; enforcing rules for air traffic; and investigating accidents, among other duties.[30] Aviation's freewheeling days would soon screech to a halt. Before then anyone could fly any machine since neither pilots nor their planes needed licensing. Orville Wright declined the honor of holding the first pilot's license, saying he didn't need the federal government to prove he was first to fly. Soon afterward, a gangly airmail pilot named Charles Lindbergh was handed his first license in St. Louis, a stop on his record-breaking, transcontinental flight to New York, and then Paris.

Oddly, the significance of her father's involvement in aviation seemed to elude Anne. Even in later years, she didn't acknowledge his participation and leadership in the early years of American aviation—a small world of well-connected men who dominated and plotted its future. Yet she must have been influenced by her father's discussions about aviation, even before she met Charles Lindbergh. In any event, his work on the Morrow Board and the Guggenheim Fund would pave the way for his introduction to Charles, when the two met in Washington in June 1927, after Lindbergh's transatlantic flight.

Heading the Morrow Board piqued Dwight's interest in politics. Restless and tired of banking, and with a multimillion dollar fortune freeing him from financial concerns, he yearned to leave private industry and move into public service. In July 1927, a few months before Anne entered her senior year at Smith, the Morrow family's course shifted significantly. President Coolidge tapped Morrow for a diplomatic post, asking him to assume the ambassadorship to Mexico. Dwight wanted the position, but early on his wife recoiled at Coolidge's request, thinking it would be "a hard job, and not much honor." Unlike London or Paris, Mexico was not a glamorous posting, and the Morgan partners scoffed at the idea of Dwight accepting this "lemon" of the Foreign Service. Furthermore, an architect had drawn up plans for the Morrows' new house, a Georgian manor in Englewood, and Betty fretted that a move to Mexico would delay its construction.[31]

Once her husband gave the go-ahead for the mansion, though, she threw herself into backing him, becoming his staunchest ally. Dwight resigned from J. P. Morgan, and by October 23, he, Betty, and Constance had taken up residence in the splendor of the American Embassy in Mexico City. Built at a cost of $150,000, the embassy was a neoclassic mansion staffed with fourteen servants, and featured red-carpeted steps leading to its white pillar structure. Betty and Dwight Morrow came to love Mexico, and the Mexicans, in turn, wholeheartedly embraced them.

A few months earlier Anne had complained in her diary of her "wasted" summer full of "petty day-to-day things." At age twenty-one, she was becoming more aware of her somewhat insulated life. After Betty and Dwight departed for Mexico, Anne praised her mother for taking on such a "tremendous challenge." In this same letter, she wrote, "I do look forward so to

Christmas." The family was planning to meet in Mexico for a vacation that "may be *much* more satisfactory than they usually are, with none of the distractions of New York and different engagements." It was in Mexico City only months later, in December 1927, that a distraction named Charles Lindbergh would enter into her sheltered world.[32]

2

A Different Drummer

Charles Augustus Lindbergh, with a pilot's unblinking gaze fixed on the limitless horizon before him, rarely looked back on his odd upbringing. Born in 1902, the child of an unconventional family, he seldom attended the same school for more than one year, and shuttled between Michigan, Minnesota, and Washington, D.C. His heritage and youth were polar opposites to those of Anne Morrow. Long-established Americans, the Morrows rose through society by working hard and playing by the rules. In contrast, the Lindberghs, newly arrived from Sweden, were forced to overcome physical hardships unknown by Anne's parents. Writing years later, Anne expressed amazement that her and her husband's diverse backgrounds led to a successful marriage. Each opened and expanded the other's world, her refinement and literary sensibility melding with his love of adventure and action.

The aviator's father, Charles August, was born in Stockholm, Sweden, on January 20, 1858, the son of Ola Månsson and his mistress Louisa Callén, a waitress twenty-nine years his junior. Månsson, an elected official of the Riksdag, Sweden's parliament, and a farmer from the parish of Smedstorp, would soon flee his homeland in the midst of a political scandal. While an officer of the State Bank of Sweden, he was accused of violating banking regulations, accepting commissions from persons for whom he had helped secure loans. Determined to carve out a new life for himself, he asked his family to emigrate from Sweden to America. When they turned him down, he gathered up the baby and Louisa and set sail for North America. Månsson took a new name, August Lindbergh, then homesteaded with his family near the town of Melrose in Stearns County, Minnesota, in August 1859. Years later, he and Louisa married.[1]

Charles August, or C. A., as he came to be called, grew up on the Minnesota frontier in a log cabin built by his father, the family struggling to survive a harsh pioneer life. Blizzards dumped snow drifting twenty feet high; for three years, swarms of grasshoppers over a hundred miles long destroyed and devoured all in their path; crops failed; Indians marauded— to name just a few of the many hardships they overcame.[2] The 1862 Sioux Uprising saw an estimated 800 white settlers killed, men scalped, women taken captive. Diseases were rampant, with cholera, scurvy, and dysentery claiming lives—as well as whooping cough, which killed three of the six children Louisa bore in Minnesota. While August farmed and branched out into local politics, Louisa worked the homestead, crushed by loneliness and yearning for Stockholm.

Children of pioneers grew up fast. At six years of age C. A. could carry a shotgun, and his father deemed him old enough to put food on the family's table. The boy fished, hunted deer, and shot ducks and other game. When he turned twelve, he started lessons in a two-room schoolhouse, all the while chafing at not being outdoors. After hit-and-miss country schooling there, he spent two years at an academy established by a Catholic priest, Father Daniel J. Coogan. Between terms he earned his tuition by hunting and trapping for muskrat and mink. He then matriculated at the University of Michigan in Ann Arbor, where he studied law and graduated in 1883.

Two years later, in 1885, after practicing law in nearby areas, he opened up shop in Little Falls, Minnesota, a fast-growing lumber town a hundred miles downstream from Lake Itasca, headwaters of the Mississippi River. Nearby tribes—Dakota, Ojibwa, and Winnebago—knew the area well, as did nineteenth-century explorers such as Joseph Nicollet, the Frenchman who had named the site "petite chutes."[3] Twenty-seven years of age when he moved there, and standing just short of six feet tall, with blond hair, blue eyes, and a dimpled chin, C. A. was by far the best-looking bachelor in town. He knew to set off his lanky frame too, wearing stylish three-piece suits. C. A. prospered in Little Falls and rose to become one of its leading attorneys. Townspeople saw him as one of their own, a man who had pulled himself up from poverty to become a trusted and hardworking Minnesotan who had their concerns at heart. Before long, he took up real estate and bought properties in the surrounding area. And soon after, he would make room for a career in politics. Few men, however, were more unsuited to this work and incapable of the diplomacy it required than Congressman C. A. Lindbergh, a crusader-turned-crank who eventually lost most of his political battles.

Two years after moving to Little Falls, C. A. fell in love with Mary LaFond, the daughter of his landlord. After their marriage in 1887, three daughters were born within five years: Lillian, Evangeline, and Edith, who died an infant. Death stalked their home again when Mrs. Lindbergh died unexpectedly in April 1898 from complications after surgery. The grief-stricken girls, thereafter shuttled between relatives and schools, never recovered from their mother's untimely death.

In September 1900, the widower C. A. moved into the Antlers Hotel in Little Falls, where he met Evangeline Lodge Land, the newly hired science teacher for Little Falls High School. Miss Land, twenty-four years old, with a trim figure, fair skin, and luminous blue eyes, was the high-spirited daughter of two distinguished families, the Lodges and the Lands of Detroit, Michigan. An 1899 graduate of the University of Michigan with a Bachelor of Science degree, she would later earn a Master's degree at Columbia University in New York. Like most educated women in her time, Evangeline turned to teaching as a career. Wanting to experience adventure outside of Detroit, she settled on teaching in Little Falls, with a salary of $55 per month.

Having the striking Evangeline Lodge Land in his life warmed C. A.'s heart after the death of his first wife. A quick courtship followed, and they married on March 27, 1901, in the parlor of her parents' Detroit home.

Returning from a ten-week honeymoon to the West Coast, C. A. commissioned a three-story house to be built on a bluff atop a west bank of the Mississippi River; about two miles south of Little Falls, the 120-acre property was heavily wooded with elm, oak, birch, and linden trees. He spared no expense with the house and its furnishings, hiring a cook, a maid, and a coachman to staff the small estate.

Less than a year later, on February 4, 1902, the couple's first and only child together, Charles Augustus Lindbergh, was born in his grandparents' home in Detroit. But the birth of the golden-haired boy didn't stem the problems his parents had sustaining their slowly unraveling marriage. C. A.'s urbane and spirited wife found Little Falls provincial while he, a tight-lipped and reserved man, couldn't understand what he considered her rash behavior, spendthrift habits, and moodiness. Like many of their Swedish neighbors in Minnesota, the Lindberghs prized reticence and indeed, C. A. had come to be known as a man who rarely smiled. His wife's close-knit family, by contrast, more readily expressed their sentiments. The age difference between them further contributed to their marital problems, as well as the stepchildren, who resented Evangeline—she was only twelve years older than Lillian—and country neighbors who frowned at her stylish dresses and mannerisms.

Evangeline lavished all her affection on her only child, a "painfully shy" boy, as one of his half-sisters described him. Charles and his doting mother cleaved to each other and would remain unusually close until he married. Their relationship differed sharply from that Anne experienced with her mother, who was an "inaccessible" parent, she would later tell her daughter Reeve. Evangeline's devotion to her son could be considered somewhat smothering; when Reeve later described their deep bond, she jokingly suggested that he flew across the Atlantic to "get away" from her. As the only child of his parents' marriage, Charles had no playmates during his early years and grew up surrounded by adults. He was happiest outdoors and if housebound, pursued solitary hobbies: collecting stamps and stones and making endless lists of his possessions.[4]

When together in Minnesota and Washington, D.C., C. A. and his son were inseparable. He taught his boy, whom he dubbed "Boss," to fish, hunt, and swim in the cold waters of the Mississippi. They bagged the Plains' plentiful game, as had C. A. in his young years. Reminiscing about his father years later, Charles wrote, "He'd let me walk behind him with a loaded gun at seven, use an axe as soon as I had strength enough to swing it, drive his Ford car anywhere at twelve."[5] And later, during his congressional career, C. A. would let Charles tag along after him through the halls of the United States Capitol, ignoring the complaints of other congressmen.

On August 6, 1905, the Lindberghs' home burned to the ground. The dream house lay in ashes: from a charred pit in the ground, only a brick chimney remained. C. A., then strapped for cash, opted to build a one-and-a-half-story, wood-frame replacement upon the basement of the original house. In this cottage, referred to as "camp" by the family, young Charles and his mother spent their summers. The boy slept in a screened-in porch overlooking a sheer vertical drop to the water's banks, stretched out on a folding cot with his dog Wahgoosh at his feet. Though Charles would forever refer to his youth alongside the river and write a slender autobiography titled *Boyhood on the Upper Mississippi,* he had to spend his winters with his parents in Washington, D.C. In 1906 his father had been elected a representative on the Republican ticket for Minnesota's Sixth Congressional District, an office he held until 1917. A leader of farmer and labor groups, the radical C. A. Lindbergh pushed for progressive reform and raged against J. P. Morgan & Co. and the other financial powers conspiring to control America's banking and currency.

In mid-1909, Evangeline asked C. A. for a divorce. Convinced that his constituents would not reelect a divorced representative, C. A. balked and suggested they keep up appearances and continue living together, but by fall of the same year, having exhausted all attempts at reconciling, they established separate residences. By this time, Evangeline's stepdaughters had left home to attend school in the Midwest; they could no longer tolerate living with their stepmother. In Washington during the school year, Charles and his mother called a series of dismal boardinghouses home, usually sharing a bedroom to curtail expenses. The friendless young boy referred to Washington as a "prison."[6]

When Charles turned eight, his mother enrolled him in a private school in Washington, the first of eleven institutions he attended until he went to college. His parents did not seem to value a normal education or empathize with the ordeal their son underwent as a loner and a misfit teased by other school children. "You and I can take hard knocks," C. A. told his young son, then attending grade school.[7] His mother, despite being a trained teacher, gave no thought to interrupting her child's school year, pulling him out of class before the spring term ended and having him start in late fall, well into the season.

Away from Washington, Charles enjoyed visits with his Grandfather Land and his Uncle Charles Land, Jr. He and his mother, trekking between Washington and Minnesota at the start and end of each school year, stopped at the Lands' Detroit home for lengthy visits. For the boy, the Land family and their house were heaven sent. Inside the house were tools, a basement shooting gallery, and Dr. Land's dental rooms and laboratories, all of which his grandfather made available to him. A curious, young boy couldn't ask for more, and he later declared, "I never had a dull moment at Detroit."[8]

And so the years continued for Charles, back and forth between Little Falls, Detroit, and Washington, a pattern broken by occasional sightseeing trips with his mother to New York City, Philadelphia, Atlantic City, and a three-week winter cruise to Panama in 1913. These were educational excursions, Evangeline always claimed. While in Washington, he and his mother also frequented cultural and historical establishments: the Smithsonian Institution, art museums, and exhibitions. In 1912 they went to their first air meet, the Aeronautical Trials at Fort Myer, Virginia. Watching the races there sowed the seeds for the ten-year-old boy's decision to later fly himself.

Charles's interest in aviation continued to grow in the following years. In 1914 the First World War erupted in Europe. What had begun with horse cavalry and brandished swords was transformed by sweeping technological advances: combat aircraft, tanks, and other modern weapons. Pilots reconnoitered, bombed, and strafed enemy lines. Meanwhile, the public's attention was captured by the dogfights—skirmishes between flying aces, who in the popular imagination had become a new breed of gallant knights. The term ace, of French origin, was an honorific title awarded to aviators after they had downed at least five enemy aircraft. (To certify the kills, other combatants were required to witness the action.) The first aces took to the skies in open-cockpit planes, shooting pistols at the enemy; later aircraft came with forward-firing machine guns synchronized to shoot between propeller blades.

Despite the glory attributed to them, few aces survived the duels. Many were shot down, while others died when their flimsy planes shed wings in flight. They were not equipped with parachutes, the military brass reasoning that they might bail out before fighting to the end, and so rather than burn to death in flight or on the ground, some aces shot themselves. Away from the front, however, a new generation of boys hunkered under bedcovers at night, savoring tales of the aces and their battles aloft. One such boy was Charles, who treasured "Tam o' the Scoots," a magazine serial about a British airman.

In the spring of 1916 the fourteen-year-old Charles put aside his books to chauffeur C. A. through Minnesota's back roads for his father's senatorial primary campaign. C. A. finished fourth, his platform of monetary reform falling on deaf ears, as well as his opposition to America's entry into World War I. With his father's congressional term soon ending, Charles retreated with his mother to Little Falls. He started high school there in the fall of 1916, only to leave in October for yet another trip, driving his mother and uncle to California. He went to high school in Redondo Beach until April 1917, when the threesome returned home because Grandmother Land was dying from breast cancer. The following fall, he began his senior year at Little Falls High School but left midseason to work the farm, along with the other farm children who were excused from classes to harvest crops, milk cattle, and do other chores during the war. Charles returned to school in June 1918 to pick up his diploma. Few students would remember him. In 1927, when interviewed about their then famous classmate, members of the graduating class of 1918 would say they were proud of him, but none could say he was their friend. They did add that he was often working with machinery, usually an old motorcycle, while other boys took part in athletics.[9]

After Charles graduated, he and his mother worked hard on the Minnesota farm stocked with cattle and sheep, among other animals. Two years later, however, distressed about ever making a go, financially, from farming, he capitulated to his parents' wishes and applied to college. He enrolled at the University of Wisconsin-Madison, majoring in mechanical engineering, and in the fall of 1920 began classes. A loner and an oddball who turned up his nose at drinking, smoking, and dating, he lived with his mother, who had resumed her teaching career in Madison. Rather than taking up with girls in his college days, Charles recollected, "I preferred to ride my motorcycle. It was also a lot cheaper."[10] However, surely he turned girls' heads. Now six feet and two inches tall and weighing about 150 pounds, he was exceptionally good-looking: sandy-haired with a chiseled face and penetrating blue eyes.

University life and its rigors did not suit Charles. An undisciplined student, he struggled with the course work, later reporting, "The long hours of study at college were very trying to me." He complained bitterly about such demands as "formulae, semi-colons, and our crazy English spelling." Instead of studying English composition, he felt he should learn to fly and not "fiddle with pencil marks on paper." What held his interest were the Reserve Officer Training Corps program and the university's rifle and pistol squads where he, a surefire marksman, aced the competition. In February 1922 the university dropped Charles from its rolls. On probation since his first midterm report, he was hardly surprised hearing the news. Enamored with flying since childhood, he was already reviewing flight school curricula and preparing for his aviation career. He had decided while a college freshman that "ten years spent as the pilot of an airplane was in value worth more than an ordinary lifetime."[11]

On the first of April 1922, Charles, age twenty, stepped off a train in Lincoln, Nebraska, and presented himself at the Hotel Savoy. Two days later he started flight school at the Nebraska Aircraft Corporation, the $500 tuition reluctantly paid by his father on the condition that he later return to college. In his two months at the school, Charles never soloed. Despite logging almost eight hours of dual instruction, flying a Lincoln Standard Tourabout, he couldn't afford to post the bond that was required if he crashed. Instead, he joined a barnstorming outfit. Originally a theatrical term used to describe troupes that performed in barns, barnstorming referred to the flying circuses of vagabond pilots who flew from town to town, taking off from cow pastures or dirt roads to give stunt exhibitions or rides. Like the aces of World War I, barnstormers helped to usher in an era of airborne romance and adventure that has never quite been equaled since. They cut dashing figures, appearing in jodhpurs, high-top boots, leather flying helmets, and wearing white scarves around their necks that trailed in the slipstream. At first, $5 or a fee of a penny per passenger pound bought a ride in their rickety planes, but as more pilots turned to barnstorming and war surplus planes became readily available, it soon became a buyer's market. Many aviators slept on fields beneath their plane's wings and came close to starving, but Charles thrived and relished the gypsy-like life. He took up wing walking and parachute jumping, activities he had regarded as "suicidal" two months earlier.[12] Gradually, he learned the ropes, sometimes literally—one of his stunts was to climb atop a plane's wing and hang from it while in the air.

Little more than a year later, Charles owned his own plane, a war surplus Curtiss Jenny open-cockpit biplane that he picked up at Souther Field in Americus, Georgia. Again his father foot the bill, lending Charles $500 for the Jenny. After coming close to crashing on his first solo, Charles learned to fly the small trainer and racked up five hours alone. It was sufficient time, he felt, to act as a flight instructor, hop passengers, and stunt fly for hire. Like other aviators, he didn't need a license to fly or to fix planes until after 1926, when the Air Commerce Act was enacted.

On May 17, 1923, Charles left Georgia, flying his Jenny north to join his father on yet another senatorial campaign. C. A. lost the Farmer-Labor nomination but marveled at the new chariot that transported him around. He was not elected when he ran in future primaries and died a disillusioned man in 1924. "In the end, like most crusaders of the masses, he lost popular victory. He lost his fight to keep his country out of war, lost his struggle for monetary reform," reported the *Post-Bulletin,* a Rochester, Minnesota, newspaper.[13]

Both Lindbergh parents liked flying with their son, but Evangeline especially thrilled to the adventure. After the 1923 campaign, Charles took to the skies with his mother, barnstorming around southern Minnesota for ten days. She had "never objected to my flying," he later wrote, "and after her first flight at Janesville, Minnesota, she became an enthusiast herself. We had been together constantly up to the start of my flying career and had both looked forward to flying around together."[14] Later his mother would fly round-trip between Chicago and St. Louis in the mail compartment of his plane.

Within a year, in March 1924, Charles had sold the Curtiss Jenny biplane and turned up in Texas as an enlistee in the U.S. Army Air Service. He wanted to fly higher performance aircraft, and the military offered him his "only opportunity to fly planes which would roar up into the sky when they were pointed in that direction, instead of having to be wished up over low trees at the end of a landing field." Lindbergh's transformation in the army school was nothing short of miraculous. While he had scoffed at the course work required at the University of Wisconsin, he now had a clear goal and knuckled down and studied, knowing a washout was a certainty if he failed two tests. For the first time, he later recalled, "School and life became both rationally and emotionally connected." For diversion he honed his skills as a practical joker; he became the lead trickster, hiding cadets' gear—and, in one instance, a bed—or putting a dead skunk on another's pillow. Life in the boisterous barracks appealed to Lindbergh, or Slim, as he was now called, as did the military regimen. He graduated first in his class—only 19 of the original group of 104 cadets finished—from the Air Service Advanced Flying School at Kelly Field in March 1925. He was commissioned a second lieutenant in the Air Service Reserve Corps.[15]

Because squadrons didn't need new pilots at the time, he turned to civil aviation for employment. Declining an offer to fly as a crop duster, he waited for an airmail pilot position to open up. Across the United States, there was no better aeronautical training than flying the mail. A pilot learned how to navigate, handle a plane, and scud-run beneath low ceilings or through clouds, if he lived to tell his stories. In the interim, Charles returned to barnstorming, basing his operations at Lambert Field in St. Louis, Missouri. By late 1925, Robertson Aircraft Corporation, a small outfit at Lambert, hired him as chief airmail pilot, at a salary of $200 a month, to fly the St. Louis-Chicago contract airmail route, or the C.A.M. # 2 line. The Post Office had handed its reins over to private industry when Congress passed the Air Mail Act of 1925, better known as the Kelly Bill, which authorized the awarding of contracts to air operators who won bids to fly the C.A.M. lines. Operators earned government subsidies of about $3 per pound of mail carried. On April 13, 1926, Charles stood before a notary public and signed the Certificate of the Oath of Mail Messengers; two days later he inaugurated Robertson's airmail service, flying reconfigured war surplus de Havilland planes, or DHs.[16]

Flying C.A.M. # 2, Lindbergh gained the skills needed for his future record-breaking flights, but the monotony and routine began wearing on him—flying the same route every week, five round-trips from St. Louis to Chicago—and he turned his mind to new challenges. In the fall of 1926, while flying the route near Peoria, Illinois, Lindbergh had a "vision born of a night and altitude and moonlight"—a solo flight across the North Atlantic.[17] In 1926 the most formidable challenge facing aviators was a nonstop flight across the North Atlantic between New York and Paris, a feat so improbable that the $25,000 Orteig prize for this flight, established in 1919, still lay uncollected. Teams of well-known, experienced airmen, armed with substantial financial backing, clamored to take the award. It was a high-stakes game, and with the odds heavily stacked against them, many aviators would perish in their quest.

Aviators had crossed the Atlantic previously. The first to accomplish the feat was Lieutenant Commander Albert C. Read, who with his crew hopped from Newfoundland to the Azores, and then to Portugal in May 1919 in an NC-4, a U.S. Navy Curtiss flying boat. One month later, two British pilots, Captain John Alcock and Lieutenant Arthur W. Brown, walked away with the London *Daily Mail*'s £10,000 prize after flying a twin-engine Vickers Vimy bomber nonstop 1,900 miles from Newfoundland to Ireland. In April 1924 the U.S. Army launched four Douglas World Cruiser biplanes from Seattle, two of which successfully circumnavigated the globe; the 26,345-mile epic flight took 175 days to complete.

In Europe, meantime, aviators were making marathon overland flights. An Australian crew consisting of Captain Ross Smith, his brother Keith, and two mechanics took off in November 1919 in a Vickers Vimy from England to Australia, competing with four other aircraft for a £10,000 purse to be awarded by the Australian government. Twenty-eight days later, the Smiths landed at the coastal city of Darwin, the only plane to reach Australia. Captain Smith had served as Lawrence of Arabia's pilot, and his desert flying experience had stood him in good stead on the backbreaking flight. The other contenders met dismal fates. Two aircraft crews died in accidents, another crash-landed in Crete, and the fourth set down in Yugoslavia, where its crew was promptly arrested as Bolshevik spies. By the mid-1920s, British, French, Dutch, and German airmen had started to pioneer routes to Burma, South Africa, Persia, and Peking.

Yet these flights paled in comparison to the supreme challenge the Orteig purse presented: 3,600 miles across the ocean. The first to try for the Orteig prize was France's World War I ace René Fonck. In September 1926 he took off from New York with a four-man crew, flying a Sikorsky-designed S-35 overloaded with thousands of pounds of fuel. Staggering into the air, the three-engine craft cartwheeled over the runway and exploded, killing two crew members.

Charles, however, had in his arsenal some 1,800 logged flight hours and experience flying the mail, day in and day out, in weather so marginal that other pilots rarely attempted leaving the ground. Unlike them, he knew how to fly "blind," using instruments, but no outside visual references. With good equipment, he considered a transatlantic flight "less hazardous than flying mail for a single winter with our Liberty-powered DHs." And in contrast to the pack of pilots vying for the prize, he would fly solo in a single-engine airplane, without a crew and their "quarreling." He used his $2,000 life savings toward the purchase of a plane and began to look for sponsors. By Christmas of 1926 he was searching for an airplane he would name for his financial backers in St. Louis, Missouri, the *Spirit of St. Louis*. By late April he had made the maiden flight in the new silver-colored monoplane, built to his specifications in sixty days by the Ryan Aeronautical Company in San Diego at a cost of $10,580. The Department of Commerce licensed the *Spirit* as N-X-211, the "N" representing an aircraft of U.S. registry and the "X" its experimental status. Although a small plane—twenty-seven feet, eight inches long with a forty-six-foot wingspan—it weighed two and a half tons with its five fuel tanks fully loaded. It was powered by a 223-horsepower Wright Whirlwind J-5C radial engine, the most reliable at that time. Inside the small cockpit Charles sat on an inflatable air cushion placed above a rock-hard, brown wicker seat, sandwiched between the instrument panel and a rear compartment. He had no forward visibility, having sacrificed a front window for a fuel tank, and either used a periscope to see out, or turned the plane to see where he was going. Slightly unstable, because he traded some lateral stability for better cruise efficiency, the monoplane was a tough bird to fly, requiring constant attention. One pilot who later flew a replica of the plane described it as a "high-workload airplane that never allows you to relax."[18]

Meanwhile, other Atlantic contenders met with disaster in April. A Fokker piloted by Commander Richard Byrd crashed on its first trial flight, Clarence Chamberlin damaged his Bellanca on takeoff, and Noel Davis and Stanton Wooster died after their *American Legion* crashed during a test flight. In early May two French aviators, Charles Nungesser and François Coli, disappeared over the Atlantic while flying toward New York in their Levasseur biplane *L'oiseau blanc* (The White Bird). Last spotted over Cherbourg, they were never seen again. Nonetheless, "Atlantic fever" continued to rage on both sides of the ocean.

On the afternoon of May 10 Lindbergh sped out of San Diego in the *Spirit,* stopped in St. Louis, then landed at Curtiss Field on Long Island, New York, on May 12. His record-breaking flight across the country was clocked at twenty-one hours and twenty-one minutes. Whereas a small group of reporters had milled around watching his San Diego takeoff, hundreds awaited his New York landing. A mob of media men pounced on Lindbergh, whom they dubbed the "Kid Flyer," "The Flying Fool," and the "Human Meteor." Amazingly photogenic, he also provided good copy: a bashful mail pilot, twenty-five-year-old Minnesota farm kid, and dark horse in the race who dared to fly the Atlantic alone. The media attention alarmed his mother, who arrived in New York on May 14, visiting for one day to reassure herself about her son's unfolding epic flight. When reporters swooped down on her and asked her to kiss Charles for a photograph, she refused, but the next day one newspaper ran a fake composite picture of the two embracing. She and her son had simply shaken hands when she departed, their usual custom.

Foul weather delayed Lindbergh's departure to Paris. But when a high-pressure system began to build over the Atlantic, he readied to leave the next morning. On May 20, 1927, at 7:52 A.M., the *Spirit of St. Louis* rumbled into the air over muddy, rain-soaked Roosevelt Field, barely clearing telephone wires. Hundreds cheered the sight captured on Movietone newsreels. Heading out, Charles tracked an east-northeast course of 065 degrees for the first hundred miles, then turned toward Newfoundland along a land-hugging route. Over St. John's some twelve hours after takeoff, he dove his plane and waggled his wings to alert people of his whereabouts. From there he turned east toward Ireland, 1,900 miles away over bleak, cold seas with no land in sight. Meanwhile, Americans held their collective breath, waiting, and praying for his success.

Blazing across the North Atlantic Ocean, he battled wing and engine carburetor icing, electrical storms playing havoc with his compass, and fog and clouds forcing him to fly blind. But it was fatigue which almost proved his undoing; he hadn't slept the night before taking off. With the plane droning on and on, and with no landmarks to break the monotony, he nodded off for minutes at a time. So severe was his exhaustion that he later said he had seen semihuman ghosts, "emissaries from a spirit world" moving through the cockpit, telling him what to do.[19]

Twenty-eight hours after taking off from New York, the *Spirit of St. Louis* reached Dingle Bay, Ireland, just three miles off course and nearly three hours ahead of schedule. Soon within range of the English Channel, Lindbergh turned his thoughts to the pioneer airmen Louis Blériot and Otto Lilienthal, whose earlier flights had paved the way for his generation of aviators. Reaching Paris, Charles circled over the Eiffel Tower and flew north to Le Bourget aerodrome, where 150,000 people clawed at each other to catch a glimpse of history in the making. Looking up, the crowd heard a rumble, the silver *Spirit* appeared over Le Bourget, and like a gilded moth descended into a blaze of bright headlights. After thirty-three and a half nonstop hours, he landed at 10:22 P.M. Paris time, and 3,610 miles from New York, on May 21, 1927. Startled, he watched the screaming, seething crowd rush toward the *Spirit,* and he eased the plane into a gentle ground loop, holding full rudder in to force a turn and stop the plane, since it had no brakes. When he pushed himself out of the cockpit he heard a "sickening noise," people tearing fabric from the plane's fuselage; souvenir hunters added to Lindbergh's dismay by stealing his flight log, too.

The next morning Charles awoke in the American Embassy an international hero. Across the globe, newspapers made his flight front-page news, and hysterical adulation broke loose. Parisians went wild honoring Lindbergh, latching onto him like a long-lost savior. They had lost Nungesser and Coli, but now they had him; it was a divine act some said, proving that their countrymen's quest had not been in vain. He gave his first speech at the Aéro Club of France, surrounded by fifty of France's leading aviators. In the audience sat Louis Blériot, the first man to pilot a plane across the English Channel, but Alberto Santos-Dumont, the first to fly in France, was ill in a Swiss sanitarium, and he sent his regrets, weeping as he scrawled his message. After more banquets, honors, and awards, Lindbergh traveled to Belgium and England, receiving a hero's welcome on par with that of Paris.

But with fame came a loss of freedom. President Coolidge wanted the hero at home, and he ordered a U.S. Navy cruiser, the U.S.S. *Memphis,* to steam toward Cherbourg to transport him and the dismantled, crated *Spirit* back to America, ending his dream to continue flying around the world. On the afternoon of June 11, the *Memphis* steamed up the Chesapeake Bay, escorted by a convoy of four destroyers. Two U.S. Army blimps floated serenely overhead, and forty planes soared high, dipping wings and diving, welcoming Charles Lindbergh home. His mother joined him for celebrations in the capital city. Praised as "the ideal mother" who had "allowed her son to shape his own destiny," she had already turned down a six-figure movie contract.[20] That same day, more than 250,000 people jostled in stifling heat behind police barricades in Washington to cheer Charles. There President Coolidge awarded him the first Distinguished Flying Cross and announced his promotion to colonel in the United States Reserve Corps.

Offers worth millions of dollars would come Charles's way within the first month of his return, and Dwight Whitney Morrow, whom he met in Washington the night of his homecoming, acted as his financial advisor until he left J. P. Morgan in the fall to become ambassador in Mexico.

Lindbergh-mania continued throughout the country. Four million people lined the streets of New York City for his ticker tape parade, and when he later flew the *Spirit* to St. Louis, a throng of 500,000 cheered him in another parade, this one along a seven-mile stretch. Back in New York, Charles holed up at Falaise, Harry Guggenheim's twenty-six room mansion on Long Island, where, over three weeks, he wrote *"WE,"* his first autobiography. On July 20 he climbed into the *Spirit of St. Louis* to begin a three-month flight tour sponsored by the Guggenheim Fund to promote "popular interest in the use of air transport." The 22,350-mile circuit covered eighty-two stops in forty-eight states and drew an estimated thirty million Americans, about one-quarter of the population.

This extensive travel only whetted his appetite for another trip in the *Spirit,* one more long-distance, nonstop flight before he retired the plane. Out of the blue, an opportunity opened up when Ambassador Morrow asked him to make a goodwill flight to Valbuena Airport in Mexico City to help cement the precarious relationship between the two countries. As soon as Mexico's President Plutarco Calles extended the formal invitation, he prepared to leave. On December 13, 1927, the *Spirit of St. Louis* sloshed through mud at Bolling Field in Washington, hopping over puddles before lifting into the air shortly after noon. The next day, as the sun beat brightly upon a crowd of 150,000 spectators, a tired Charles landed at Valbuena Airport, twenty-seven hours and fifteen minutes after launching. One week later, while a guest of Ambassador and Mrs. Morrow at the American Embassy, he met their daughter Anne Spencer Morrow.

3

A Whirlwind

An aviator never forgets her first flight, when a new dimension unfolds below and above. On the morning of December 26, 1927, Anne Morrow was sitting in a silver-colored Ford trimotor, NC-1077, listening to its engines gunned for takeoff. When the plane lifted into the air over Mexico City, Anne shook with joy. Looking below, she eyed the shimmering metropolis and a patchwork of brown and pale green fields. As the plane ascended slowly above the high-altitude city, Anne left her rear wicker seat and moved forward in the cabin, watching Charles Lindbergh pilot the trimotor, one hand on the wooden control wheel while he scanned outside. On her first flight she had fallen in love with flying and with the handsome man flying the plane.

On December 21, only five days before her first flight, Anne had moaned about having to meet Charles. "All this public hero-stuff breaking into our family party," she complained to her diary. How could "Lindy"—the "baseball-player type . . . not at all 'intellectual' and not of my world at all"— possibly fit in with her scholarly family? Yet that same evening when she first saw him, her heart raced. Dressed in evening wear, he stood in a reception line atop the American Embassy's red-carpeted steps, leaning his lanky frame against a stone pillar. Tall and vibrant, with a "refined face" and fair coloring, he wasn't the grinning thrill-seeker she had expected, or the man the media portrayed. When Anne's mother stepped forward to introduce her daughters, Charles turned to Anne, and without a smile, bowed and shook her hand. He was so unlike the college boys she knew and deserved the hero worship heaped on him, she wrote a few days later.[1]

While staying with the Morrows at the invitation of Anne's father, Charles came to relish the close-knit family and its pretty daughters. One excursion, on Christmas afternoon, found the Morrows, Evangeline Lindbergh, and Charles poling through the floating gardens of Xochimilco on a covered barge; although Anne thought he might prefer solitude, he had jumped at the chance to join the family. When the Morrows threw a Christmas Eve dinner party, though, both Charles and Anne seemed befuddled: while looking for their place cards at a table festooned with poinsettias and candles, they bumped into each other, blushing and stammering apologies. After dinner Anne danced to Spanish music and a Virginia reel, whirling around with a red carnation in her hair and a mantilla and a shawl, until she saw Charles eyeing her. Embarrassed, she pulled the carnation out of her hair. "She should have been born in Spain, shouldn't she?" an onlooker asked Charles, who mumbled a yes.[2] Hearing this, Anne nodded and retreated into silence for the rest of the evening.

Her quiet demeanor impressed Charles. Even though she seemed to stand in a "shadow thrown by the sparkling vivacity of her older sister, Elisabeth," he would write years later, he most remembered that Anne didn't make small talk the way other girls did. But Elisabeth's good looks and charm appealed to him, too. Always at ease with men, she flirted with Charles, while Anne, who stumbled trying to talk to him, found herself falling into an "*odious* envy" of Elisabeth. After flying with Charles in NC-1077, Anne and her sisters had asked him if they could learn to fly. What man could ask for a better opening? Laying plans for a rendezvous, he promised to take them for another flight after he returned home.[3]

On December 28, a clear, cool morning, Charles shook his hosts' hands, fastened his leather helmet, and clambered into the cockpit of the *Spirit of St. Louis*. The little plane rumbled down the runway at Valbuena Field at

6:35, and Anne looked up as Charles waggled his wings in a final salute, steering the plane southward. On its last, long flight, the *Spirit* would make a two-month goodwill flight through Central America, Colombia, Venezuela, and the Caribbean, much of it territory over which no plane had ever flown. "My little embroidery beribboned world is smashed," Anne confessed to her diary after he left. She had known him only one week but in that time he had "swept out of sight" her "arty" male friends, and her "frivolous" world had come crashing down. Reminiscing about first meeting him, she later said, "He filled some kind of hunger in me to break out of the pattern which was neatly laid out before me." In December 1927, however, she still felt far too shy to think she stood a chance with him.[4]

In January 1928 Anne returned to Smith College to wrap up her senior year, and the magic of Mexico quickly evaporated. Reality continued to snake its way into the walled garden of her youth: that semester she would experience two traumatic events that subsequently gave her serious insomnia and "nights of terror."[5] The first event was the disappearance of Frances St. John Smith, an eighteen-year-old heiress worth $2 million in her own right, who as a lonely and alienated Smith freshman had been befriended by Anne. In mid-January Frances vanished from Smith's campus, leaving no note and her dormitory room window wide open. Within days, a wide search began for her, and reporters and detectives descended upon the campus, grilling Anne and other classmates. Characteristically, Anne blamed herself for not foreseeing Frances's disappearance. And though her distraught parents were certain that their daughter had been kidnapped, Anne and the police suspected otherwise. In June a boater on a nearby river found her decomposed corpse; the police ruled the death a suicide.

Around the same time, Anne's nineteen-year-old brother, Dwight junior, suffered his first serious bout of mental illness while a senior at Groton. He had become severely depressed, the result of a breakdown brought on by a manic episode a few months earlier. Of the family members, Anne would come to be the most sympathetic to his illness. Betty Morrow, then in Havana with her husband on a diplomatic trip, hurried home to Englewood, where she and Elisabeth nursed him for a month. He then departed for a short stay at Southern Pines, a resort-sanitarium in North Carolina. Few people were aware of the boy's troubles, but Charles Lindbergh stopped by Englewood to cheer him up. It also gave him a chance to see Elisabeth, who invited him to later visit the family's new summer mansion in North Haven, Maine. Upon hearing that Charles had seen Elisabeth at Englewood, Anne again lost hope. She was certain he had stopped by solely to see her sister, and she lamented that he would "get on with Elisabeth and avoid me."[6]

With spring and her graduation nearing, however, Anne's spirits lifted and she focused on writing. She wanted to win the Mary Augusta Jordan Prize, awarded by Smith for the most original work of prose or verse. But Anne was a perfectionist who carefully crafted each and every word, and her struggle with writing persisted well into her career. She dragged her feet preparing for the Jordan Prize, dismissing her "vain ambitions to work for it or to expect it." Mina Curtiss, her writing instructor, encouraged her to enter the competition. Writing a book review in March, Anne "*writhed* and *agonized*" over her inarticulateness. "I could not write decent English and didn't know the meaning of words," she confessed to her diary. Only months later, by the end of her senior year, Anne's hard work came to fruition. She was awarded the Jordan medal and the Elizabeth Montagu Prize for the best essay, "Women in Dr. Johnson's Time." The awards delighted her family. "You'd think I'd given birth to triplets," wrote Anne of their reaction.[7]

Filling her time between school projects was her new obsession with flying—and with Charles Lindbergh. She pored over aviation magazines and in Northampton went to see a popular newsreel: "Forty Thousand Miles with Colonel Lindbergh." When she wasn't dwelling on the Colonel, she wrote emotional letters to her sisters. To Elisabeth she wrote that she wanted to "go to Germany this summer if I thought we could *really* learn to 'glide'. . . . But I am afraid it is entirely outside of my world."[8] Nonetheless, Anne's blossoming confidence won out, and she took three flights at a local field near Smith. The simple fact that she alone had arranged the flights thrilled her.

If Anne had knowledge of women aviators at the time, she did not mention them in her diary. Few women piloted planes then, but those who did received press coverage—especially if they crashed. (Following Laura Bromwell's 1921 death in the crash of a Curtiss Canuck biplane, the public outcry led to a *New York Times* editorial defending women's right to fly.) Female barnstormers in particular enjoyed attention. In the 1920s Mabel Cody ran her own flying circus, stunting as a wing walker and transferring from a car to a plane at high speeds. Phoebe Fairgrave could not find a willing flight instructor—a perennial problem for women—so she purchased her own plane, asked an airman named Vernon Omlie to train her, and then took up parachute jumping and other stunts to pay her expenses. She, too, formed a flying troupe, and after marrying Omlie, the two barnstormed together until earning enough money to open a flying school in Memphis. Bessie Coleman, the world's first licensed black aviatrix, learned to fly in France, because American flying schools refused to teach her. Like Fairgrave, she wanted to open a school and an aviation business, and used barnstorming as a means to achieve it. At the height of a successful career, while practicing for an air show in 1926, she fell to her death when her plane flipped over in midair.

When Amelia Earhart rose to prominence in the late 1920s, women pilots gained more attention. In June 1928 Earhart crossed the Atlantic by air, the first woman to do so. Although a licensed pilot at the time, she flew as a passenger in a Fokker trimotor plane owned by heiress Amy Phipps Guest, whose family had refused to let her make an Atlantic crossing. Amy insisted a woman replace her and formed a committee headed by publisher George Palmer Putnam to find a surrogate. In stepped Amelia, whose blonde hair, boyish figure, and tall, slender frame made her look like a female Lindbergh. Upon landing in Wales, "Lady Lindy" claimed she had been nothing more than mere "baggage" over the seas, and her modesty endeared her to millions.[9] Abroad and stateside, she became a heroine and would soon begin making record-breaking flights herself. Just over a year later, she and Anne would become friends, joined together by their common love of aviation.

After graduating from Smith with honors, Anne was at loose ends, questioning where her future lay. Like her mother before her, she wanted a writing career and returned to her family when college ended. She joined the Morrows at their new summer estate in Maine, while continuing to fret about Charles Lindbergh, who had yet to honor his promise to take the Morrow girls on another flight. He told them to expect him in June, but rain and fog forced his plane down, news that left the entire Morrow family brooding and discouraged. He called to reschedule a flight, but instead visited Elisabeth in New York.

Hearing this, Anne was crestfallen. Trying to hide her disappointment, she joked with Constance about an elaborate and inevitable wedding between the Colonel and Elisabeth. By this time, the press, too, was forecasting their imminent engagement. Whether Charles romanced Elisabeth in New York is subject to speculation, as is the depth of his infatuation with her. She was a beautiful woman who dressed in the latest styles, and her wit dazzled her suitors. On the other hand, her childhood illness had left her sickly; she suffered relapses that required bed rest and that would worsen in time. If Charles had strong feelings for her, he had buried them by the fall of 1928 during what he called his "girl-meeting project."[10]

Twenty-six years old and lonely, with no one to share his life, Charles wanted to marry, and he needed a strong wife beside him as a companion and to bear his children. Decades later, while reminiscing about his wife selection process, he wrote that he had looked for a healthy woman. In addition, she had to like flying "because I would take her with me on the expeditions I expected to make in my plane. That ought to be great fun." Anne Morrow was such a girl. She returned to Englewood in the fall, and Charles laid plans to meet her: First, he would invite her to go flying, a surefire way to entice girls, according to his fellow barnstorming pilots. A ground date would soon follow, if all went as planned. In early October he telephoned Anne with the invitation. She was flabbergasted at his offer, but stammered that she would love to go. She then cautioned Constance, "Please don't write Mother that I might go up with Colonel L . . . she might telegraph me not to go!" Their father didn't want further publicity, and Anne was afraid the press would report another rumor about Charles and Elisabeth.[11]

Charles carefully arranged details of the flight, planning every move to seduce Anne. He dropped by Englewood to "settle a few points" about the forthcoming flight. What type of plane would you like to fly in? he asked her. "An open one!" she cried. Charles had chosen Falaise, a close friend's Long Island estate, as the backdrop to the first flying date on October 15. Owned by Harry Guggenheim, a World War I pilot and a son of Daniel Guggenheim, it came complete with a twenty-six room Norman mansion featuring an enclosed cobblestone courtyard, a round tower, and steeply pitched roofs. Tucked inside the manor were sixteenth- and seventeenth-century antiques, sculptures, and Renaissance paintings, while outdoors peacocks strutted across a lush lawn. Anne would later gush about Falaise and Charles's "poise of centuries of luxury."[12]

From a horse pasture at Falaise, Anne and Charles took off in a silver de Havilland Moth plane, the "kind that Lady Somebody flew to South Africa," Charles told Anne. (That "Lady Somebody" was Lady Mary Bailey, daughter of an Irish peer, who flew solo in a Moth from England to South Africa in 1928, setting a female distance record of 8,000 miles.) In a log entry dated October 15, 1928, Charles scratched in Anne's first training flight, which ran a total of fifty-five minutes. Like most first-time students, Anne was heavy handed with the flight controls during the lesson, pushing the plane across the sky as if it were a "stubborn elephant." But the flying was "glorious," and after spending the day with Charles, she found him "kind and absolutely natural." Charles, meanwhile, was thoroughly enchanted with Anne, and after she told him she wanted to learn to fly, he grinned. They were both comfortable with each other, and their mutual physical attraction was giving rise to a growing sense of intimacy.[13]

The whirlwind had begun—a blur of flying, romance, and adventure. On October 18, only a few days after Anne's first training flight, Charles put her and Jo Graeme, Betty Morrow's secretary, into a Ryan Brougham plane and flew them from Teterboro Airport over the Jersey coast to Long Island,

and returned to Teterboro. As the plane barreled through fog and cottony clouds and skimmed over treetops, Anne and Jo squealed with delight. The press was hot on their trail, however, having seen them at the airport. Back at Englewood, reporters milled around, trying to sniff out which Morrow girl had gone flying with America's most eligible bachelor. The Mexican press added fuel to the fire by reporting that Charles's flying date was Elisabeth, who was then abroad. "It wasn't Elisabeth, it was Anne—isn't it funny," Ambassador Morrow and his wife joked to the embassy staff. The news spread like wildfire through Mexico City, and her parents' indiscretion infuriated Anne, who recoiled at the publicity.[14]

The evening of October 18, Charles returned to Englewood, concerned about the press dogging Anne. After supper, the countryside thick with a dense fog, he and Anne drove around in his black Franklin sedan and shared intimate conversation. Charles talked optimistically about aviation linking nations, and Anne told him she wanted a literary career. To her amazement, he replied that he wished he could write. As the hours-long drive came to a close, Charles turned to Anne and asked her to marry him. Astonished, she thought he was teasing her, but when he reaffirmed his proposal, she accepted at once, and they vowed to tell no one until he spoke to her parents in Mexico City. Anne returned to the embassy there, awaiting his arrival. Oddly, she deleted any mention of his proposal in her published diaries, though she did write about the drive and their conversations.

On November 9, 1928, Charles landed his blue and orange Curtiss Falcon biplane at Valbuena Field in Mexico City. The next day he accompanied the Morrows to Casa Mañana, the family's vacation retreat in Cuernavaca, fifty miles south of Mexico City. This small estate featured adobe bungalows with red-tiled terraces and roofs, set amid terraced gardens of oleander, heliotrope, banana trees, blue plumbago, and datura, and it had come to be Dwight Morrow's favorite hideaway. There Charles told Anne's parents he wanted to take their daughter as his wife.

"I think that I can never be surprised again," Mrs. Morrow confided to her diary that same night. "I am stunned." No husband was good enough for his daughters, and Dwight Morrow grumbled to his wife, "What do we know about this young man?" Though not opposed to the match—he had earlier described Charles as a "wonderful boy"—he urged the young couple to postpone the engagement announcement. They needed time to better know each other, he said. Charles agreed, and fearing publicity, he suggested they keep the news a secret from all but a few close friends and relatives. Even Anne's siblings would be told only weeks before the official announcement.[15]

Of further concern to Ambassador and Mrs. Morrow was their future son-in-law's profession, since pilots lived perilous lives at the time. How would their daughter cope with her life as an aviator's wife? Anne's aunt, Mrs. Jay J. Morrow, had earlier told reporters if Colonel Lindbergh wanted to marry a Morrow, "he'd have to give up flying." Certainly, Charles was aware of their fears, and during his two-week stay in Mexico, he tried to allay Mrs. Morrow's anxieties about flying by taking her aloft for one hour over the volcano Popocatépetl. Anne, too, flew with him in the Falcon for her second training flight. Circling to 17,000 feet over the snow-capped volcano, she found flying easier, the plane now obeying her. In a letter to Constance she described flying over pine trees and craters while marveling at the scenery.[16]

One month later, in December, the Morrows left Mexico for Englewood and their recently completed mansion. In a play on the surname Morrow (as she had with Casa Mañana) Betty dubbed the new estate Next Day Hill. The red-brick, twenty-four-room Georgian residence, built by European craftsmen at a cost of $400,000, included a cathedral-like formal library with thousands of books and a morning room. A staff of twenty-nine servants—chauffeurs, valets, maids, private secretaries, and cooks—tended to the Morrows' needs. Boosting the cost by another $225,000 were the furniture and the landscaping of its seventy-five acres of wooded property. On New Year's Eve the family threw open the doors for a housewarming, receiving nearly a thousand guests.

Although Americans were at the forefront of pioneering flight in the early twentieth century, the birth of commercial, or civil, aviation took place in postwar Europe. Visionaries there saw an immediate use for the thousands of available war surplus planes: providing transportation over bombed-out rail networks as well as the bodies of water that separated countries. Furthermore, several European nations governed far-flung colonial outposts and foresaw a day when aircraft could cover much greater distances, linking colonies to the motherland. By the mid-1920s, seventeen European nations offered some sort of air service, a phenomenal growth that was often boosted by hefty government subsidies. Meanwhile, back in the United States—the country that had given the world flight—civil aviation languished. The public and the government remained skeptical of its benefits, given the country's excellent rail network, which boasted inexpensive transportation that offered coast-to-coast service in seventy-two hours. That, combined with the public's and the government's aversion to granting subsidies, along with the scarcity of larger-sized, passenger-carrying planes in the United States, led to a general disinterest in developing commercial aviation.

Fortunately, not all Americans were shortsighted when it came to aviation. In 1918 the U.S. Post Office's airmail pilots began service between New York and Washington. Gradually, routes were added using relays of airmen; they flew DH-4s during daylight hours and navigated by "iron compass"—railroad tracks. In February 1921 they added night flights, sometimes navigating by bonfires lit by appreciative townspeople. A few years later, some airmail routes were operating twenty-four hours straight, complete with flashing beacons, weather-reporting stations, and a network of emergency fields positioned along the courses. These advances had come at a great cost, however: during the time the Post Office provided aerial service, forty-three pilots died in crashes and another twenty-three suffered critical injuries.

As revenues increased, railroad companies became uneasy about the government's role in transporting mail. Political pressure resulted in Congress passing the Air Mail Act of 1925, which turned over the service to private industry. The legislation opened the contract airmail routes to competitive bidding by airlines, also known as operators, whom the government paid to fly the mail. As a result, the Air Mail Act became the springboard America's fledgling airlines desperately needed. Early airmail players included Western

Air Express, National Air Transport, and Henry Ford's Ford Air Transport. Of Ford's contributions to aviation, the most famous were his all-metal trimotor (dubbed the "Tin Goose" by reporters, this was the type of plane that carried Anne Morrow aloft on her first ride) and his construction of the world's first concrete runway in Dearborn, Michigan, in 1926. Another early player was a little-known outfit in St. Louis, the Robertson Aircraft Corporation, whose pilot Charles Lindbergh flew the contract airmail route known as C.A.M. # 2.

Commercial aviation in the United States was finally beginning to catch up with that of Europe's. Still, the country lagged behind in passenger air transport until Charles Lindbergh's transatlantic flight in 1927, an event that served as a catalyst for the American aviation industry. Combined with a growing public interest in air travel, his flight spurred businessmen to heavily invest in the future of flying, and aviation stocks became a favorite of Wall Street. In one year, from 1928 to 1929, passenger traffic on American airlines more than doubled, from 60,000 persons to 160,000.

By 1929, Charles was working for both Pan American Airways and Transcontinental Air Transport (TAT) in the role of technical adviser. When hired by TAT in 1928, he received a signing bonus of $250,000 to use for the purchase of company stock, along with a promise of a $10,000 annual salary. From Pan Am, he earned the same yearly salary, and, similar to the arrangement he had with TAT, the right to purchase shares of company stock at below market prices. In addition, he acted as a consultant to the Pennsylvania Railroad, the Guggenheim Fund, and the U.S. government. Though he turned down many lucrative offers after his transatlantic flight, by 1929 Charles had earned over one million dollars from consulting work, royalties from *"WE,"* salaries, and investments.

Charles didn't squander his time and reputation, however. He took seriously his mission to lay the foundation for the commercial success of American aviation. He laid out air paths, advised on and tested new equipment, and helped establish a nationwide meteorological network. When he wasn't inaugurating international routes for Pan Am, he planned Transcontinental's domestic routes and operations. Historians would later call this era aviation's "golden age," or its "wild west" phase. It was a heady time in which the sciences of aerodynamics and meteorology came into their own, and Lindbergh played a key role in their development.

While airline business occupied Charles's time, Anne had returned to Mexico City, where she assumed the role of a jittery bride-to-be. "I went through such agony of indecision before I married Charles," she later confided to a friend, "that I sometimes think I learned everything there was to learn in those months." She realized the marriage could be fraught with problems because of their diverse backgrounds and different outlooks on life. She and Charles shared few interests apart from aviation. How could he possibly appreciate the subtle humor of the *New Yorker* or converse with her sophisticated friends? In what she later described as "weariness and anger," she snapped to her mother, "I wish the man had never crossed my horizon!" Her mother responded, "That is only because you are tired of the conflict." Anne was "not only tired of it," she remembered, she was "afraid of it and afraid of life." After much deliberation, Anne decided to discard the "nice comfortable box"—the security she could expect from marrying someone in her social set. Putting aside a rational approach to the marriage, she determined to marry Charles because he was "real life, like pure sunshine or pure fire."[17]

At four in the afternoon of February 12, 1929, reporters lined the embassy office in Mexico City, where Ambassador Morrow, his face lit with pleasure, announced his daughter's engagement. The press went wild, broadcasting the news over the airwaves and in print. Charles encountered the media frenzy when he landed in Havana at 8:00 P.M., after opening the first airmail route between the cities of Belize and Havana. "I have nothing to say," he told reporters. His curt responses would continue to annoy newspaper correspondents, all of whom felt that as a public figure, he owed them more. Charles thought otherwise. Exasperated with the press before his engagement, he "found them next to impossible thereafter," he later wrote.[18]

In contrast, Anne, in Mexico City, had to deal with a deluge of congratulatory telegrams, letters, and presents. "Unlike most brides-to-be," she later wrote, "it was *I* who was congratulated, not he."[19] Thrust into the public eye, waiting for Charles to join her, Anne got a taste of her future life as Mrs. Charles A. Lindbergh. Reporters, with cameras and cars at the ready, stood watch at the embassy gates. They tried to bribe servants, printed false anecdotes, and at one point climbed the roofs of nearby buildings at Cuernavaca to photograph the couple.

Charles turned up in Mexico City the last week of February, flying a Travel Air plane from Texas. Just several days later, on February 27, he and Anne again made headlines when the plane, having lost a wheel on takeoff, somersaulted onto its back on landing, thirty miles northeast of Mexico City. Charles dislocated his shoulder, but Anne was unharmed. Wisely, Charles took Anne aloft the next day, before a fear of flying set in and she lost her confidence. Borrowing a Consolidated Fleet plane, with his arm in a sling, he took off on February 28 and logged four flights instructing her.[20]

Charles spent two weeks in Mexico, and he and Anne gloried in their time together. "He has come into the family so, and we have so many jokes and he and Elisabeth tease each other," Anne wrote to Constance.[21] He left to inaugurate another mail route, then returned to Mexico City in his Curtiss Falcon, and on April 4 treated each of the three Morrow girls to a flight. During the month of April Charles also firmed up plans for his future bride's continued flight instruction, paying $1,000 to become a charter member of the Long Island Aviation Country Club, a posh flying club at Hicksville, New York, near Roosevelt Field.

Favored by society types and well-known aviators, the club was modeled after European ones and was the first of its kind in America. Flying was fashionable, and the country club setting offered the best of all worlds, according to those who spread the concept in America. "In aviation, just as in other sports, such as yachting, golf and tennis, the place to develop one's game is at one's club," wrote aviatrix Ruth Nichols in the *Ladies Home Journal.* (She was one of several women pilots hired as regular contributors by national magazines.) Initiation fees and annual dues granted members the right to rent, for an hourly fee, any of the club's planes. Others hangared their own planes there, as Anne Lindbergh would in the early 1930s. When members weren't in the air, they sprawled in lawn chairs fronting the four-bedroom clubhouse, or dallied by the swimming pool or tennis courts. One long-time member, describing the club's first decades, said, "In those days people wore helmets and goggles and nice white linen suits. They talked aviation, drank beer and tea, and whatnot. There were a great many women pilots; it was just fun." In 1930 another club sprang up in Los Angeles, where Douglas Fairbanks and other high-flying movie stars took to the skies.[22]

Until the end of April, Anne remained in Mexico City, and, with her mother, rehashed plans for a small, private wedding ceremony. Charles had insisted on such a service, and he was working on other strategies to get the press off the scent. He hangared his Curtiss Falcon at a New York field because reporters assumed they would honeymoon by airplane, after they married in Maine. On May 18, he flew an amphibian to North Haven, Maine, with the Morrow women and Amey Aldrich, Betty's college class-mate, aboard. There he instructed Anne in water landings, after which the group quietly commemorated the anniversary of his Paris flight.[23] On May 22 they returned to Next Day Hill at Englewood, where a few days later the family celebrated Betty Morrow's birthday.

The following day, the Monday afternoon of May 27, 1929, Anne and Charles were married at Englewood. As twenty relatives and family friends looked on, Anne descended the stairs wearing a shoulder-length lace veil, a crème white chiffon gown run up by a local dressmaker, and blue heeled slip-pers; her bridal bouquet was made from flowers cut by her sisters the same morning. A minister officiated as Charles, wearing a blue business suit, slipped a ring made from gold nuggets onto Anne's finger. After refreshments of fruit-cake and punch, the newlyweds departed to start their honeymoon on the *Mouette*, a thirty-eight-foot motor cruiser anchored in the Long Island Sound.

That evening, several hours after the couple had left, Dwight's secretary announced the marriage. The plan had worked, and the press was dumb-founded. Reporters immediately began searching for the Lindberghs and dis-covered them one week later, cruising in the Sound. In one instance, photographers circled the *Mouette* in a speedboat for over six hours, rocking their cruiser. Two weeks after the wedding, the *New Republic* labeled their honeymoon a "game of hide-and-seek, with bride and groom trying to keep out of sight" as they attempted to avoid reporters and photographers; it was as if the couple had committed "murder instead of matrimony."[24]

By any standards, the three-week honeymoon on the *Mouette,* during which the Lindberghs ate canned goods and drank ginger ale, fell far short of the luxury their wealth allowed. Moreover, any of their friends would have jumped at the chance to provide the privacy of their opulent estates to the newlyweds. It is unclear why Charles chose such a honeymoon. Perhaps he wanted to prepare his wife for their forthcoming expeditions, when they would endure difficult conditions and rely only on each other, away from civilization. Yet other than the occasional "terrifying drone" of planes and boats hunting them, Anne would write that the honeymoon was "a great deal of fun."[25]

After their honeymoon ended, the Lindberghs settled into the Hotel Berkshire in mid-Manhattan, a temporary home. From here, Anne and Charles would go on to become one of America's most-loved couples. Together they would blaze air paths and break records while promoting aviation across the globe. Anne would fly more than 30,000 miles within the next year—and many more miles in following years. It was the beginning of an entirely new life for her—one of fame, adventure, and a conviction that she had at last joined the outside world.

4

The Good Ship Anne

On the morning of June 19, 1929, Anne and Charles Lindbergh made their first public appearance as man and wife, attending the Safe Aircraft Competition at Mitchel Field on Long Island, New York. This was by no means entertainment: Charles had turned up to test-fly entries in a Guggenheim Fund-sponsored contest awarding $150,000 for a "fool-proof" aircraft that would not spin when stalled.[1] Anne watched her husband, a contest judge and a Fund trustee, fly a Brunner Winkle Bird biplane, a craft so safe and maneuverable that she herself owned one by fall of the following year.

The competition at Long Island ushered in Anne's new role, that of accompanying her husband wide and far over the States and across continents. Writing to her mother about the contest, she said that they would rise at six and deal with "crowds, reporters, pictures, etc.—and we won't get back till after lunch; then to a conference. . . . It will all be quite an ordeal, but I don't mind." One week later Anne and Charles left New York, blazing their way across the country in a Curtiss Falcon biplane on a hectic two-week inspection tour, checking airfields and equipment for Transcontinental Air

Transport. The Falcon's open cockpit made this an arduous business. Flying long distances in most small planes is hard work, but even more difficult in the open, exposed to the elements. Winds lashed the Lindberghs' faces like fine wires. They were cold at altitude and hot near ground level, and air currents buffeted the lightweight plane from side to side. They dodged storm buildups, climbing above clouds or skimming over treetops close to the ground, and they made a dismal run through fog over the Allegheny Mountains, which early airmail pilots had dubbed the "aviator's graveyard," because of its storms and sudden unpredictable weather.[2]

At each of the eleven stops, the Lindberghs unbuckled their parachutes and hoisted themselves out of the tandem-seat cockpit to face a horde of journalists and hangers-on. Idolized by the public, they were quickly becoming America's golden couple. They made headlines whenever they flew, and articles described every move they made, every word they spoke, every item they wore. On all but a few flights, Anne appeared in knee-length dresses topped with a leather jacket, while her husband wore a suit and tie; on their heads were snug leather helmets.

Anne found she usually liked meeting everyone on the route, from mechanics to small-town folk. Once painfully shy, she was starting to shed her self-consciousness, taking on "poise and dignity," as she called it, in her new role as the hero's bride. Nonetheless, as the trip dragged on, occasions arose when spending time with people didn't sit well with her. She began to buckle under the ceaseless demands of journalists, radio announcers, and Movietone men who circled hungrily at the Lindberghs' public appearances. Worse, some determined reporters pretended they were airline officials to get comments from Anne, or invented stories to satisfy readers. It was a harsh awakening for such a private person as Anne, who later said that fame could be just as insulating as the "walled garden" of her youth. Exhausted, she wrote her sister Constance, "I have to keep *so* reserved and taut and on edge for pitfalls." And when she couldn't evade answering ridiculous questions, Anne put on a "Bright-Insane Smile."[3]

Charles, on the other hand, had developed a knack for handling fans and wasn't above being rude if necessary. Early in their courtship, he had cautioned Anne, "Never say anything you wouldn't want shouted from the housetops, and never write anything you would mind seeing on the front page of a newspaper." These were serious restrictions for a woman who from early childhood had wanted to write and who treasured the ability to communicate above all other skills. Regardless, Anne didn't write in her diary for three years after she married, and even her letters home were phrased cautiously. Deeply in love, and having left behind the "gentle life" as an ambassador's daughter, she was turning to Charles to lead her. "Charles is Charlemagne," she told her family, and she a "devoted page" to the knight. While it was probably not the best foundation for a marriage, Anne later wrote, "It was a role I could play until I grew up." And as time went by, she would become more independent.[4]

On July 7 the Lindberghs reached Los Angeles, having completed the tour, and Charles authorized Transcontinental Air Transport to begin its service, a combination air-rail link from New York to California. Because air travel at night was still perilous, passengers boarded night trains for portions of the journey. Passengers who ponied up $290 (about the cost of a new car) could hop from coast to coast in forty-eight hours by train and TAT's airliners—weather permitting, of course. With so many flights later grounded by fog, storms, and ice, airmen sarcastically labeled TAT "Take a Train."

On the morning of July 8 movie star Mary Pickford christened the *City of Los Angeles,* a TAT Ford trimotor plane, at Grand Central Air Terminal in Glendale, California. With the aplomb only "America's Sweetheart" could muster, Mary climbed a short ladder to the plane's nose, then swung a bottle of grape juice (Prohibition was still in force) on it. When the festivities ended, Charles prepared to inaugurate TAT's service from the West Coast. Made of Duralumin coated with corrosion-resistant pure aluminum, Henry Ford's state-of-the-art trimotor planes cost nearly $50,000 each, cruised at 105 miles per hour, and were equipped with three 400-horsepower Wasp engines. Whatever the hype about these modern airliners, the facts pointed to a downright uncomfortable and noisy ride for passengers. In those days planes weren't pressurized and flew at low altitudes in turbulent air, leaving queasy passengers reaching for sick bags—or gasping for air as they crossed high-altitude mountain ranges.

A white-uniformed attendant ushered ten passengers, including Anne— the only woman—aboard the trimotor, which was flown by Charles and a copilot. Hours later, after flying over desert and foothills, they stopped briefly in Kingman, Arizona, before heading east across the mountains to Winslow. This second leg lasted one hour and forty minutes, during which the attendant put a portable tray before each pampered passenger, serving a lunch of cold chicken or tongue, salad with sliced pineapple, cake, and hot coffee.[5]

Meanwhile, passengers traveling west were in transit to Winslow. The next day, Charles flew the westbound legs back to Glendale after taking on new passengers. One of the people on board was Amelia Earhart, who had been recently hired by TAT as an "assistant to the general traffic manager," her job to promote flying to women. It was the first meeting between Anne and Amelia, and the genesis of a friendship that continued until Amelia disappeared in the Pacific in 1937 during her attempt to fly around the world. In a letter to Elisabeth, Anne described Amelia as "*very* likable and very intelligent and nice and amusing."[6]

Despite the hullabaloo attending the inauguration of TAT, which was also known as the "Lindbergh Line," the public would shy away from flying across the country. Few people could afford the princely sum for a ticket, and they were afraid of flying. Within a short time, their fears proved justified. In September 1929 a TAT plane slammed into the Sierras, and in January 1930 a second TAT trimotor crashed in fog on a California beach and burst into flames. In both incidents, all aboard were killed.

On July 21, 1929, Charles and Anne left California, flying the Falcon. During their leisurely flight home, they stopped again in Winslow, where Anne's flight training started in earnest. She logged nine instruction flights of aerobatics and landings on a dry lake bed northwest of the city.[7] She learned dead reckoning navigation, calculating an estimated time of arrival based on the plane's ground speed while flying from one point to another. More important, in an era when flying was still mostly an art, Anne developed the intuitions needed for piloting: learning pitch angles and bank angles, getting a feel for differences in airspeed, and knowing when a stall was imminent.

The couple continued their homeward jaunt with photo flights over archaeological digs, canyons, and mesas in Arizona. When they weren't taking hundreds of photographs, they passed penciled notes back and forth in the Falcon cockpit, using slips of paper or writing in the plane's logbook. "Compass is completely out. Don't know where we are but I'm hopeful," wrote Charles in one entry. "Looks like Grand Canyon region. This compass says east," penciled Anne.[8] They playfully commented on the topography and their flights, and Anne penned ditties such as the following:

> When I first rode a Franklin with Gus
> I would shrink and silently cuss
> But now in a biplane
> When you can't see the sky plain
> I am feeling decidedly wuss.[9]

The trip was not without its dangers, of course. When landing in Columbus, Ohio, the Falcon turned and skidded after a main tire blew. After replacing the tire, the Lindberghs continued to Newark, New Jersey, where the plane ground looped a sharp, uncontrollable turn again, this time bending the propeller and damaging the wing. Charles downplayed the two accidents, telling reporters they were no worse than a car "skidding into a curb on a wet day and breaking a wheel."[10] Even so, the second incident grounded the plane until costly repairs were made.

No sooner had Anne and Charles returned to New York than they began another blur of air travel, taking two trips to Washington, D.C. at the invitation of President and Mrs. Hoover. From there they flew a Curtiss Robin plane to Cleveland, where they visited Grandma Cutter and Aunt Annie. "Grandma worships Charles, says, 'That boy lives in a higher plane' (no pun intended)!" Anne wrote home. Next, they stopped by Detroit, where they spent time with Charles's mother, Evangeline, and his uncle. During this first trip to her mother-in-law's home, Anne was impressed by her spunk and her "quick, sharp Irish wit," as well as her husband's playful and "small-boyish" manner when he was with his family. She admired their close relationship with Charles, whom they obviously adored. On the seventeenth of August, Charles, Anne, and Evangeline flew to New York, where Anne soon began a grueling schedule of flight instruction.[11]

On Friday morning, August 23, 1929, Anne made her first flight alone. A few days earlier she had received a student pilot's permit and now dressed the part of a true aviator, wearing riding breeches with black boots, white shirt and necktie, blue leather jacket, blue helmet, and brown kid gloves. Her husband stood nearby, watching her open-cockpit Curtiss Fledgling biplane rumble down the grass runway at the Long Island Aviation Country Club. As the engine surged and the plane's airspeed nudged higher, Anne gently eased back on the stick. She took the Fledgling to 500 feet, then entered a landing pattern. Minutes later, she made a perfect three point landing, the two main wheels and the tail skid touching down at the same time, while she flew at minimum airspeed, just above a stall. After two more short flights and successful landings, Anne closed the throttle and then climbed down from the cockpit.[12]

Charles darted to the plane, an ear-to-ear grin crossing his face. Anne had passed the first benchmark for a private pilot's license. The morning after her first solo, newspapers across the country ran the story with headlines such as "Bride Tries Lone Eagle's Realm." Over the last five days, Charles had put his wife through a nine-hour-and-twenty-minute course of flight instruction, rigorous by anyone's standards, whether male or female. But in an age when people frowned at women taking part in men's sports, the *Post Dispatch* claimed that the credit for Anne Lindbergh's solo success belonged to her husband: "When one recalls how few women are able to learn such a simple thing as driving an automobile from their husbands, with whom they are in other matters (with the possible exception of bridge) able to get along perfectly, one begins to suspect that as a teacher Lindbergh must have had unusual tact and patience." Either way, there was plenty of publicity: when the Lindberghs returned the following day to fly at the club, their two-and-a-half-hour session was cut short when a photographer's airplane persisted in buzzing their plane.[13]

Anne still was not keeping a diary, and her letters home frequently omitted details of her flight training. However, decades later she wrote that her marriage and her flying had made her more confident. Undoubtedly she was exhilarated after her first solo, yet she also may have been frightened, a not uncommon feeling among beginning students. Regardless, her husband was quite proud of what she had accomplished, and he would continue to celebrate her achievements in aviation and, later, in her writing career. Likewise, Anne strove to meet his expectations. "When Charles Lindbergh believed in you, you could do anything. His assurances made me try my hardest to rise to the occasion," she later told an interviewer.[14]

Two days after Anne's first solo, the Lindberghs flew a de Havilland Moth to the National Air Races, a blockbuster ten-day aviation fair in Cleveland, Ohio. Held annually, the races drew nearly 100,000 spectators who paid a dollar a day for the thrill of watching pilots compete for prestige and prize money as they stunted, sped around pylons, or crossed the finish line after long-distance flying contests. One of the biggest draws was Charles, who flew loops and barrel rolls with a team of Navy pilots called the High Hats. The event also included the first Women's Air Derby; sitting in the visitors' box, Anne and Charles saw the black-and-white checkered flag drop as the winner, Louise Thaden, screamed by in her Travel Air plane. After several accidents and one fatality, ten more women, including Amelia Earhart, would land their machines in Cleveland, ending the 2,800-mile course that had begun August 18 in Santa Monica. They were serious aviators, not the amateur "Petticoat Pilots" depicted by male journalists. When reporters asked Charles his opinion of the women's derby, he responded that he saw "no reason why women should not be successful transport pilots," the transport license being the highest commercial license granted at the time.[15] The male pilots fared worse than the derby women: five men died while flying a cross-country competition from Los Angeles, and at Cleveland another plane crashed and burst into flames, killing its pilot.

The National Air Races were considered a working laboratory because of their new and innovative planes, and they drew the industry's designers and engineers. There Charles met with Jerry Vultee, Lockheed Aircraft's chief engineer, to design a new airplane, a state-of-the-art, long-distance machine. While "pylon polishers" roared around the track, the two men scratched out specifications for a low-wing monoplane on hotel stationery.[16] Lindbergh's new plane would be built by late 1929 and was named Sirius, after the brilliant Dog Star in the constellation Canis Major.

Anne liked the autogyro and glider demonstrations, but overall she begrudged their week at the races, missing her family and their summer retreat in Maine. She, along with her mother-in-law, who attended two days, sat outside in heat and humidity and watched the stunts, including Charles's antics. Perhaps seeing him and others fly unnerved Anne, since she dubbed the races "deadly."[17] In any event, the next week she wrote her mother that Charles regretted having interrupted her vacation. To mollify her, he was making plans for a four-day visit to North Haven starting September 11.

First, however, an emergency cropped up. The Lindberghs sped westward in a Vega to Albuquerque, where Charles joined the search for a TAT airliner that had disappeared after takeoff. It was soon found in pieces: it had slammed against a mountain and there were no survivors. Distraught, Anne grieved for the victims and found the accident personally upsetting, triggering feelings of hopelessness she compared to those she felt during the search for Frances St. John Smith in 1928.

Nonetheless, another trip loomed, and the Lindberghs busied themselves in preparation. Beginning in late September, they would inaugurate the Pan American Airways airmail route to Paramaribo, Dutch Guiana, and inspect Caribbean air paths and ground stations. It would be Anne's first flight with Pan Am, which was on its way to becoming the most important and powerful airline in the history of American commercial aviation. Detractors later criticized Pan Am for its political influence and its decades-long monopoly over international routes. Over time, the airline came to be called the "Chosen Instrument" because of its close alliance with the U. S. government, and for many foreigners it was identified with the American flag fluttering atop overseas embassies. The fact is, however, that Pan Am laid the groundwork for America's overseas airways. Charles Lindbergh was instrumental in pioneering all its innovations, serving for forty years as adviser and technical consultant to the airline.[18]

It was on this survey flight that Anne first met Juan Terry Trippe, Pan Am's founder. Trippe was a former U.S. Naval Air Reserve aviator and a Yale University graduate who guided the airline for four decades, building an empire through both persistence and political sophistication. Husky and dark-haired with brown, almond-shaped eyes, he ran Pan Am like a private fiefdom, working secretively and leaving no paper records for its board. Trippe was born in 1899 and named for his grandmother's second husband, Juan Pedro Terry, whose father, a Venezuelan of Irish extraction, had made his fortune in Cuba. Trippe's parents were American-born; his father's forebears had settled in Maryland in 1663. He forever disliked his distinctive name, though its Hispanic origin eventually proved useful in his business dealings with Latin American power players.

Juan Trippe started his first aviation business with five war surplus Navy seaplanes in 1923, ferrying socialites to resort areas. His family and wealthy Yale colleagues—including Cornelius Vanderbilt Whitney, the only son of financier Harry Payne Whitney and Gertrude Vanderbilt Whitney, granddaughter of railroad baron Commodore Cornelius Vanderbilt—chipped in to fund the charter business. A year later it folded, and he moved on to merging an organization he had just founded, Eastern Air Transport, with Colonial Air Transport, a charter service based in New England. (On more than one occasion, Dwight Morrow helped him to secure a meeting with Second Assistant Postmaster General W. Irving Glover to discuss airmail contracts.) When internal feuding—Colonial's president thought Trippe too ambitious and fast-moving—led to his resignation eighteen months later, he again recruited his friends to form yet another new company: Aviation Corporation of America. More company mergers ensued, and at age twenty-eight, Trippe emerged as the president and general manager of Pan American. In January 1928 it carried its first passengers, who paid $50 for a one-way fare from Key West to Havana.

A month later, Trippe met Charles Lindbergh in Havana, one of the aviator's stops as he swung through Latin America and the Caribbean after leaving the Morrow family in Mexico City. The 9,000-mile course he blazed in the *Spirit of St. Louis* was the beginning of an air link between the northern and southern continents of the Western Hemisphere, and Trippe saw that Lindbergh could potentially play an important role in expanding Pan Am's reach. He tried to press Charles into a formal relationship with Pan Am, but the pilot remained noncommittal until 1929, when he signed on as a technical adviser. The airline, meantime, continued to successfully bid on foreign airmail routes. A superb lobbyist, Trippe had helped craft the Foreign Air Mail Act of 1928, legislation that awarded Pan Am a subsidy of two dollars a mile for routes such as the one the Lindberghs were opening from Miami to Paramaribo.

Anne and Charles flew to Paramaribo in a Sikorsky amphibian S-38. Of the many craft they flew, the Sikorsky looked the strangest. Its hull resembled a huge, elongated slipper, atop which sat two sets of wings, two engines, and twin tail booms, making it seem a mix of fairy tale and science fiction. Inside the luxuriously appointed cabin, passengers sat on one of two wicker chairs or on upholstered seats that paralleled the hull, as on a subway car. On September 22, 1929, the Lindberghs, a radio operator, and a copilot boarded the S-38 in San Juan, Puerto Rico. From there they began what would become a 7,000-mile loop around the Caribbean, the northern coastline of South America, and Central America, a tiring journey to sixteen nations in twenty days. In addition to inaugurating airmail routes, Charles would inspect the new radio equipment for communications between ground stations and aircraft. By its end, the survey flight would pave the way for Pan Am's commercial air routes to Latin America.

Juan Trippe and his wife Elizabeth "Betty" Stettinius Trippe, daughter of a former J. P. Morgan partner, joined the Lindberghs on the second day. At each stop the foursome deplaned looking as if they had stepped from the pages of a fashion magazine, like smartly attired socialites embarking on high adventure across the seas. The media added to the froth by billing their jaunt as an "air cruise." Anne wore a straw hat and pastel dresses, while her husband appeared in a gray business suit with tousled hair, his helmet clutched in his hand; Juan looked downright tropical, wearing a white linen suit and brown-and-white saddle shoes. Nonetheless, the schedule was arduous, with their awakening at five o'clock and flying until dark, after which they were fêted in "hot crowded rooms with champagne, roses, and long speeches," or paraded through towns' streets. Most of the fanfare and hysteria were accorded the Lindberghs. Not that the Trippes minded: Betty, a confident and extroverted woman, took the more timid Anne under her wing. Together they compared notes about the trip, wrote letters to their families, and enjoyed their roles as young matrons. "The Trippes have been such fun, and wear so well," Anne wrote her mother.[19]

Though Anne didn't crew on this Caribbean survey flight, it served as a diplomatic forerunner to the survey flights she and her husband later undertook. She worked hard as a goodwill ambassador—trying to bridge cultures, speaking French when needed, while adding a dash of élan and romance. She was constantly sent flowers, and people clamored to talk with her. It was not always pleasant: at a private dinner one reporter posed as a guest and engaged Anne in conversation, which was soon sold as an interview, even though most of it was "sheer rot," as Anne put it.[20] Still, the trip was successful and Anne's reassuring presence helped convince the public of the safety of air travel.

By the fifth of October, the Trippes returned to the States. The Lindberghs devoted the next five days to an aerial/archaeological exploration of the Yucatan peninsula, using Belize City as their base of operations. Joining them on the S-38 were two scientists from the Carnegie Institution. Anne, the only woman along, tramped around ruins and roughed it with other expedition members. They returned to Miami on October 10, having flown more than seventy-seven hours total since leaving San Juan.[21]

Returning to New York, the Lindberghs stepped up their search for a permanent home. They were still living in their suite in the Berkshire Hotel in New York, dropping by Next Day Hill in Englewood for weekend visits. But like many young wives, Anne wanted her own home—and she wanted to stay close to her family. Further, she needed a break from the peripatetic lifestyle she and her husband lived. In fall 1929, Anne wrote her mother-in-law that they were "terribly sick of hotels and the Berkshire and wanted to get some place, however temporary, of our own—where we could at least unpack and leave our things." Even though they had looked at apartments, she added that they "*hate living in New York.*" Her husband couldn't get "relaxation or isolation or exercises" living in an apartment, and the city's dirty air bothered them both.[22] Charles had left the Minnesota farm nine years earlier, but he missed country living and wanted any property they bought to include enough acreage to farm. (His first choice was to move back to Minnesota, but Anne nixed the idea.)[23] Living in the country brought its own set of problems, however. Having grown up with people around her, Anne didn't like the thought of living far removed from her family. She cringed at the possibility of people spying on them and felt more protected in an urban setting. By this time, she found their public life brutal and wearying, a never-ending circus where people openly violated their privacy. As she explained years later, "Life on the ground married to a public hero was a full-cry race between hunter and hunted. We were the quarry."[24] This vital, wealthy young couple had been forced into a semireclusive life.

More than a desire for a home preoccupied Anne. In the first week of November, her doctor confirmed that she was pregnant, news that surprised her because she did not "feel married," she told her family. Beset with nausea in the first months, she couldn't keep food down, and although Charles wanted a large family, he made few concessions for a pregnant wife, expecting Anne to accompany him during his trips. She would continue to fly throughout her pregnancy, but between October and January she logged only one hour of flight instruction, in a de Havilland Moth.[25]

By mid-November Anne felt well enough to have her long hair bobbed, after months of nagging from Charles. "Oddly enough, I like it *very* much and Charles *adores* it and says he'll never let it grow again," she told her mother. Even more odd, of course, was her saying that he controlled her hair length. Often she dressed to suit his tastes, and he wasn't above asking her to change outfits at the last minute. When Charles crooked his finger, Anne dutifully followed—in the first years of her marriage at least. He could be an

Flying this open-cockpit Curtiss Falcon in January 1930, Anne and Charles hopped across the country on an inspection tour for Transcontinental Air Transport. Lindbergh Picture Collection, Manuscripts and Archives, Yale University Library. Reproduced with permission.

autocratic, forceful man, as his children would admit. His daughter Reeve later wrote, "In his presence we became much more completely, and more perilously, alive." At the same time, there were ways in which their marriage could be considered liberating, and Anne would later write that her husband was more of a feminist than she. During one flight layover he told reporters that "woman's part in aviation will parallel that which she assumed with automobiles. There's no reason why she shouldn't have a place in the field." Unlike most men then, he encouraged his wife to participate in all his activities.[26]

Two days after spending Christmas with the Morrow brood at Next Day Hill, the Lindberghs departed New York in the open-cockpit Curtiss Falcon for yet another transcontinental hop: their newly built Sirius was ready at Lockheed's factory in Burbank, California. Across the country snow stretched out white beneath them. In the dead of winter, flying in the open plane, a freezing cold wind blasted them and coated their goggles with frost. Encased in bulky, fur-lined flight suits, helmets, gloves, arctic boots, and thick woolen socks, they looked like Eskimos, according to the press. (One reporter added that Anne's nose jutted like a "red grape" from the back cockpit.)

Before leaving, Charles had told Anne that three weeks on the West Coast was more than sufficient time to inspect and to test-fly the new plane. If all went as planned, they would return to New York in the Sirius, aiming for a transcontinental speed record. On Sunday, January 5, 1930, the Lindberghs arrived in Los Angeles, where they hangared the Falcon. The next day Anne and Charles took to the skies in the Lockheed Sirius for fifty min-utes: four test flights over Los Angeles. On her first flights in the black-bodied and orange-winged plane, Anne described the machine: "smooth as syrup and sensitively obedient." Its technology surpassed that of anything she had flown. Heralding unlimited possibilities, the dual-control plane could be flown from either cockpit and would eventually usher in a new world of long-distance flights around the globe. Wisely, Anne asked Charles to modify the

Sirius after the first flights. She wanted the comfort and easier communication an enclosed cockpit offered, having flown so often in open planes, exposed to the elements. Made of isinglass (a semitransparent material), the innovative sliding canopy was the first of its kind and completely covered the front and rear cockpits when fully extended. Although the cockpit design wasn't patented, it would come into common use.[27]

On long flights the Lindberghs wore electrically heated flying suits powered by a wind-driven generator: the unpressurized craft was extremely cold at higher altitudes. Much larger than the planes Anne had previously flown, the Sirius—which cost $22,000—had a wingspan of nearly forty-three feet and weighed 4,289 pounds empty, without a crew, baggage, and fuel.[28]

While waiting for the Sirius, the Lindberghs stayed with a business associate, Jack Maddux, and his wife Helen at their sprawling house at 49 Fremont Place in Los Angeles. Wiry and energetic, Jack had founded the Maddux Air Lines, a regional airline linking California cities that merged with TAT in 1929. (It was folded into Western Air Express in October 1930, which later became Transcontinental and Western Air, then TWA.) Jack, like many aviation pioneers, was a maverick. Fearless, self-made, and having little formal education, he moved forward with business ventures regardless of people's opinions. "The man who never made a mistake never done anything!" he wired a critic of his airline management. By contrast, Helen was a college graduate who stepped in to run her husband's various business interests when needed and was a pilot, too. She had a suave, polished manner; Anne described her as "keen" and "bright" and became fast friends with her and her young son Jack.[29]

During their first week at the Madduxes, the Lindberghs again saw Amelia Earhart, who had been staying at the Fremont Place home for the previous two months. Amelia and her secretary, Norah Alstulund, had traveled the West Coast on business for TAT, working out of what Amelia called her "itinerant office" of thirteen pieces of baggage, which included parachutes and emergency rations. On the other hand, the Lindberghs limited themselves to only one suitcase. When Charles saw Amelia's mountain of baggage, he asked: "And what might that be?" He then told Anne with a grin, "Don't you get any foolish ideas from this!" Amelia got a good laugh out of this and included it in an article she wrote. She and Norah soon departed, flying east in Amelia's newly purchased Vega. Amelia again made a favorable impression on Anne. "It startles me how much alike they are in breadth," Anne wrote when comparing Amelia to Charles. "She has the clarity of mind, impersonal eye, coolness of temperament, balance of a scientist . . . I like her."[30]

A study in opposites, Anne and Amelia differed in every way, including appearance, personality, and background. The daughter of an alcoholic railroad lawyer and a genteel mother, Amelia was forthright and brazenly independent. Amazingly photogenic, in contrast to Anne, whose pictures rarely did her justice, she cut a dashing figure with her short, tousled hair and rakish, masculine flying suits. Unlike the moneyed Lindberghs, Amelia had to support her record flight attempts, her business ventures, and her family with nonstop rounds of lecturing, working for airlines, and penning books and magazine articles. For a time she was aviation editor for *Hearst International-Cosmopolitan* magazine.

In 1929 Amelia helped found the Ninety-Nines, an international organization for women pilots named for its number of charter members. (In early 1930 the Department of Commerce listed only 138 licensed women pilots in the United States.) Anne didn't join the Ninety-Nines, or other professional women's organizations related to aviation or exploration. Perhaps she lacked the time to participate, as she later told Amelia (her hectic traveling schedule and family obligations would interfere with most memberships), or perhaps Charles discouraged his wife's involvement, or Anne was fearful of meeting their standards.

In a letter dated January 30, 1930, Amelia wrote to Anne: "Despite the pleasure it gave me to do so, I really shouldn't have visited the Maddux family at the same time as you and the Colonel. For I have been asked by *Cosmo* to write something of you for publication. I flatly refused at first, and then decided to check off the pros and cons (to you). . . ." She sent Anne a draft of the article, asking her to comment on its content. "I wish I could write adequately of you," she wrote, "but I have neither the skill nor, in this instance, an opportunity to do you justice." Whether Anne made changes to the draft or the galley proofs sent her in March is uncertain, but Amelia's article, titled "Mrs. Lindbergh," appeared in the magazine's July 1930 issue. About Anne,

Amelia wrote, "She is an extremely feminine, gentle person, essentially modest, totally lacking mannerisms, pretenses, superiorities." What particularly struck her were Anne's "pluck" and the "fine courage" with which she met "both physical and spiritual hazards with understanding." Amelia pointed out that, during their January visit with the Madduxes, Anne confided to her that she had wanted to learn to fly *before* she met Charles Lindbergh. About the famous couple, Amelia wrote that their "habit of doing everything together" impressed her. But their togetherness may have startled her, too. In 1930 the thirty-three-year-old Amelia was single and wrote to a friend: "I am still unsold on marriage. I think I may not ever be able to see it except as a cage."[31]

Hollywood stars and politicians also sought the Lindberghs' attention during the winter of 1930. On January 17 they dined at Pickfair, the eighteen-acre estate of Douglas Fairbanks and Mary Pickford, the movie stars who had founded United Artists. The popular humorist and social commentator Will Rogers, a Dwight Morrow and Lindbergh fan, also hosted the couple. Two years earlier, this promoter of aviation had greeted Lindbergh after his goodwill flight to Mexico City, having been invited by the canny Ambassador Morrow to win over Mexican politicians.

Never one to waste time when he could experiment with aircraft and champion aviation, Charles took up glider flying in California. The sport of motorless flying, or soaring, had gripped Germany after World War I, when the Treaty of Versailles severely curtailed German military air power and its development. In 1922 Hermann Goering, a World War I ace and later Hitler's Air Marshall, told Eddie Rickenbacker, America's top WWI ace and later chairman of Eastern Airlines: "Our whole future is in the air. It is by air power that we are going to recapture the German Empire."[32] By the late 1920s news of German record-setting soaring flights reached America, and San Diego, with its temperate climate and favorable terrain, emerged as western America's premier soaring spot. After taking instruction at a local glider training school, on January 19, 1930, Lindbergh soared along Point Loma's ridge

In January 1930 Anne soared in this Bowlus glider near La Jolla, California, and earned a glider pilot's rating, becoming the first woman and the tenth person awarded the first-class license. Lindbergh Picture Collection, Manuscripts and Archives, Yale University Library. Reproduced with permission.

in a Bowlus S-18 sailplane, earning the ninth first-class glider license in the States. After landing, he told reporters that he saw a great future for gliding because it was safe and cost less to train in than power flying.

Rather than idly standing by while her husband had fun, Anne, too, jumped on the bandwagon. To get the rust off her piloting skills, Charles first gave her instruction in a Curtiss Fledgling biplane, and she logged eleven flights totaling fifty minutes on January 27. Two days later, just after sunrise, Anne arrived at the training field accompanied by her husband, glider instructor Hawley Bowlus, Helen Maddux and her son, and a throng of glider enthusiasts. Her logged hours in airplanes stood her in good stead: in ten short flights she breezed through a primary course, towed behind a car in "Tillie the Toiler." (Beginner pilots trained in Tillie, a glider on which two wheels were mounted for landing on a dirt runway, to better get a feel for flight.) After quickly mastering the basics, Anne was deemed ready for a solo flight. She would launch from Mount Soledad, an 800-foot promontory just north of San Diego, close to the coastline. Within an hour, the news spread, and a mob of Movietone men, photographers, and reporters headed toward the site to see the Lone Eagle's wife fly.[33]

Early in the afternoon at Mount Soledad, Anne appeared, dressed in men's-sized, loose white coveralls, her hair secured with a wide white headband. Jittery, she calmed herself thinking about her many flying dreams: "The mountain is just the same, steep, way down, and you just flap and glide off."[34] As if from a huge slingshot, Anne's glider was catapulted into the air, pulled by a four-man crew who manned ropes attached to the craft's nose. The glider whooshed aloft, and Anne turned right and left, soaring six minutes over the cliff. She then glided down to a bean field beside the ocean and jumped from the glider, ecstatic with joy.

"Where did you come from?" demanded onlookers standing next to their cars, which were scattered helter-skelter along the highway.

She pointed upward, beaming with pride. Out of the crowd, a woman cried, "She's all right! She's all right! This little girl came all the way down from that mountain, and she's all right!" Flabbergasted, other passers-by stared at Anne and her craft.[35]

Whether it was whimsical or daring, Anne had shown her flying prowess and bolstered her ego with the flight. She was the first woman and the tenth American to earn a first-class glider pilot's license. Though she had been frightened right before her launch, she later wrote that she felt strong and invulnerable, and she never regretted or forgot the wonderful experience. It seemed to be a turning point in her flying career also, because she enjoyed the flight and the public recognition. The day after her flight, the *San Diego Union* headlined "Who Says Lindy's Wife Can't Fly?" and the *San Francisco Chronicle* ran a piece titled "Anne 'Lindy' Qualifies as Glider Pilot." The front-page article reported that "Mrs. Lindbergh's takeoff was as good as though it had been done by the Colonel himself," then noted her "perfect landing in a field beside the State highway."[36] Her flight also made the front page of the *New York Times*.

The Lindberghs' interest in gliding stoked the fever for soaring, and Anne's flight galvanized local and national female pilots into action. One local admirer was twenty-year-old Peaches Wallace, who held both a private pilot's license and a newly issued third-class glider pilot's license. A tall, athletic woman named for her father's favorite racehorse, Peaches was introduced to aviation in 1929 when she won a contest—open to unmarried women only—sponsored by the *San Diego Sun* and the Ryan Flying School; the prize was a complete flying course worth some $1,300. Inspired by Anne, she formed the first women's glider club in the West, the "Anne Lindbergh Gliders of San Diego." Elected honorary president of the club, Anne told newsmen that, though flattered, she didn't feel worthy of the tribute. Strapped for cash to buy a glider, the club held a benefit dance at the U.S. Grant Hotel on February 20. With their profits and donated funds, members purchased a Bowlus S-20 glider, which they dubbed "The Good Ship Anne." They asked Charles Lindbergh to fly its maiden flight, and on February 24, 1930, he would soar twenty minutes along Torrey Pines's cliffs.[37]

Earlier in the month, before Charles's flight in the S-20, the Lindberghs, Bowlus, and a cadre of glider aficionados escaped to the hills at Lebec, California, near the Tehachapi Mountains. During their week there, they tried to elude journalists, but again crowds pursued them; one flight was witnessed by thousands of people. Anne cooked meals, washed dishes, and overall, was a "smiling, helpful, but unobtrusive member of the camp," reported one woman journalist. She didn't fly gliders at Lebec, saying, "I wouldn't think of interfering in any way with the progress of the important experiments which are being carried on here."[38] In fact, she never had the opportunity to fly gliders again, although her daughter Reeve later said that her mother preferred soaring over any other flying—quiet and ethereal, it fascinated Anne. More than likely, Charles's glider flying also ended in 1930, since his logbooks didn't show any sailplane entries after that date.

It seemed an optimistic time for gliding and for aviation in general, and a February issue of the *Literary Digest* commented: "Among believers in the glider is the Detroit Aircraft Corporation, which predicts that by 1935 there will be 1,000,000 licensed glider pilots in the United States."[39] However, the euphoric forecast fizzled away in the face of the Great Depression: in the year following Black Tuesday, many factories would declare bankruptcy, never to open again. By 1933 one-third of the nation's work force was unemployed, and starving families groveled for food in soup kitchens, desperate for any work. This, combined with several tragedies in 1930, soon sounded the death knell for the Anne Lindbergh Gliders of San Diego. Following complications from appendicitis, Peaches died in June. Then, in September, her friend (and sometimes rival) Ruth Alexander, who was America's first female glider instructor, died during a transcontinental record attempt in a Barling NB-1 airplane. Within half an hour of an early morning takeoff into low-lying clouds and fog from San Diego's Lindbergh Field, Ruth's plane spiraled to the ground. She died instantly, still strapped in her seat.

Week after week after week, Anne waited in California while her husband's promised "three weeks" stretched into three months. Charles saw personally to every detail of the Sirius's final assembly, then made countless modifications before and after the ongoing test flights. At one time, he had wanted a retractable landing gear installed, a feature he rejected after deciding he would later equip the plane with pontoons. While he worked on the plane, talking shop and tweaking designs in the Lockheed plant, Anne waited outside in their large touring automobile parked next to the factory airstrip.

Her patience was wearing thin, however. "I am so tired of waiting for planes and husbands and babies!" she wrote her sister Elisabeth on April 3, 1930.[40]

During their last month in California, the Lindberghs learned celestial navigation. Their instructor was the Australian-born Harold Gatty, the "Prince of Navigation" who would navigate for the one-eyed aviation legend Wiley Post on their 1931 around-the-world flight. Celestial navigation was then the primary method for checking position over seas and uncharted territory. (It's occasionally used by sailors and aviators today.) Using a sextant, a navigator would measure the angle of the sun and moon or stars above the horizon. With this calculation, a chronometer set at Greenwich mean time, and prepublished trigonometric tables, he could then plot a line of position to get a fix on his exact location. Typically, Anne deprecated her abilities. "I *can't* multiply *at all*. . . . I'm no good at hours, minutes, and seconds," she fretted about having to measure longitude and latitude.[41] In her day, women were actually encouraged to utter such dismissive statements about their skills in mathematics. While it is true that she disliked arithmetic, Anne had studied algebra, geometry, and physics in school; she was not as incompetent as she said.

Finally, on Easter Sunday, April 20, at 5:26 A.M. the Sirius lifted skyward from Grand Central Airport, near Los Angeles. The Lindberghs made only one stop, for twenty minutes to take on fuel in Wichita, Kansas. Shortly after 11:00 P.M., the Sirius swooped in to land at Roosevelt Field in New York, having flown coast to coast in fourteen hours, forty-five minutes, and thirty-two seconds—three hours under the previous speed record. At altitudes between 14,000 and 15,500 feet, the Lindberghs had taken advantage of tailwinds and observed the effects of high altitude on aircraft performance: higher airspeed, less fuel consumption, and the possibility of stronger tailwinds. Flying high was downright dangerous, said old timers, but Charles had thought, and then proven, otherwise. Certainly, he wasn't the first pilot to fly at what were then considered high altitudes, but whatever feats he performed in the air served as a catalyst for the growth of aviation because the public and pilots looked up to him as the ultimate pioneer. Time and again, he followed his own instincts, to great success.[42]

Anne served as navigator and copilot on the record-breaking flight. She was then seven months into her pregnancy, and the last four hours of the long flight taxed her. Flying without supplemental oxygen, and with gasoline fumes leaking into the cockpit, she felt nauseated. She suffered in silence, though, because she didn't want Charles to end the flight short of the goal. She, too, took seriously her part in promoting aviation, and she didn't want people to know she had been airsick, or have them consider her a "weak woman."[43]

With this flight, Anne once again captured headlines across the country and triggered the public's awareness of her achievements aloft. One woman journalist observed, "During a period when many another woman would spend her time complaining . . . the flying colonel's wife has chosen to model her life along radically new lines, showing a rare courage, an extraordinary will and unusual skill."[44] Anne Lindbergh was fast becoming a role model for American women.

5

A Challenge Met

Their transcontinental flight behind them, Anne and Charles returned to the splendor—and safety—of Next Day Hill, where Anne awaited the birth of her firstborn. Yet living at the Morrow mansion was hardly a respite, with Dwight Morrow campaigning in the New Jersey primaries for the U.S. Senate, and Elisabeth recuperating from a mild heart attack brought on by the work of opening the Little School in Englewood, a progressive nursery school established by her and a friend. "There has been so much tension here," Anne wrote her sister Constance. Even as her due date neared, Anne did not stop flying with her husband, going on three local flights, the last in the Sirius on June 17.[1]

Away from the Morrows' enclave, Charles kept busy. He piloted a Sikorsky to Panama, opening a new airmail route, part of a run to Buenos Aires. Back in New York, he and Juan Trippe talked about aerial surveys needed to implement Pan American's transoceanic air travel. Charles itched for adventure and laid plans for an around-the-world flight in the Sirius, exploring and charting air routes for Pan Am. The odyssey would take place in 1931, Anne serving as copilot, navigator, and radio operator. Other than radio equipment provided by

86

Anne comforts her firstborn, Charles A. Lindbergh, Jr., in the gardens at Next Day Hill. Lindbergh Picture Collection, Manuscripts and Archives, Yale University Library. Reproduced with permission.

Pan Am, the Lindberghs planned and financed the survey flight themselves. At that time, there were no scheduled passenger flights across either the Atlantic or Pacific Oceans, and several years would elapse before aircraft technology made them possible.

In Pan Am's Chanin Building office, Lindbergh and Trippe looked at air paths, moving a piece of string across the turquoise and gold patches of a huge freestanding globe. The great circle route over the top of the world was the shortest distance between North America and the Orient. The route was far shorter than flying across the mid-Pacific, and as Charles pointed out, a shorter hop between Alaska and the Siberian coast involved fewer risks. Less distance between land masses typically ensured a safer flight. The chance of surviving a forced landing at sea was slim; to rescuers, a plane bobbing in the water could be compared to looking for a needle in a haystack.

At Next Day Hill, attended by a nurse and three doctors, Anne gave birth to a seven-pound, six-ounce boy on June 22, 1930, her twenty-fourth birthday. Throughout her eleven-hour labor, Charles held one of his wife's hands and Betty Morrow the other. When Anne first saw the newborn she fretted that it looked like her, with "dark hair and a nose all over its face," but after seeing that the infant had his father's mouth and chin cleft, she fell peacefully asleep.[2] The couple named him Charles Augustus Lindbergh, Jr., though Anne soon called him Charlie, or her "fat lamb." Worldwide, the birth of the "Little Eaglet" and "Baby Lindy" made front-page headlines, and at Next Day Hill telegrams, letters, and presents poured in, sometimes from strangers.

Gradually, Anne settled into motherhood, but like many new mothers, she was at first uneasy tending to the infant's needs. A painful breast abscess and a minor illness of Charlie's added to her distress, but her mother and nurses stood by to help. While convalescing, she raided her sister Elisabeth's bookshelf for child rearing topics, reading *The Montessori Mother* and other books. Most of them advocated the theories of popular child psychologist Dr. John B. Watson, who urged mothers to treat their children as adults.

"Never hug and kiss them, never let them sit in your lap," Watson admonished in his 1928 book, *Psychological Care of Infant and Child.*[3]

Less than one month after giving birth to a healthy boy, Anne found another reason to be thrilled: she had purchased a new Brunner Winkle Bird biplane, registered under the name of Mrs. Charles A. Lindbergh. The blue-colored aircraft was powered by a ninety-horsepower Kinner engine; in it, Anne would eventually complete the training needed for her private pilot's license. She gushed to Constance about the Bird, describing it as a "light open plane that you can 'sit down anywhere'—will land *easily* in the Maine field—not very fast—but we could get to Maine in five hours I think."[4]

In the first week of August Anne's recuperation from childbirth ended, and she resumed flying with her husband. "I jumped from bed into a plane, almost," she wrote to Charles's mother. After flying the Lockheed Sirius to aerial survey property near Princeton, New Jersey, and after leaving the baby at Next Day Hill, the Lindberghs winged north in the Bird to North Haven, Maine. There four days, Anne and Charles gave rides to Betty Morrow and Constance. Another streak of air travel followed their return—visits to Washington, Detroit, and the 1930 National Air Races in Chicago, where thousands stood to cheer the Sirius as it swooped in to land. Unfortunately, the press and autograph seekers hounded Anne and Charles so aggressively that they were forced to escape to the roof of their grandstand box.[5]

On September 2, 1930, the world's attention turned to a pair of gallant French flyers named Dieudonné Coste and Maurice Bellonte. Landing at Curtiss Field, they had achieved aviation's ultimate goal, flying nonstop westward across the Atlantic, against the prevailing winds. They had flown just over thirty-seven hours from Paris to New York, and Anne and Charles were on hand to greet and congratulate them on their arduous flight. While the Lindberghs, of course, could not personally meet every record-setting pilot, over the years they made certain to wire congratulations. Typical of the responses they received was one from Britain's Amy Johnson who, on June 25, 1930, wrote thanking them for the "message which you so thoughtfully sent to me on the termination of my flight from England to Australia, and to assure you how delighted I was to receive it."[6] In an open-cockpit Gipsy Moth, Amy had battled her way from London to Darwin in nineteen days, becoming the first woman to fly the 10,000-mile course from England to Australia alone.

Barely had Anne settled in back at home than Charles started training her in her new Bird. To pass the flight test for her private pilot's license, she needed to demonstrate proficiency in stalls, spins, spirals, steep turns, pylon turns, and spot landings. On Thursday, September 25, 1930, Anne logged sixteen instruction flights. That same day she flew her first flights alone in the Bird at the Long Island Aviation Country Club, where she kept her plane.[7]

The second half of 1930 was an exciting time for Anne: a new baby, a new Bird biplane—and a new home. In the fall of 1930 the Lindberghs purchased a 425-acre parcel of land, ten miles north of Princeton, New Jersey. Located in the Sourland Mountains, the area was uninhabited other than by a few farmers nearby. The property was 500 feet above sea level, with a brook and woods of old oaks, and was "practically inaccessible except by air," according to newspapers; from its high point, the Lindberghs looked down onto a wide, rolling valley. Finally, some sixteen months after her wedding, Anne had a home and a family. "Our own home—imagine it!" she wrote her mother-in-law Evangeline, to whom she had grown closer since giving birth.[8]

Anne and Charles hired Chester Aldrich, architect of Next Day Hill, to draw plans for a new house whose construction was expected to take about a year. In the meantime, they rented a plain, two-story furnished farmhouse near the property site. Uncertain about her domestic skills, Anne asked Charles's mother to visit and show her how to "run a house"—though the request was mostly for Evangeline's benefit, since help had already moved in. Elsie and Aloysius "Olly" Whateley, an English couple, served as butler and cook for Anne and Charles, and a nurse tended the baby. Anne would round out a blissful year in her temporary home, where the family ate "farm fashion," serving themselves from the kitchen table, and Charles took his adorable, curly-haired baby "ceiling flying." So content was Charles in the farmhouse that he later told an interviewer, "It has been so quiet and peaceful down here—even better than we dared hope."[9]

At the same time, sequestered in the country, away from culture and society life, Anne still pined for the rest of her family, and the Lindberghs continued to make weekend treks to Next Day Hill. Years later, Anne expressed embarrassment over her attachment to her family, calling it "incredibly naïve for a young wife, and rather hard on a young husband."[10] If Charles had any misgivings about her homesickness, he didn't say so; the many flights they shared alone kept her close to him.

Even with the baby, Anne's training in the Bird, and their new home, Anne and Charles kept up a frenetic schedule, flying to events in Washington, Boston, and other cities. When Anne stayed home, Charles returned to his pressing business matters: in late October he surveyed a new section between New York and Columbus, Ohio, a Transcontinental and Western Air route that had formerly used trains across the "aviator's graveyard" in the Alleghenies. On October 25, 1930, Transcontinental began its all-air service, which would spirit passengers from New York to Los Angeles in thirty-six hours—like a "new magic carpet," according to the *New York Times*.[11]

By spring of 1931, the Lindberghs' global flight was approaching, and Anne worried about leaving her baby, and for good reason, since strangers had disturbed their farmhouse haven from time to time. One woman had appeared at the door, insisting that she must see Charlie, and occasionally other crackpots stumbled onto the property. Moreover, newspapers reported the Lindberghs' whereabouts whenever they flew, leaving a very real possibility that someone could take advantage of their absence. As Anne explained to her mother-in-law, neither the Whateleys nor the newly hired Scottish nurse Betty Gow was experienced with the press or publicity, and so Anne arranged to have her mother and Betty take care of Charlie in Maine and Englewood. "My, how I hate to leave that baby!" she wailed in a letter to Evangeline.[12] Throughout the next decade, Anne would remain torn between her roles as wife and mother, trying to balance flying with Charles along with her family obligations.

With the flight nearing, Charles put his wife through the final stages of her crew training so she could earn licenses to fly airplanes and to operate the airborne radio. During the month of May, she flew sixty individual flights on her own, totaling about six hours of solo flight. Most of these were in the pattern, one takeoff and landing after another. When she wasn't flying solo, she took instruction from her husband in air work—including spins, spirals, and figure eights—and cross-country flying. Years later Anne would remember being "challenged, frightened, and infuriated" while trying to satisfy Charles, who demanded perfection in her flying. Nonetheless, her training, which included fifteen hours of dual instruction and fifteen hours of solo flying, paid off on the morning of May 28, 1931, when she passed both the written and the flight tests for a private pilot's license. The Aeronautics Branch of the Department of Commerce, predecessor of the Federal Aviation Administration, issued her license #20169.[13]

Afterward, Anne continued to fly alone, logging several local and cross-country flights around New Jersey and Long Island. On her first solo cross-country flight she flew her Bird over the Manhattan skyline, from the Long Island Aviation Country Club to Teterboro Airport. (In those days the airspace over Manhattan was uncontrolled and required neither a clearance nor a flight plan.) This flight was her "dream as a young girl at last come true," she later wrote, and on another solo flight from Newark to Long Island, she "felt like a queen."[14]

In the spring Anne and Charles also trained in Morse code and radio technology, earning their licenses as third-class radio operators. In 1931 radiotelephone communications had just come into use, and then only over a few well-traveled routes. So mariners and aviators communicated with Morse code, telegraphing dots and dashes over a set radio frequency. A high level of skill, developed by hours of practice, was required to transmit and receive the code and to translate it into understandable words. The aircraft's noise and vibration added to the difficulties. Learning the theory and the operation of the radio's vacuum tube apparatus proved to be challenging for Anne; she recalled the instructor speaking to her "very gently, as though talking to a child."[15] Eventually, of course, she mastered the program and passed the examination, and went on to achieve awards and accolades for her skill in radio operation. Among these, in 1934 she became the first woman awarded a gold medal from the Veteran Wireless Operators Association.

Charles designated Anne radio operator, and on the Sirius the bulk of the radio equipment was placed in her rear cockpit. Using a modified telegraph key, Anne tapped out "dits" and "dahs" to send messages. When receiving transmissions, she translated the code into letters or numbers and wrote them on a note pad. Working with various frequencies required the use of one of six different transmitting and receiving coils, which she had to manually change. In order to improve the radio range, she also had to crank in and out by many turns a trailing radio antenna, which had a ball weight attached to the end. On top of all that work, she was sometimes jolted out of her seat by a 400-volt shock from the radio.

By June the Sirius sported a new landing gear, having become a seaplane with the addition of metal Edo pontoons needed to set down on lakes and seas along the route. Pontoons opened up other possibilities too, because they could withstand a landing on ground, if need be. With the 900 pounds of fuel each pontoon held, and with more fuel in the fuselage and wing tanks, the Sirius's range extended to 2,000 miles—a considerable distance at the time. With the installation of a new 600-horsepower radial engine, the seaplane could cruise up to 180 miles per hour, though the best fuel efficiency was achieved at about 125 miles per hour.

Between trial flights testing the pontoons and the radio equipment, Charles took care of the mountains of paperwork required for the flight. Flying in foreign countries, the Lindberghs needed clearances and visas from embassies, and liability insurance against property damage. Charles also arranged for fuel to be cached in northern Canada and in Siberia. As July rolled to a close, all was ready for the epic flight.

About the planned flight, the *Scientific American* observed, "The opinion is often expressed that Colonel Lindbergh is tempting fate by his many bold flights . . . and that an accident to him and Mrs. Lindbergh would be a disaster for American aviation in particular and for the country in general." The article concluded, however, that Charles exercised "the greatest care in all his plans." All in all, the Lindberghs had spent months getting ready for their July launch, making preparations that Anne called "back stairs"—the work required before one could experience the magic of flying. Anne and Charles would be away from civilization over much of the route, and thus had to carry aboard food rations, a full medicine kit, a rubber boat, a rifle and a pistol, sail, oars, tools, spare parts for the Sirius, and countless other articles. Only those prepared for emergencies—forced landings and parachute jumps—could survive the wilderness they would soon traverse.[16]

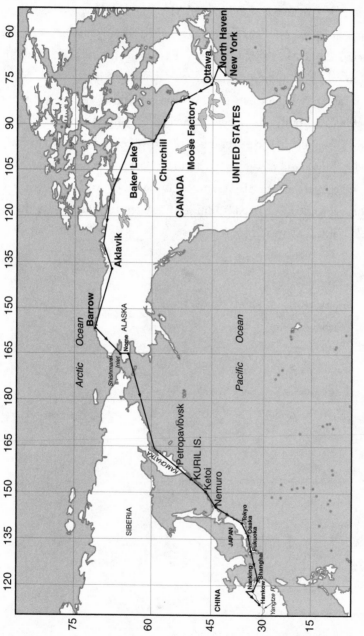

Survey flight to the Orient, 1931. Map by Chris Robinson.

6

The Land of the Midnight Sun

On the sweltering afternoon of July 27, 1931, a throng of reporters and Movietone men stood watch at the Edo Aircraft Company's gate in the borough of Queens, New York. When a brown sedan snaked past at 2:00 P.M. they snapped to attention. Inside the car, Anne Lindbergh looked out at the exploding camera flashes. The car came to a stop near the factory's entrance, and Anne and Charles stepped out. Ahead, their orange and black Lockheed Sirius, looking like a great gull on its silver pontoons, lay cradled in a wooden frame.[1]

While Charles took care of loading the seaplane and supervising the workmen, Anne escaped into the sanctuary of the factory office—but there, too, a reporter nosed his way in. He asked if she thought it was an especially dangerous trip. She managed a halfhearted laugh and tugged at her tan blouse, while replying that she had nothing to say. Anne knew all too well the dangers of flying and could name many lost souls killed in planes that had slammed into fog-cloaked mountains or into the ground. The chances of surviving a forced landing were slim in the no-man's-land she and Charles would be flying over.

Undeterred, the reporter continued his questioning until a friend of Anne's intervened. As soon as she was outside the stifling office, however, two women reporters peppered her with more questions. One asked about her clothes, while the other wanted to know about housekeeping in the plane, including where she put the lunch boxes. Although Anne considered these questions slightly insulting, she felt sympathy for female journalists, who often chafed when they were assigned these trivial topics. Nearby, male reporters, wearing the trade uniform of dark suits and fedoras, were elbowing closer to Charles, asking him technical questions about the flight. Sighing, Anne told the women she had no comments.

After lingering farewells with her small circle of friends, Anne climbed the fuselage to her rear cockpit, but she stopped cold when a radio announcer began describing her flying costume: "Mrs. Lindbergh is wearing a leather flying helmet and leather coat, and high leather flying boots."[2] This was nonsense—she wore a blouse, lightweight riding breeches, and rubber sneakers. It was simply more proof that the media fed the public whatever suited their fancy, whether fact or fiction.

Ready to launch, the Lindberghs put on their flying helmets and goggles. Turning to Anne, Charles asked, "All set?" Hearing her say yes, he signaled the mechanics, and the seaplane rattled down a ramp into the East River. As the engine rumbled, Charles checked his gauges, then taxied east for a mile, clearing the area and getting enough distance for a takeoff run. He gunned the throttle, and the engine roared; the plane sped ahead, trailing a foamy wake, spray lashing the windshield and wings. Suddenly, the vibrations stopped, Charles eased back on the stick, and the Sirius soared up into the clear blue sky. It was just after 4:00 P.M.

When the altimeter read 600 feet, Anne and Charles looked out to see a lone photographer's plane peeling away from their wingtip. Over the Edo factory Charles waggled his wings in a parting salute, then turned south toward Washington, D.C., where visas awaited them. Reporters rushed to file stories, Movietone trucks scattered, and the same evening, an estimated one million listeners tuned their radio sets to hear the National Broadcasting Company air coverage of the Lindberghs' departure.

This leg of the flight was Anne's first chance to become more familiar with the equipment packed around her. Within reach of her right hand was a transmitter key; below that, a box of the transmitting coils that she plugged into the radio set to change frequencies. Ahead of this box was the receiving set. She passed notes and sandwiches to her husband from a shelf atop the set. Squeezed in just to the right of her head was a condenser for the fixed-loop, direction-finding apparatus. At the left side of her cockpit was an aluminum case she used to store gloves, helmets, maps, pads, pencils, and extra sandwiches. Ahead of the case sat the transmitter; below it, the reel used to crank the trailing antenna in or out. Behind her seat lay the radio's dynamotor.

As radio operator for KHCAL, the Sirius's call sign, Anne sent their position, along with weather reports, to ground stations. She also received news of weather ahead, which could make go or no-go decisions for them. The direction-finding loop antenna jutted from the bottom of the plane's fuselage, and it enabled the Lindberghs to receive radio signals from ships or stations to determine bearings used for homing. Along the sparsely settled routes they flew, however, there were few stations to give weather reports or signals. Anne would strive to improve her speed and accuracy in sending and receiving, knowing that a good part of the flight's success would hinge on radio communications from KHCAL. Later, as her skills with Morse code improved, she would begin to hear words when she listened to transmissions, as if in a regular conversation.

Anne's first introduction to the radio equipment filling her cockpit was abrupt and unpleasant. Trying to send a message to WOA, North Beach, in Queens, she put in the 3130-kilocycle coil, then cranked out the antenna. After turning on the keyboard switch and hearing nothing, she tried more switches. Seconds later, she felt a powerful electric shock run through her. Charles handed back a note, telling her to take out the fuses. "I would if I knew what a fuse looked like," she retorted. In the front cockpit, a hand rose up, holding a spare fuse. She brooded while pulling out the fuses, chiding herself for her lack of mechanical skills. Would people say she couldn't work the radio because she was a woman? Charles was sure the problem was nothing but a short circuit, which could be easily repaired in North Beach on their way north. He passed back another note: "Don't look so gloomy."[3]

Two hours and twenty minutes after leaving New York, in skies laced with fleecy cumulus clouds, Charles circled the naval air station at the Anacostia River in Washington, D.C. Waiting to cheer the Lindberghs' arrival were 200 onlookers flanking the shore. After an overnight stop there and in North Beach for radio repairs, the Sirius took off with the wind on its tail and pushed to North Haven, Maine. There Charles and Anne said good-bye to thirteen-month-old Charlie and left him in the care of Betty Morrow and Betty Gow.

The next day, bathed in brilliant sunlight, the Sirius roared northward from Maine to Ottawa, Canada, the next stop on its long journey toward Alaska. Three hours and thirty minutes later they landed at Ottawa, ending a flight during which Anne's spirits had been buoyed by her frequent radio transmissions. But her confidence disappeared when, after landing, she was told that Canada's foremost radio expert would sit beside her at the evening banquet to be held in their honor. "Your husband says you have entire charge of the radio," Ottawa's hosts declared, adding that she and the expert could "just have a splendid talk about everything." She had been wrestling with the radio set for only three days, still saying she needed *four* hands to operate it. A sort of stage fright came over her, she said, when she tried to send and receive messages in Morse code. Whatever could she, a rookie operator, say to a radio expert? As she walked into the banquet hall in Ottawa that evening, she coached herself: "Don't say *coil* when you mean *tube,* and try not to speak at all."[4]

In the hall's back room, a beleaguered Charles had his own problems. On the floor lay his maps, marked with black lines showing his proposed route across the wilds of Canada. A group of baffled bush pilots, surveyors, and scientists—all seasoned explorers—threw up their hands looking at his course. They could not understand why he was considering flying over this perilous virgin territory of fog, glassy water, quicksand, and swarms of mosquitoes—near a magnetic pole that made a compass nearly useless. Far removed from civilization and established routes, Anne and Charles would not survive a forced landing, they told him. Surely, a course along proven routes was safer.

Slipping into the room, Anne looked on with amusement at the scene unfolding between her obstinate husband and the explorers. One of the pilots eyeballed Anne, then pointed to the Lindberghs' route, saying, "I wouldn't take *my* wife over that." Charles smiled at his wife, then responded, "You must remember that *she* is *crew*." Anne's face flushed at this, the highest praise her husband could bestow. She was a full partner, not an accessory or a wife or a passenger, and thought, "Have I then reached a stage where I am considered on equal footing with men!"[5]

That settled, Charles continued to argue for his shorter route, telling them that, when flying, he liked to draw a straight line between two points and follow it. He preferred to prepare for difficulties, rather than have to deviate from them en route, he said. Weary of the debate, the other explorers eventually gave up, saying they knew he would get through just fine.

Leaving Ottawa on August 1, Charles and Anne winged north to Moose Factory, a fur trading settlement near James Bay that had been founded in 1673. They flew over flat land sprinkled with hundreds of lakes, all fringed by spruce and pine forests, before landing on the Moose River on a warm evening. Hordes of mosquitoes flitted everywhere. Lining the shore to greet Anne and Charles were Cree Indians, Hudson's Bay Company men, and four white women—a far cry from the throng of voyageurs and traders who had once lived there. After a late supper of fresh moose, lettuce, and canned goods provided by a Scottish couple, the Lindberghs called on the Mounted Police and visited an Anglican mission school. Overnight, they billeted in an old Hudson's Bay Company house, built of wide, white-washed timbers.

The next day, the Lindberghs took off for Churchill, Manitoba, covering a distance of 750 miles. At one point, Anne spotted beluga whales splashing in Hudson Bay, but otherwise, the flight traversed barren, bleak land. En route Anne noticed the North Star blazing almost directly above them as they neared the Arctic Circle. Over Churchill, they circled the ruins of the Prince of Wales Fort, where the English and French had battled for supremacy over Hudson Bay in the eighteenth century. Upon landing in Churchill, the Lindberghs shivered in the brisk autumnal air—quite different from the warm and humid weather in Moose Factory.

Pushing farther north the next day, they flew some 400 miles to Baker Lake. As the Sirius streaked across the afternoon sky, Anne looked down at the vast boreal forest, woodland, and wetland riddled with ponds and marshes. There millions of ducks and shorebirds nested, while wolves, lynx, caribou, musk oxen, bears, and moose meandered through fens and bogs. But soon the terrain again took on a disappointing gray color. Anne was startled by the forlorn-looking and damp Baker Lake settlement, which had only three houses. She wondered how anyone or anything, including animals, could live there. Inhabited by Eskimos, fur trappers, and missionaries, the isolated trading post received supplies only once a year, by boat; the next one was due in two weeks. The Lindberghs had been told that planes often dropped in and were surprised by the shortage of provisions. They handed over three plums, a pear, and fresh meat sandwiches they had carried from Ottawa. During dinner the burly, bearded trappers shared the sandwiches with each other, carefully doling out quarter portions. Meantime, Anne and Charles feasted on salmon, which was standard fare there.

Soon, a red-coated Mountie, two foremen from Hudson's Bay Company, a game warden, and an Anglican parson joined the dinner party. "What's it like outside?" one of them asked the Lindberghs. Seeing them hesitate, the trappers explained that they received newspapers only once a year. Proudly, they told the Lindberghs that some of them were "bushed" and "inside" for life—away from civilization, as they preferred.[6] They spent their time trapping, fishing, playing cards, and watching the missionaries—a Catholic priest and the parson—compete for converts among the Eskimos. Having arrived earlier at Baker Lake, the parson was ahead, but as Anne noted, the priest was inside for as long as he lived, and would probably win in the end.

The next morning, Baker Lake Eskimos gawked at the Lindberghs and their plane, the first that they had laid eyes on. Two shy boys peeked at Anne, the first white woman they had seen, following her everywhere. (Because she wore trousers, she was certain she disappointed them.) The most isolated station the Lindberghs had stopped at so far, Baker Lake chilled Anne's heart, and as she looked at the Sirius, still tethered to the shore, she prayed that it would soon take them out.

On August 4, a cold gray evening draped with low-lying clouds, the Lindberghs set off for their longest leg to date, beginning the dangerous course the Canadian explorers had warned against in Ottawa. After leaving Baker Lake, they intended to fly 1,115 miles nonstop to Aklavik, in the Northwest Territories. On this twelve-hour night flight, they flew above the Arctic Circle into "the land of the midnight sun," where the sun never sets in summer. Crossing over tundra, they looked down to see a herd of caribou thundering beneath them, looking like cloud shadows. When they reached the Arctic Ocean's Amundsen Gulf, a white cloudbank rose up from the ice packs and hovered just off the plane's right wingtip. To their left was a bleak, gray treeless land. The flight went on and on, and only the engine's hum kept Anne from sinking into a trance. When the sun sank toward the horizon, Anne saw "a strange green glow, like that from a partial eclipse" light the sky.[7] At that point they turned west-southwest toward Aklavik and took turns flying and napping until one of the pontoon fuel tanks coughed dry. The starved engine sputtered and the plane's nose dropped, jolting Anne awake. Charles promptly switched selector valves, and the engine growled to life again.

At 3:00 A.M. they found Aklavik, a small town on one of the many meandering channels slithering across the delta of the great Mackenzie River. Despite the hour, all the townspeople turned out to greet them, standing on the glassy river's shore, snapping pictures in the middle of a night that never turned dark. There were thirty houses, two churches, two mission hospitals, and a school for the Eskimo children in Aklavik, the largest settlement the

Lindberghs had seen thus far. Stepping onshore, they heard for the first time packs of howling Huskies, eerie sounds present at all their stops in the North.

The next day, children's shouts echoed through the town. "The boat is coming—look!—the smoke."[8] A white paddleboat, the year's last supply ship, was chugging its way downstream toward Aklavik. Later, the town's residents formed a procession slinking up the gangplank to the purser's office, waiting for their precious cargo as if it were Christmas in August.

On the evening of August 7 the Sirius winged westward. Charles and Anne were leaving Canada behind and heading for Barrow, Alaska, on what would become a harrowing six-hour-and-thirty-minute flight. Midway, the ceiling fell lower and lower, like a sheet of gray steel, squeezing the Sirius between fog above, behind, and before them—and the sea below. They were trapped. Could they land at Barrow, or was it, too, blanketed in fog? Frantically, Anne worked the radio, trying to raise WXB, Barrow's station.

With rain pelting the Sirius, Charles flew blind in the clouds, relying on the instruments alone. Then, spotting a hole in the fog, he shoved the stick forward to skim the sea, while signaling Anne to reel in the antenna—if its ball weight hit the water, they would lose the antenna and any chance of communicating. Suddenly, the fog thickened into a solid wall around them. They could either make a forced landing at sea, or land at Barrow. The Sirius climbed, and Anne again cranked out the antenna, trying once more to raise WXB. At last, the signals she had been desperately waiting for came in: "KHCAL," Barrow's radio operator tapped in code, "fog lifting fast, visibility two miles."[9] An exuberant Anne poked her husband and relayed the good news.

At 1:00 A.M. in the dim morning light, they landed on a lagoon near Barrow, a small town with several houses, a hospital, a Presbyterian church, and various shacks and tents. Located near seventy-one degrees latitude, Barrow looked like it stood on the edge of the world, perched between the Arctic Ocean and the hummocks rising from the vast tundra. The Arctic ice pack, composed of gray floes, isolated the town like a fortress most of the year. Only in summer could a northeasterly wind drive away the ice, opening a path for supply boats to come ashore. This year's boats, the *Bay Chimo* and the *Patterson,* stood watch off the coast, waiting for the winds to shift. Still another ship, the cutter *Northland,* hovered a hundred miles out to sea at Icy Cape while waiting to unload its cargo that included fuel for the Sirius.

While the marooned ships lay off the coast, a quiet desperation wracked the townspeople, whose supplies were dwindling by the day. But the Lindberghs' arrival on August 8 gave rise to a festive mood, a welcome break in a life of hardships and bitter cold. Residents scrambled to arrange a feast, calling it a "Thanksgiving Dinner." Pooling their scarce food resources, they served up canned sweet potatoes, peas, and beets, reindeer and goose meat from their cellars, and a sprig of parsley lovingly grown in a window box with imported soil. With fog in Barrow and storms lashing Nome, their next stop, Anne and Charles laid over several days. In the downtime, they saw a reindeer rodeo—Eskimos herding the animals across the tundra—and went to services in the white frame church. Wearing furs and wrapped in robes, they raced across the tundra on their first dog sled ride.

When the fog began to lift in Barrow, Anne trudged to the radio station, receiving word of clear skies ahead. The *Northland* was still marooned, and with it the fuel to fill the Sirius's tanks. Nonetheless, Charles decided they would press south to Nome. They put on their heavy flight suits and pulled on sealskin boots sewn and chewed into shape by Barrow's native women. On the evening of August 10 they took off for what they thought would be an uneventful flight—one that would become a close call with disaster.

After flying above the Arctic Circle for a week in twenty-four-hour sun-lit days, both Anne and Charles had forgotten about the night. Nome lay 518 air miles south of Barrow. Though not far, the change in latitude was sufficient to shut the doors on the never-ending days.

Skirting the coast, the Lindberghs flew over the *Northland* and headed southward. While the needle on the fuel gauge continued its dip toward "E," a lavender twilight fell softly around them. Anne tried to raise WXY at Nome but heard no reply. Soon, they passed the point at which they could no longer make it back to Barrow. Nor could they land the Sirius at night because of unseen hazards—logs or other debris in the water. In the distance Anne saw only desolate, rugged terrain and fog-shrouded mountain peaks. Again, she tapped in code to WXY, "What time does it get dark at Nome?"[10]

After repeated attempts to raise Nome, Barrow, and the *Northland,* Anne finally heard from WXN, Candle, a coastal station. WXN relayed Nome "reported overcast and getting dark."[11] But with Nome still far, and dusk turning into blackness, Charles had to make an emergency landing. He shouted back to Anne, telling her to radio that they would land for the night and go into Nome in the morning. He cut the power, pitched up the plane's nose, stalled the plane, and kicked in the rudder. It spun down and around toward a sliver of misty lake below.

"Hurry up! Going to land!" he yelled. Her heart racing, her arms aching, Anne hurriedly cranked in the antenna as if she were "reeling in a gigantic fish from the bottom of the sea."[12] Pushed by a tailwind, the Sirius glided to a landing on a shallow lagoon, its pontoons almost scraping bottom, scooting along before stopping in three feet of water. They were safely down in the Shishmaref Inlet, on the Seward Peninsula, about a hundred miles northwest of Nome.

Charles jumped onto a pontoon and tossed out the anchor. Bunking in the baggage compartment, he and Anne slept soundly until 3:00 A.M., when Eskimo hunters in kayaks, holding lanterns, awoke them. "We—hunt—duck," they stammered in English to Charles, who shook his head in wonder at seeing unexpected company in the wilds.[13]

Overnight, the fog lifted, and after sliding back the hatch, Anne and Charles looked up to see a panorama of snow-capped mountains. After taking off, they passed over green valleys and the sparkling blue Bering Sea, a kaleidoscope of changing colors so unlike the drab Arctic flights. With fuel tanks nearly dry, they arrived on August 11 at Safety Harbor, a lagoon twenty-five miles from Nome. They refueled the Sirius with a Pan American cache of gasoline in barrels, brought to the plane by Huskies pulling sleds.

Storms and pouring rain pummeled Nome during the Lindberghs' August layover, time enough to attend festivities that had been arranged in their honor. Among these events were a kayak race and a seldom-seen wolf dance put on by visiting Eskimos who had paddled their walrus-skin boats from King Island, a spit of land eighty miles northwest of Nome in the Bering Sea. (The islanders' chief won the kayak race, of course. "When he ceased to excel, he would cease to be Chief," Anne noted.)[14]

While in Nome, Charles finally disclosed his plans for the rest of the trip. He informed the press that they would circle the globe, flying across Asia, Europe, and via the Azores over the Atlantic. This surprising news made headlines across America, because the media—and the Lindberghs' friends— had assumed their journey would end in Tokyo. Ever since the famous couple left New York, accounts of their escapades had appeared in the newspapers, along with a running history of the flight and maps. Americans were still thrilled by the adventures of aviators, and they considered the Lindberghs— along with other pilots, like the globe-trotters Wiley Post and Harold Gatty, who had made an eight-day, around-the-world flight in July—to be almost mythical figures, the stuff of Greek legends.

The alluring Far East beckoned, and Charles and Anne were anxious to leave, having waited for a break in the weather. On August 14 the day dawned clearer, and the ceiling lifted high enough to allow a takeoff from Nome, their last stop on the North American mainland. They turned the Sirius toward their next destination—the land of the smoking volcanoes, Siberia's Kamchatka Peninsula.

7

Into the Raging Yangtze

On the morning of August 14, the Sirius soared gracefully into the air, its bright orange wings glistening in the sunlight breaking through the low-lying clouds over Nome. Charles dipped the wings to salute the crowd below, then set course across the Bering Strait to St. Lawrence Island. Anne put on her headphones, logged the 9:00 A.M. takeoff, and listened for the naval radio station on St. Paul Island, part of Alaska's Pribilof Islands. Thirty minutes after liftoff, Anne reported unlimited visibility and an altitude of 500 feet. But an hour later, they were flying over a blanket of milky white fog at a speed of 110 miles per hour.[1]

Nearly eleven hours after leaving Nome, having covered a 1,067-mile course across the Bering Sea, the Sirius approached Karaginski Island. The island, a fur trapping settlement, lay just east of the Kamchatka Peninsula, a 750-mile long scimitar of land pockmarked with a hundred-plus volcanoes and steaming geysers. Anne looked down at a stretch of green trees and shrubbery, a sharp contrast to Nome's grays and browns. She had talked with St. Paul Island every half hour, and later, a Russian station and an American ship, the S.S. *President Cleveland.* Now she could reel in the antenna.

Waiting to greet the Lindberghs on the island were a circle of natives, two Russian women wearing short skirts, and several men dressed in conventional Russian costume—blue smocks and high boots. Their pet, a little brown motherless bear named Dunka, skittered behind them. In a log cabin filled with red fox, ermine, and bearskin furs, Anne and Charles put in for the night. The next morning the two Russian women—a zoologist and a fur trapper's wife—gazed at pictures of Charlie, and Anne felt that her "boy seemed nearer." The zoologist's young son lived in Moscow, and Anne promised to carry a letter to him to be posted in Tokyo. Such experiences left Anne with fond memories. Years later she told an interviewer that one of the favorite parts of her flights was the "human warmth" of people she met in foreign lands after dropping in from the sky.[2]

On August 16, as a light northeast wind ruffled cloudy skies, the Sirius winged south toward the city of Petropavlovsk. There the Lindberghs toured an experimental farm, and visited schools and stores—"all the things that one is supposed to do in Russia before one writes about it," said Anne. But it was the Russian people who impressed her, not the communist government's propaganda and its plans for revitalizing the country. Of all the destinations on this survey flight, Russia and its inhabitants would spark the most curiosity back in the United States. At the time, Americans were fascinated by the social experiments of communist Russia. When they later asked Anne what she thought of "it," she protested, "It isn't *It*; it's *Them*, and I like them." She had grown to admire the warmhearted, raucous Russians who touched her with their humor and generous spirit.[3]

Next on the Lindberghs' course was Nemuro, on Hokkaido, Japan's northernmost major island. The Kamchatka Peninsula and Hokkaido were linked by the Chishima, an archipelago containing the Kuril Islands. Later owned by Russia, the Kurils—the "black hole" of the Chishima—were frequently ravaged by quick-forming fog, rough seas, and rain. Nemuro's weather station, JOC, reported clear skies before Charles and Anne left Petropavlovsk on the nineteenth of August. Expecting an eight-hour flight through the Kurils, they blithely set off. While eyeing a fog bank just east of their course, Anne radioed JOC for its forecast, which was still clear.

They pressed onward, flying past Buroton Bay (about midway on course), when suddenly, the fog bank oozed over their plane. Rolling waves of mist scudded across the islands' volcanic peaks, and ahead black storm clouds brewed. Behind the Sirius, murky fog closed in, forcing Anne and Charles to make an emergency landing. Anne relayed to JOC, "fog on sea . . . we are turning back . . . will land." Charles throttled back, slid the canopy aft to improve his vision, and put on his helmet and goggles. Anne dubbed this the "buckling-on-of-armor," procedures she had come to know well after many hazardous flights with her husband.[4]

Grim-faced, Charles moved forward in his seat to see outside. Anne cranked in the antenna, cinched tight her seat belt, and shuddered as the plane's nose dropped. Charles had spotted a hole in the fog and was diving toward a patch of glistening water scuffed with whitecaps. Then clouds wrapped around the seaplane again like a cocoon, and the ocean and the horizon disappeared. Charles pulled the stick back and the Sirius soared to blue sky. It lurched like a roller coaster, down and up again. A terrified Anne compared it to "tobogganing down volcanoes," and she vowed to herself she would stop flying for good.[5]

His jaw clenched, Charles corkscrewed down again. The plane barely cleared bushes and rocks on the volcanic slope of one of the islands before it leaped over a fifty-foot cliff to the sea. Slapping down hard on choppy waves, the Sirius bobbed like a cork in rough swells. Charles turned around and looked at his wife, whose face was blanched with fear. He asked what was bothering her, and she replied she was happy to be down. "We weren't in much danger," he said, before throwing back his head and laughing.[6]

They plowed through tangled seaweed to reach the island's lee side, and then radioed their location: 200 meters southeast of Ketoi Island. JOC replied that they would send the *Shinshiru Maru* to help them, though Charles insisted Anne tell the operator that they did not need assistance. His was a typical male attitude, Anne thought, while wondering what exactly was a *Shinshiru Maru*. They slept aboard the Sirius and awoke the next morning to chanting sounds coming across the water. Rounding the bluff was a skiff manned by eight singing Japanese sailors whose small, two-masted naval cutter, the *Shinshiru Maru*, lay anchored only 200 meters away.

After coffee on the Japanese cutter, the Lindberghs readied for takeoff. The seaplane's engine coughed and sputtered, despite repeated attempts by Charles to get it going. Looking out the cockpit, they saw the Sirius was drifting toward the rocky shore, less than 100 feet away. Charles jumped onto the wing and pulled up the anchor rope, only to see it fall apart in his hands—it had been shredded overnight by rocks. Yelling for help, Anne and Charles saw the sailors straining at their skiff's oars to rescue them. The crew pulled alongside, caught the fast-drifting plane, and tethered it to the naval cutter's anchor.

The Lindberghs bunked in their plane a second night, tossed about by a raging windstorm. In the morning the Sirius was towed to Buroton Bay's sheltered harbor by the naval cutter, whose crew worked "like horses to help the Lindberghs," said its captain to reporters.[7] Happy to be ashore, Anne and Charles slept overnight in a fox farmer's bungalow. In the morning, Charles and the cutter's crew cleaned the Sirius's spark plugs, and the Lindberghs roared off toward Nemuro. But en route, JOC warned of bad weather, and again they landed short of their destination. After setting down on a lake full of water lilies at Shana, Etorofu Island, they stayed overnight in a Japanese inn. The following day they reached Nemuro but thick fog and driving rain prevented a landing. Making a 180-degree turn, they spied a hole in the overcast and coasted to a landing on a small inlet, where the reeds parted to reveal a small sampan poled by a bare-chested fisherman. Where were they? Charles pulled out a map, and the fisherman pointed to Kunashiri Island. Anne strung the antenna out on the wing and relayed their location to JOC.

Gesturing and smiling, the fisherman invited them into his thatch-roofed hut, which was also home to his son and aged father. When Anne tried to use a Japanese phrasebook to ask for food, they looked perplexed. Charles resorted to his tried-and-true method of communicating in foreign languages: sketching the request. He drew a fish in profile, then pointed to his mouth. Jumping up, the Japanese smiled and scurried to place bowls of fish and potatoes in front of Anne and Charles.

The following morning, August 24, they made another try for Nemuro, their fifth attempt in five days. After a twenty-eight minute flight over calm seas and in fair skies, they arrived safely. Journalists and a crowd of well-wishers lined the harbor, where they greeted and interviewed the long-overdue celebrity flyers. Anne and Charles wore oil-stained shirts and looked "tired and dirty" when they deplaned in Nemuro, according to the *Japan Advertiser*. Anne had long since put aside her heavy flying garb and now wore breeches and high boots. The couple promptly bathed in a hotel, their first bath since leaving Nome more than a week earlier. Anne later described the bath as "divine," writing, "We poured basins of nice hot water over each other and washed everything—hair, teeth—and soaked under the water to get fleas off!"[8]

✈

On August 26, after flying almost six hours, the Lindberghs landed at Kasumigaura, Tokyo's naval base, where an assembly of 30,000 joyfully cried "*Banzai! Banzai!*" (or "May you live 10,000 years!") Photographs wired worldwide showed a beaming, sun-tanned Anne dressed in riding breeches, her head crowned by a white flying helmet. Since leaving New York one month earlier, she and Charles had flown 7,132 miles. Now they would break for vacation and sightseeing, though like all their endeavors, business would be mixed with pleasure.

Dignitaries meeting them at the base included America's ambassador, W. Cameron Forbes, and Japan's Minister of the Navy, Admiral Kiyokazu Abo; plus 150 invited guests. Also on hand were the American aviators Clyde Pangborn and Hugh Herndon, Jr., who had recently been fined $1,000 each for flying over restricted Japanese airspace. Japan was at war with Manchuria and did not look kindly at their transgression, so the aviators were cooling their heels, awaiting permission from the Japanese government to fly their plane out of Japan. On October 5, 1931, they would win the $25,000 prize for the first transpacific flight, after flying their Bellanca Skyrocket airplane nonstop 4,900 miles from Sabishiro Beach, Japan, to Wenatchee, Washington.

The Lindberghs took Japan by storm. The *New York Times* reported that the Japanese were delighted with the couple's "friendly ways," and added that observers thought Charles was "more like an Englishman than an American," not the "typical aggressive go-getter but was rather considerate, quiet and gentle." The article went on to describe Anne as possessing "all the virtues which the Japanese esteem most in wives. She is gentle and attentive to her husband, always helping him with his kimono."[9]

An exhausting mix of tourism, social events, and official visits took place during the Lindberghs' stay in Japan. The day after arriving they stopped by two shrines before Charles headed back to the naval air station, where Japanese mechanics were overhauling the Sirius. Besides routine maintenance, the plane required repairs for a damaged pontoon strut and an oil leak from its tough trip through the Kuril Islands. The next day Charles called at various governmental departments, while Anne joined diplomats' wives at a tea house ceremony. Later the parties met at the Imperial Aviation Society, which awarded both Lindberghs medals for their aerial accomplishments. And with awards went speeches. Japan's communications minister pointed out that Mrs. Lindbergh had "assisted her husband in his work of advancing aviation. Her own flight record covers the distance of over 80,000 kilometers." He concluded, "We are, indeed, happy and proud that this distinguished couple of the air has flown to our land from the other side of the Pacific. . . . May they long continue in their service as the Ambassadors of Friendship and Good Will."[10]

The relentless pace continued later that same day at the Tokyo Club, where Ambassador Forbes and his sister, Mrs. James Russell, hosted a late afternoon reception for the Lindberghs, attended by nearly a thousand guests. A lavish dinner at the Imperial Hotel capped the day's activities, which had lasted for twelve hours, in stifling humidity.

Anne's weeks in Tokyo opened her eyes to Japanese philosophy and poetry and gave her a new appreciation for the country's culture. "In every Japanese there was an artist," she wrote, while admiring their ability to see "beauty in the smallest things." She was especially impressed with their use of metaphor—such as the plum for courage because it blossoms while snow is still on the ground. If she stayed there longer, she thought that perhaps she could learn to see the world as they did. To her hostess Mrs. Russell, Anne wrote that their time in Japan had been a "rich and stimulating month." Still, Anne wrote her mother-in-law from Tokyo that she was homesick and missing her baby, "But I can't fuss too much before Charles—it is such poor sportsmanship—when this *is* a marvelous experience."[11]

On September 19 the Lindberghs left Japan and set course over the Yellow Sea toward Shanghai at the mouth of the Yangtze. Many miles ahead of the Chinese coast, they spotted a brown maelstrom of mud and debris: the flooded Yangtze meeting the blue seas. Anne and Charles had heard about the flood, but its enormity shocked them. The swollen Yangtze had swallowed cities and crops in its path; it would go on to leave 30 million Chinese homeless and cause disease and starvation that would kill 3.7 million people. The Lindberghs continued toward the walled city of Nanking, looking down at the great river speckled with barges, junks, rafts, and sampans. The Sirius swooped in to land on Lotus Lake, near Nanking's eastern gate. Inside the noisy city bustled rickshaws, long-gowned men and women, and vendors and workmen wearing blue coats and balancing their wares on bony shoulders.

Immediately, the Lindberghs canceled all prearranged social events and put their seaplane to service, aerial surveying submerged areas that were equal in size to New York State. The maps they made proved invaluable to China's National Flood Relief Commission. "Our first surveys we did alone, I doing the flying and C. the sketching and mapping," Anne explained to her mother. On September 21 Anne piloted the Sirius for more than four and a half hours, covering an 8,000-square mile area; the next day, she flew for over seven hours, while her husband charted flooded areas. In just two days, she flew nearly twelve hours, flying low and often putting the plane in steep banks so Charles could photograph flooded areas.[12]

Taking a much needed break from relief work, Anne and Charles met General and Madame Chiang Kai-Shek for tea on the afternoon of

September 25. The general's wife, who later played a key role in the Nationalist party led by her husband, was a graduate of Wellesley, and, Anne noted, "quite beautiful and very clever, not at all second fiddle to him."[13] The next morning, General Chiang awarded Charles a medal commemorating his flight to China and in appreciation for his relief work.

One day later Charles and two passengers aboard the Sirius, Dr. J. Heng Liu and Dr. J. B. Grant, came close to losing their lives in the Yangtze. Anne had stayed behind to make room for the doctors. On a mission to deliver serum and vaccines, Charles landed near the city of Hinghwa. Suddenly, from out of nowhere, hundreds of sampans appeared and surrounded the seaplane. Desperate and starving, the Chinese mistook the package of medicine for food and frantically tried to board the plane. One person climbed onto one pontoon, then another onto the second one, with more coming near. A few more, and the Sirius would capsize. Charles pulled out his .38 revolver and shot it into the air. As soon as the Chinese jumped from the pontoons, he revved up the engine and the Sirius roared off dead ahead, leaving behind a wake of sampans. Their mission cut short, Charles and the doctors returned to Nanking.

The Lindberghs hoped to make one last aerial survey on October 2, but again the Yangtze thwarted their flight plan. With the couple aboard, the Sirius was lowered to the river from the deck of the *Hermes,* a British aircraft carrier. Slack in the line caused a wingtip to dip and hit the water. Just before the plane overturned in the Yangtze, Charles hollered "Jump!" to Anne. She leaped overboard into the foul waters "without the slightest hesitation or fear," as she described it in a letter to Elisabeth. Her husband dove next, and when he came up he saw his wife "perfectly happy paddling along like a little mud turtle."[14]

Anne looked tearfully at the Sirius, sure it would be destroyed like a "little match box crushed in a giant's hand," but Charles and the *Hermes* crew salvaged the seaplane, hoisting it to the carrier's deck.[15] Although there were gaping holes in a wing and the fuselage, repairs could be made in Shanghai and the *Hermes* set sail toward the port city.

Several days later, though, all hopes for continuing the global flight withered when Anne received a telegram aboard the *Hermes.* Her father, Dwight, had unexpectedly died at his home from a cerebral hemorrhage. Though Betty Morrow wired the couple not to change their travel plans, immediately the Lindberghs made plans to return home. At Shanghai Charles arranged to have the Sirius shipped to Lockheed Aircraft in California for a rebuild. From Yokohama, he and Anne set sail aboard the S.S. *President Jefferson* to Victoria, B.C., Canada, and from there they would fly home in a borrowed Lockheed.

The Lindberghs' great adventure came to a close two and a half months—and 10,000 miles—after their launch from New York. Although they had not achieved their original mission of circumnavigating the globe, they met their objectives on the Arctic survey flight. They had surveyed routes, looked at potential bases for aircraft, and evaluated weather conditions. Their discoveries led Pan American to shelve its plans to fly the polar route across the Bering Sea to China. The brutal climate and unpredictable weather, pervasive fog, desolation, and lack of adequate facilities for airports and flying boat terminals prompted Lindbergh to conclude that Arctic routes to Asia would be the last ones developed. Instead, five years after the Lindberghs' survey flight, Juan Trippe turned to the mid-Pacific to transport Pan Am's passengers with a twenty-three ton flying boat, the Martin M-130, known as the *China Clipper.*

A few years after the flight to the Orient, Anne described the trip as having "a quality of magic—a quality that belongs to fairy tales." She would call it a "collision of modern methods and old ones; modern history and ancient; accessibility and isolation." What had started as a dream shared by Charles Lindbergh and Juan Trippe in Pan Am's offices had become a reality. And after World War II, airlines began flying the Arctic air route the Lindberghs and other aviators had pioneered. As Anne Lindbergh would one day write, "Yesterday's fairy tale is today's fact."[16]

8

A Time of Mourning

Late at night on October 23, 1931, a cream-colored Vega touched down at Newark Metropolitan Airport, ending the Lindberghs' exhausting cross-country flight from Victoria, Canada. Anne and Charles climbed down from the cockpit and gathered up their small bundles: two packages wrapped in Chinese silk and tied with twine, their sole baggage since leaving Shanghai. Charles appeared in a gray business suit, his wife in a short-skirted, blue silk suit. Meeting the celebrity flyers was Betty Morrow's chauffeur-driven limousine, which whisked them to Next Day Hill in Englewood.

Some three weeks had passed since Anne had heard of her father's death, a period of initial grief made easier thanks to her husband's support—though even strangers helped steel her, she wrote Constance en route. Her father's death was the first in her immediate family, and Anne clung to the idea of him alleviating her pain: "Daddy, who would be the most magnificent about death, cannot be here to explain and show us its reality," she wrote.[1] Doubtless, the family took solace in the respects shown his memory. Among the dignitaries attending his service at the First Presbyterian Church in Englewood were former president Calvin Coolidge, Vice President Charles

Curtis, and a quarter of the United States Senate. Dwight would leave an estate valued at more than $10,000,000, and after various bequests and estate taxes, his wife inherited the remainder—almost $9,000,000. Mrs. Morrow declined an offer to complete her husband's term in the Senate and in the future would dedicate her time to philanthropic causes.

Her father's death left Anne in a tailspin, struggling to make sense of her emotions. "I cannot come to any realization of the knife-edge between life and death—and without that I don't think I can ever accept my father's death," she confided to a friend months later. Her own life demanded attention, fortunately. Over the winter she focused on caring for Charlie, whom she described as a "strong independent boy swaggering around on his firm little legs." Just starting to talk, the golden-haired baby mumbled words and toddled from room to room. A cheerful boy, he played hide-and-seek with his stuffed lamb and pussycat at bedtime, giggling when he hid them under his covers. More and more, Charles was taking an interest in his growing son too, playing with him and feeding him at mealtimes.[2]

In Anne's remaining free time, when she wasn't caught up with selecting wallpaper and paints and looking for fabrics for her new home near Hopewell, she was working on an account of the Orient survey flight. Both she and her husband had been urged to do so, but Charles had turned the task over to her—the writer in the family. They planned to look for publishers when Anne had enough material written.

Anne took a hiatus from flying during the winter. She had sold her Bird biplane on October 29, 1931, after her return from China. Although the plane had passed its annual inspection in August, between then and the beginning of October the Bird suffered an accident, possibly at the hands of Henry Breckenridge, an attorney, personal adviser, and friend to the Lindberghs. It is unclear what caused the accident—Anne did not write of it and its maintenance file did not include many details—but as a result of the crash the plane's wings were replaced. It is possible that Anne didn't want to own a reconditioned airplane; whatever her reasons for selling, it was the last aircraft she would have registered in her name only.[3]

Although Anne temporarily retired her wings, her critical role on the Orient survey flight motivated women aviators even more than her glider flight had in 1930. One month after her return home, the Women's National Aeronautical Association asked Anne to become an honorary member and serve on its advisory committee. The association counted pioneer pilots the Stinson sisters and Lady Mary Heath among its roster of legendary women aviators. Anne's joining would inspire members, wrote the president, who expressed the "deep pride of our membership in your fine aeronautical achievements in the interest of aviation."[4]

Another request followed shortly after, on January 9, 1932, when Amelia Earhart suggested that Anne join the Society of Women Geographers: "The group feels you are sufficiently geographical through the Tokyo flight, and should adore to have you join. . . . I don't know how much you care about clubs of any sort—I'm not very strong for them myself." Anne replied one week later: "I ought not to accept the membership." Even after her recent successes, she was humble and preferred to disclaim any honors. She explained to Amelia, "I do not feel that I am a woman geographer in my own right. And I think one ought not to join a club unless one has the time and strength and interest to be involved actively in it." Nonetheless, she regretted losing the chance to see Amelia, and in the same letter Anne invited her to tour Elisabeth's nursery school and dine with her and Charles during a scheduled January 25 visit to Englewood. Because of prior commitments, Amelia declined the dinner invitation but squeezed in time to stop by Elisabeth's Little School with Anne.[5]

Whether Anne had sufficient interest to become an active member of the Society of Women Geographers is uncertain, but her energy was certainly taken up by writing and taking care of Charlie. She also had just learned that she was pregnant with her second child, which delighted her but promised to consume more of her time. "I've been in bed for the last month with plenty of time to wonder *what induced* me to think that Charlie needed a 'little playmate,'" she joked to a friend in a mid-January letter.[6] Moreover, her husband expected her to accompany him on a flight to the West Coast. Recently

Lockheed had invoiced Charles $4,696 for the Sirius's repairs, and he wanted Anne to fly with him to Burbank in late February, combining a Transcontinental and Western Air aerial inspection with retrieving the plane. (The trip was ultimately canceled and another year would pass before it took place.)

Yet another opportunity came Anne's way in February when Charles persuaded her to speak on behalf of flood relief in China. Despite complaining about her fear of public speaking, she made her radio debut over the networks of the Columbia and National Broadcasting systems on February 21, 1932. During her short speech, a pleased Charles sat nearby, beaming at her. Anne's plea for aid helped the relief efforts and brought her new fans who wrote of their support and appreciation.[7]

Back in America, there was need for relief, too. Thirteen million people were unemployed in 1932, the worst year of the Great Depression. Breadlines snaked around city blocks, thousands took to panhandling, and shantytowns dotted the landscape outside cities. Rich Americans weathered the bad times as best they could, laying off servants while closing their estates or selling them at rock-bottom prices. Those whose wealth survived the stock market crash watched their portfolios and dividends dwindle to pennies on the dollar. Like their contemporaries, the Lindberghs experienced a decline in net worth, but Charles's consulting fees, their investment income, and Anne's annual trust income helped cushion their losses. And in contrast with others of her social standing, Betty Morrow lived lavishly at Next Day Hill. Endowed with a superhuman energy and the means to live as she chose, she continued her philanthropy and enjoyed a wide network of friends and interests. On the other hand, Anne seemed more sensitive to the plight of those Americans less fortunate. Her mother's house seemed an "anachronism," she later wrote, adding, "I would cringe, under a plush lap robe, being driven into New York by a uniformed chauffeur in a limousine, anticipating over-dramatically that at any moment a brick might come crashing through a window."[8]

Yet whatever misgivings she had, she continued to live in luxurious surroundings, tethered to her mother's estate. Three years into her marriage, Anne still kept close ties with her family, and she and her husband continued to use Next Day Hill as a primary residence. The Lindberghs' new house near Hopewell on Sourland Mountain, though virtually finished in October, was isolated and a two-hour drive from New York. Although the couple didn't want to live in New York, the city was the center of many of Charles's business activities and also offered Anne the museums, concerts, and readings she so loved.

The property on Sourland Mountain became a weekend retreat, with the Lindberghs and their son driving out every Saturday and remaining there until Monday, when they returned to Next Day Hill. The house, made of whitewashed fieldstone, sat behind a gravel driveway and a low stone wall. In the two-storied structure, which had cost $80,000, were servants' quarters, five bedrooms, a nursery, and four bathrooms, along with modern heating, cooling, and plumbing systems designed by Charles. Olly and Elysie Whateley stayed behind in the servants' quarters.

It is possible that Charles envisioned the new house recreating his idyllic childhood along the Mississippi's wooded riverbanks. He certainly believed it would provide privacy for his family. Nonetheless, the property's very isolation, along with the Lindberghs' reluctance to hire guards, would lead to tragedy. On Leap Year Day, Monday, February 29, Anne broke from the normal schedule, postponing a return to Next Day Hill because she and Charlie suffered from colds. Never before had the Lindberghs deviated from their set routine of returning to Next Day Hill on a Monday. On Tuesday, March 1, Anne called Betty Gow, requesting she leave Englewood and help out at Hopewell. That evening, at 7:30, she and Betty put the baby to bed, an hour before Charles returned from New York. When Betty made her usual 10:00 P.M. check, she found the baby's crib empty and the second floor nursery window open. The twenty-month-old Lindbergh baby had been kidnapped.

After Charles alerted authorities, detectives from the New Jersey State Police, led by Colonel H. Norman Schwarzkopf (the father of the renowned Gulf War general), swarmed around the house. Outside, they found a broken ladder, chisel, and footprints. The ransom note, demanding $50,000, had been left on the windowsill. Crudely written, it was barely legible:

> Dear Sir!
> Have 50.000 $ redy 25 000 $ in 20 $ bills 1.5000 $ in 10$ bills and 10000 $ in 5 $ bills. After 2–4 days we will inform you were to deliver the Money.
> We warn you for making anything public or for notify the Police
> the child is in gut care.
> Indication for all letter are singnature
> and 3 holds.[9]

The style of the handwriting suggested an author of German or Scandinavian origin. At the bottom of the note was an odd design of interlocking circles (the "three holds"), a mark that would be used to verify further contacts. Four days later, on March 5, another note arrived, demanding an additional $20,000 and promising to deliver the baby safely. The note added that the couple would have to wait for further instructions.

The Lindbergh kidnapping promptly grabbed worldwide headlines. Desperate, the Lindberghs promised not to prosecute the kidnappers if their son was returned unharmed. While churchgoers prayed for the baby's deliverance and thousands of people sent letters to the couple or swamped the police with useless clues, posters describing the boy and requesting information about his whereabouts went out to 1,400 American communities. Terrified parents cautioned their children never to talk with strangers and to stay indoors, and wealthy Americans and their employers, such as J. P. Morgan, hired bodyguards to protect their families. Foolish theories abounded—some people accusing Elisabeth or Dwight junior as having a hand in the deed.

Single-mindedly, Charles supervised the search efforts, turning his house into an auxiliary police station, a "bedlam: hundreds of men stamping in and out," as Anne described it to her mother-in-law. Detectives, police, and secret service men slept on mattresses scattered across floors, when they weren't routing Anne out of bed in the middle of the night to use her room for a conference. In the "terrifically unreal" confusion, Anne often felt numb. After a three-year hiatus from keeping a diary, she resumed the practice, which helped preserve her sanity, she later wrote. Days after the kidnapping, Betty Morrow moved in to comfort her daughter, making sure she rested and providing solace. Charles's mother remained in Detroit, teaching, but Anne wrote her almost daily, keeping her up to date as the tragedy unfolded.[10]

The search continued day after day—a mayhem of bungling police, false leads, and newspaper headlines. Family servants and neighbors were aggressively grilled, and a nationwide dragnet established, but nothing turned up. Soon a circus-like atmosphere hung over the Lindberghs' house, with sightseeing airplanes zooming and diving overhead and crowds congregating nearby.

Convinced that gangsters were involved in the crime, Charles asked two underworld figures—"Salvy" Spitale and Irving Bitz—to serve as intermediaries for the child's safe return. In Chicago, Al Capone, then serving a jail sentence for income tax evasion, issued a statement in which he offered $10,000 for information leading to the child's recovery. (Rumors percolated that Capone wanted to barter the baby's release for his own freedom.) Schwarzkopf and his men, however, believed that all signs pointed to amateurs having committed the kidnapping.

Despite Charles's efforts, a man unknown to him would serve as the go-between. He was Dr. John F. Condon, a seventy-two-year-old former school principal, athletic coach, and well-known resident of the Bronx whose articles frequently appeared in the *Bronx Home News*. Angry that his hero Colonel Lindbergh was forced to work with criminals, Condon asked the *News* to print his letter offering "to go anywhere, alone, to give the kidnapper the extra money and promise never to utter his name to any person."[11] Surprisingly, he received a reply to his letter, a note including the interlocking circles. On March 12, at the entrance of the Woodlawn Cemetery, he talked with the kidnapper, who called himself "John," and who said he was Scandinavian and only one member of a gang. On March 16 Dr. Condon received a package at his home with a child's sleeping suit inside, which Charles later identified as his son's.

Now certain of John's involvement with the kidnapping, Charles had his bankers at J. P. Morgan assemble and package the ransom money. Acting on the advice of Elmer Irey, head of the Law Enforcement Division of the Internal Revenue Service, Charles agreed to pay the ransom with gold certificates whose serial numbers had been recorded. On Saturday, April 2, Condon, following new instructions from John, made the drop in St. Raymond's Cemetery in the Bronx, while Charles waited alone in a nearby car. Condon, a blustery, assertive man, took it upon himself to hand over only $50,000 in bills, telling John that Lindbergh couldn't afford the extra demand. John then handed Condon a note, which reported that the boy was safe on a boat named *Nelly*, between Martha's Vineyard and the Massachusetts mainland.

When the sun set the next day, after a fruitless aerial and naval search of the waters, Charles knew he had been double-crossed. Yet he continued a wide search on his own the following day, flying far and wide, looking for any signs of the *Nelly*. Anne's optimism waned, and she began to fear that she would never see her son alive, despite assurances from the police to the contrary. The days passed slowly, with no more news from John.

Little Charlie's body was discovered by chance late in the afternoon of May 12, 1932, about six weeks after the kidnapping. A truck driver stopping to relieve himself in a thicket some five miles from the Lindberghs' house found a partially decomposed corpse. The tiny, blackened body lay face down in the dirt, portions of its limbs eaten by animals, but the golden curls and facial features firmly established its identity. Police officers determined that the probable cause of death was a violent blow to the head.

To Anne's newly widowed mother fell the task of telling her daughter the "baby is with Daddy." By evening, all major radio networks aired the news. "BABY DEAD" screamed a tabloid headline. At the time Charles was aboard a boat on another search, having been told the kidnappers would contact him there. Hearing of his son's death, Charles rushed home. He arrived at 2:00 in the morning, and he and Anne spent a sleepless night together. In her anguish, Anne had "no control over tears, no control over the hundred little incidents I had jammed out of sight when I was bargaining for my control." Her husband never cried but gave Anne "great courage" by speaking calmly about death. What little consolation they found came from knowing that the baby had been killed immediately and realizing none of their efforts would have kept him alive.[12]

According to Anne, their son's death brought the couple closer and "made something tremendous" out of their marriage that couldn't be changed.[13] They drew strength from each other when many marriages would have dissolved from the stress. At the same time, however, despite Charles's vow that they would build new lives and put the past behind them, the couple couldn't help but be marked by the tragedy. Charles was burying his sorrow, feeling that America's greatest hero had failed to protect his wife and son. He rarely spoke about his son's death in the years to come, though in a later autobiography he briefly detailed the crime. It shattered Anne's faith in people and further aggravated her husband's relationship with the press, whom he felt had been partly to blame.

Even in death, little Charlie was without peace. Warned that sightseers would trample his grave, Charles had his son's remains cremated. Several months later, flying alone off the Atlantic coastline, Charles scattered his ashes from a plane. The following year the Lindberghs deeded the Sourland Mountain house and property to the State of New Jersey for a home "to provide for the welfare of children, including their education, training, hospitalization and other allied purposes without discrimination in regard to race or creed."[14]

During the summer the Lindberghs retreated to the safety and seclusion of Next Day Hill, but family tragedy continued to dog them. On Friday, June 10, the Morrows' English maid, Violet Sharpe, swallowed poison, then fainted and died near the pantry at Next Day Hill. Recently she had been grilled by police investigating the kidnapping, and Anne questioned if Violet had known something about the crime. Whatever precipitated the suicide remained a mystery. Anne wondered if the "train of misery" following the crime would ever cease: "I feel as though the consequences would ripple out into an ever widening circle. There is no end."[15]

Even harder for Anne was when doctors told Elisabeth Morrow, then a semi-invalid living at Next Day Hill, that she had an irreversibly damaged heart valve. The life expectancy for patients with her condition was less than five years. Despite ill health—or perhaps because of it, knowing her short-ened life span—Elisabeth set sail for England. Soon joining her were Betty Morrow, on her first trip abroad since her husband's death, and Constance and Dwight, on summer break. While recuperating in Somerset, Elisabeth renewed her romance with Aubrey Neil Morgan, the scion of a Welsh depart-ment store owner. She had first met him in January 1930 when she went with her mother and father to England.

While visiting Elisabeth, Mrs. Morrow brought a whirlwind of activity that proved difficult for her daughter to handle, and her precarious health took a turn for the worse in July, when she suffered a relapse following a weekend party. Anne begged her sister to conserve her energy; she wrote to Elisabeth, "You are not just a weaker edition of Mother but *different.* Please don't think that Charles would say you were weak in character. (He thinks you stronger than I—and rightly.)" Anne added that she felt "terribly for Mother, too, because I know she is not living a normal adjusted life yet. She is still living Daddy's pace and *for* Daddy and especially over there—it must have been a sacred duty."[16]

Charles had been concerned about Elisabeth's deteriorating health for some time, and had hoped to design a mechanical heart for her, to be used during an operation. His initial interest in science and medicine had begun two decades earlier, following in the tradition of the Lodges and Lands of Detroit. In fact, during his youth he had entertained thoughts of becoming a doctor but didn't think he could master the required Latin. In 1930, after expressing his interest in a mechanical heart to several doctors, he was intro-duced to the brilliant French surgeon Dr. Alexis Carrel, winner of a Nobel Prize in 1912 for physiology and medicine. Carrel headed the department of experimental surgery at the Rockefeller Institute for Medical Research and offered Charles full use of his laboratories. A devout Catholic, the doctor believed in miracles and considered himself something of a mystic and a philosopher. He often held court at the Century Club in Manhattan, where his admirers gathered around to pay homage to his philosophy and political beliefs. He became a mentor of sorts to Charles, whose work at the Institute often occurred well after midnight, after he had concluded a day's worth of aviation business. In 1935 Charles would invent a perfusion pump, which could keep an organ alive after it was removed from a body. A first in medical history, it would bring him further acclaim—and more unwanted publicity.

The year would end on a high note for Elisabeth: on December 28, she and Aubrey, having decided to ignore the doctors' grim prognosis, married at Next Day Hill in Englewood. A radiant bride, flushed with happiness, she appeared somewhat healthier after a recent vacation. Constance led the wedding march into the candle-lit library, where a few dozen guests waited. On Dwight's arm came Elisabeth, dressed in a satin gown with a train, her hair held back by a band of orange blossoms. After a honeymoon in France, the newlyweds settled near Cardiff, Wales.

On August 16, 1932, with her husband and her mother at her side, Anne gave birth to her second son after a short, four-hour labor at the Morrows' Manhattan apartment. The baby's birth renewed Anne's energy and hope for the future. She had feared the ordeal of giving birth, still grieving for her first-born. "The spell was broken by this real, tangible, perfect baby, coming into an imperfect world and coming out of the teeth of sorrow—a miracle. My faith had been reborn," she described to her diary.[17] The couple named their second born Jon, a name that Anne had found in a book of Scandinavian fairy tales.

Less than a month later, on September 13, Anne returned to the air, flying with her husband in a rented Bird biplane from the Long Island Aviation Country Club to North Haven, Maine. At the controls on the Portland to North Haven leg, Anne was thrilled to be flying again. In Maine they took a sixteen-day vacation, during which they sailed and played tennis, then flew back to Long Island. Aboard their biplane on the return flight were Mrs. Morrow and Bogey, Elisabeth's Scottish terrier.[18]

With the start of the New Year Anne and Charles accepted more social invitations, while continuing the painful process of picking up the pieces of their lives. Friday, January 13, 1933, found them attending a banquet in New York, where the government of Romania awarded Charles and Amelia Earhart medals for their aeronautical achievements. In the presence of Amelia and other beautiful women, seeming like players in an unreal world, Anne described the event as a "glazed and perfect moment of its kind."[19] Only eight days later, on January 21, the Lindberghs went to a small dinner party at the Rye, New York, home of Earhart and her husband, George Palmer Putnam, or G. P., as friends called him. The party honored Auguste Piccard, the Swiss-born balloonist and scientist famous for his record-breaking balloon ascent to an altitude of 51,775 feet in 1931.

Putnam, a publisher and a public relations whiz, had created the Earhart legend, beginning with the "Lady Lindy" image he developed for her in 1928. Handsome and tall, with flashing dark eyes and close-cropped dark hair, he exuded charisma and confidence. Ten years older than Amelia, G. P. had badgered her for two years to become his wife after his divorce from socialite Dorothy Binney Putnam. Many people, including Amelia's friends, considered theirs a marriage of convenience. Certainly, G. P. was an extraordinary promoter, but his manipulation of ballyhoo did not sit well with some of Amelia's rivals. Aviators of both sexes resented the publicity the media showered upon Amelia. Elinor Smith, a celebrity pilot herself, claimed that G. P. threatened to end her flying career when she did not cave in and sign a contract with him. Perhaps motivated partly by jealousy, some pilots scoffed at Amelia's feats. While it was true that she had more than a fair share of what she called "incidents," or accidents, she was an accomplished pilot who by 1933 had flown solo across the Atlantic and had made record-breaking transcontinental flights. (In January 1935 she would become the first pilot, man or woman, to fly solo from Hawaii to California.)

By contrast, Anne Lindbergh downplayed her own flying skills and cringed at life in the limelight. As the wife of the world's champion aviator, Anne couldn't expect to share his glory just because she herself flew. Her piloting abilities weren't on par with those of celebrated women flyers, who flew competitively, for records and in contests, and who flew long distances alone. But she did count Amelia and other women flyers among her friends, and eventually she would find her own success by transforming her flying experiences into exceptional writing.

Anne was an artist whose creativity was evident in other areas, too. In a letter to Amelia written less than a week after the January dinner party, Anne described her idea for a women's clothes department in Macy's, or another department store. Geared to female pilots and air travelers, the air shop could carry lightweight clothes and all-purpose shoes, along with crushable hats and compact drug kits. Anne added, "For shameful or not as it may be, women are interested in what to wear flying."[20]

In all America, there was probably no woman more qualified to explain the clothes and personal items a woman pilot or traveler needed than Anne Lindbergh. While racking up thousands of air miles stateside and abroad and living in a seaplane, she had been limited to small parcels of carry-on baggage, including a mere eighteen pounds on the Orient survey flight. About a year after her January letter to Amelia Earhart, Anne's idea for an air shop came to fruition. In December 1933, Macy's announced it would carry a line of women's clothing for travel and sportswear, designed by Amelia Earhart.

Even though the birth of Jon had revitalized Anne, she still experienced periods of mourning for Charlie during the winter of 1933. With the approaching anniversary of his murder, she became depressed and struggled over what she called the "eternal baffling mystery of death." She had few people to whom she could confide her emotions; when she tried to talk with Charles, he cut her off: "I went through it last spring—I can't go through it again." Although Jon, a brawny, healthy baby, thrived at Next Day Hill, the Lindberghs feared for his safety and hired an armed guard to provide around-the-clock protection. A sensationalist press that rehashed the crime only added to Anne's misery.[21]

Worried about his wife's depression and the relentless pressures from the press, Charles suggested they take a brief vacation. In mid-March, the couple slipped away for a ten-day motor trip to visit family in Cleveland and Detroit, wearing disguises and using aliases. Cheered by the impromptu trip and the success of their camouflaged appearance, Anne savored the "hidden reserve" they had uncovered. "We *can* get away!" she effused to her mother.[22]

Flying continued to give Anne a feeling of freedom and contentment. On a late March flight, she compared the engine throbbing to music; looking below, she saw everything moving with "slow grace."[23] This short flight preceded a cross-continent marathon, an aerial inspection trip for TWA, which continued to bill itself as the "Lindbergh Line." Upon reaching Burbank, California, Anne and Charles would retrieve their Lockheed Sirius, reconditioned after its 1931 accident in the Yangtze. It was refitted with a wheeled landing gear for a return home—when preparations would begin for another global survey flight.

In 1933 American aviation leaped into the era of the modern airliner with the introduction of the Boeing 247, which sliced coast-to-coast travel time to less than twenty hours. Meantime, Douglas Aircraft had built the all-metal, twin-engine DC-1 for TWA. One year later, in 1934, the superior Douglas DC-2, first flown in service by the "Lindbergh Line" on May 11, would eclipse both those aircraft. Shortly afterward, the DC-3s went into service; by 1939 they were transporting two-thirds of all the nation's air passengers. A mere thirty years after the Wright brothers' *Flyer* hopped over sand dunes at Kitty Hawk, transcontinental airline service was no longer a novelty. During the TWA inspection, Charles would survey the line's routes and equipment, while looking toward its future needs by spending time at the Douglas factory in Santa Monica.[24]

On April 19, as the clock struck a few minutes after noon, the Lindberghs began the long flight toward California. Their borrowed Lockheed Vega lifted off from Newark into a murky mist of low ceilings that blanketed the eastern seaboard. After a stop at Camden, the Vega swooped under a 400-foot ceiling to land at Baltimore, where Anne and Charles overnighted with Louise Thaden, winner of the 1929 Women's Air Derby and holder of altitude, endurance, and speed records. Her young son, observed Anne, was "just the age of little Charles." Leaving Baltimore, the Lindberghs then stopped at Washington, Harrisburg, Pittsburgh, Columbus, St. Louis, Kansas City, Springfield, Wichita, Joplin, Tulsa, Oklahoma City, Elk City, Amarillo, Albuquerque, Winslow, Kingman—among other cities—before arriving in Los Angeles on April 28.[25]

The Lindberghs' transcontinental flight, in many ways, became a homecoming for the "first couple of the air." Mobbed at airports and showered with adulation, they had returned to the white glare of publicity. In Los Angeles the couple took refuge with airline executive Jack Maddux, whose wife Helen had died the previous year. Jack's loss profoundly affected Anne, stirring up memories of Helen's friendship and an earlier visit when she was carrying Charlie, but she found time to relax, too. While her husband met with Douglas Aircraft and TWA officials, Anne found solace at the beach. Walking the Pacific shore, listening to the roar of breaking waves, she was reminded of the beaches in Nassau. To her delight, she was able to blend in with the crowd while roller-skating on the concrete walkway above the palisades.

The Lindberghs left Los Angeles in their Lockheed Sirius on Saturday, May 6, as a morning haze pressed down over distant mountains. Pushed by a fierce sixty-knot tailwind, the plane streaked eastward. In the rear cockpit sat Anne, feeling comfortable and at home in her "little room," at long last. Looking around, she took stock of her cockpit, reliving the Orient flight and her part in it.

Her contentment was short lived, however. After leaving Las Vegas that afternoon, the Sirius became caught in a ferocious dust storm. During the 1930s, across the drought-ravaged Plains, huge amounts of topsoil were blown away, burying farms and ranches with a mile-high wall of dust. On the flight eastward—toward Albuquerque—sand billowed up, swallowing the Sirius even as it climbed to 14,000 feet. Rocked by turbulence, the plane's wings flexed like bows. Anne closed the sliding canopy hatch, yet a fine grit filled the cockpit, threatening to clog and shut down the engine.

Cut off from landmarks, Charles steered south looking for safe haven, then let down over the Texas Panhandle, inching closer to tumbleweeds roaring across a ground murky with thick yellow dust. Frightened, Anne put on her goggles and unbuckled her parachute, knowing that the plane was too low for a successful bail out. Charles landed on a patch of prairie and cut the switches. The couple climbed down from the plane, then dug holes to anchor the plane's main wheels and tail wheel while a gale-force wind blew. They overnighted in the Sirius, conserving water, drinking ginger ale, and eating sandwiches. By the following morning the dust had cleared to allow a takeoff.

Their disappearance set off a flurry of rumors, search parties, and all-night vigils across airfields in the Southwest. Straggling into Kansas City near noon on Sunday, May 7, dusty and tired, they deplaned from the Sirius to meet relieved officials. The hysteria annoyed Charles. Exasperated, he told reporters, "People shouldn't worry. It's liable to happen any time in the Western country."[26] Nevertheless, the next day the couple's sandstorm escape made front-page news.

Anne's return home in mid-May brought her no respite from activity, as preparations began for a lengthy survey flight across the Atlantic, to start in early July. The Lindberghs' mission—work on behalf of Pan American Airways—was not easy, by any means. They would scout airport and seaplane sites, and look at potential air lanes. They would also evaluate the Atlantic's capricious weather, a bane to centuries of mariners and recent decades of intrepid aviators. Along the way, Charles would drum up future business for Pan Am, talking shop with military staff and the officials of Europe's leading airlines, including K.L.M. Royal Dutch Airlines and Imperial Airways. Back in 1933, no aircraft, other than dirigibles, flew scheduled passenger flights across either the Atlantic or the Pacific. Laying out and implementing transoceanic routes presented the "last major barrier" world airlines then faced, Charles wrote.[27] For North Atlantic crossings, he considered three routes: the most northern across Greenland and Iceland, the great circle route from Newfoundland to Ireland, and the most southern route from the East Coast to Bermuda and the Azores to Europe. As on the Orient survey flight, the Lindberghs self-financed and planned the mission.

For safety and economics, both Charles Lindbergh and Juan Trippe realized that Pan Am had to use flying boats on its transoceanic routes. At that time, airplanes were not capable of carrying the heavy weight of the fuel needed for an ocean crossing, plus the weight of enough passengers to turn a profit on the flight. Instead, flying boats—aircraft with hulls that set down on water—would be used for the task. Although aircraft capable of both water and land landings (amphibians) were used on Pan Am's shorter routes to Latin America, the first ocean crossings would be made in flying boats. But it wasn't clear where these lumbering behemoths would refuel (technicians talked of stringing floating platforms across the ocean as refueling stops) or what ports would serve as bases.

International politics were a factor in considering potential aerial gateways, with European governments holding monopolies and landing rights for air and seaplane terminals. Indeed, most potential bases were under foreign control, with Britain holding rights in Bermuda, Canada, and the Irish Free State; Portugal with its mid-Atlantic islands; Denmark with its colony of Greenland, among others.[28] Trippe understood the necessity of cooperation among air carriers in different countries. Of course, landing rights had to be reciprocal, a fact that concerned the then isolationist United States. Thus, diplomatic aspects were important to the Lindberghs' flight, and Charles would work to facilitate international agreement.

While Anne realized that the survey flight would advance commercial air travel, in itself sufficient reason to go, there were other reasons for accompanying her husband. She was still flattered that Charles counted on her to crew, knowing that almost any pilot would want to fly with him. A June 26, 1933, *New York Times* article pointed out that the Lindberghs worked "well together in the air," with his crew-wife giving "great value" to her husband. As she acknowledged, their flights together brought them great happiness and compensated them for the burden that fame caused. The flight would also offer another opportunity to spend time with Charles and grow together with him, and in many ways, it would mark a turning point in their marriage. Twenty-seven years old when it began, she later wrote that she shed her status as a "page" to her husband by the time the survey ended, nearly six months later. She had long left her sheltered youth—after marriage, flying, and the tragedies of her father's death and her son's murder. She was maturing as a person in her own right, continuing to grow and learning to express her own desires.[29]

At the same time, Anne grappled with balancing her roles as a wife and as a mother. "I *hate* to leave him," she said of Jon before she departed.[30] Charles's mother, on summer break from teaching, would tend to little Jon at the family's Maine retreat, along with Betty Gow and a guard, until Mrs. Morrow returned from traveling abroad.

Preparing for the flight, Anne brushed up on Morse code and took care of the countless demands such a long trip entailed. Besides updating her skills, Anne read books about Greenland, sent to her by the polar explorer Vilhjalmur Stefansson, an early advocate of Arctic flight and himself a consultant to Pan American.

Charles, meanwhile, took care of upgrades and modifications to the Lockheed Sirius. He also arranged the necessary paperwork. Unlike the Orient flight, he did not have to have fuel cached in remote places—until later in the flight. The *Jelling*, a Danish tramp steamer chartered by Pan Am to support the Lindberghs' aerial exploration in Greenland, would carry fuel and even provide meals and berths, when needed.

The Sirius was refitted with its Edo pontoons and outfitted with new Pan Am radio equipment, a new 710-horsepower Wright Cyclone engine, and a controllable pitch propeller that helped the plane's efficiency. (The propeller could change pitch from "climb" to "cruise" settings.) Also installed, next to Anne's rear cockpit seat, was the navigator Harold Gatty's newly designed drift and ground speed indicator. Further enhancements included an artificial horizon and a directional gyro, instruments used in blind flying and navigation. Every addition helped. As Charles would later write, the Atlantic survey was even more perilous than his own 1927 transatlantic crossing—the most dangerous flight of his and Anne's aviation careers.

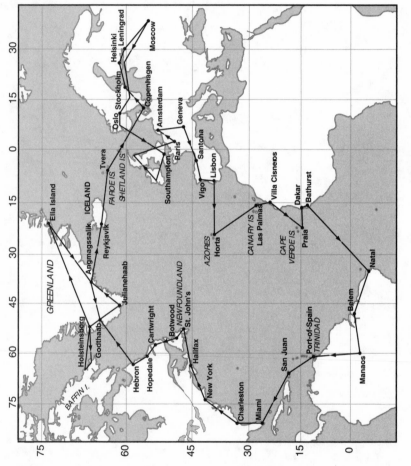

Atlantic survey flight, 1933. Map by Chris Robinson.

9

An Enchanted Land

Charles Lindbergh spent the late morning of July 9, 1933, searching the horizon above Flushing Bay, New York, frowning at skies scudded with a squall line of thunderstorms. Soon the sky blackened and rain pelted down, but after drenching the Glenn Curtiss Airport, the storm roared onward. Overhead, the clouds cleared and the sun shone brightly onto the field. That same afternoon, as planned, he and Anne would take off on their Atlantic survey expedition.

Their Lockheed Sirius was at the airport, awaiting its descent down the ramp into Flushing Bay. Ringing the seaplane were Movietone trucks and an army of reporters who circled round and round like hawks, pinpointing their prey. At 3:00 P.M. Anne appeared with several friends, then talked briefly with Charles Winters, Pan American Airways's radio technician.

Anne climbed aboard as Charles readied for takeoff in the forward cockpit. After starting the engine, he advanced the throttle while scanning the instrument panel, watching as the needles flickered around the dials. Once the Sirius slipped into the water, Charles taxied into position, then gunned the engine. The floats began to plane through the water, spray splashing the fuselage. Wind gusts surged through the open Sirius cockpit, lashing Charles's face and tossing about one of Anne's maps. The plane accelerated to its takeoff airspeed and lifted skyward around 3:30, tailed by chase planes loaded with photographers. In the days of uncontrolled airspace, pilots had free rein and could even execute dogfight-like maneuvers over Manhattan. When a flash of wing caught Charles's eye, he snapped his head to the side and saw a plane closing in on his left. He jammed the stick right and saw two other planes near his right wing. He climbed to avoid them, while Anne trembled at the near miss. "Never again on our entire trip did we come as close to having a serious accident," she would later write.[1]

Anne slid the canopy hatch closed, put on her headphones, and jotted the takeoff time on her note pad. The altimeter wound smoothly around until they reached cruising altitude, and Charles set the power to cruise at 115 miles per hour. Anne then cranked the reel located at her feet, unwinding the antenna. Within minutes a hundred feet of copper antenna wire dangled outside the plane.

The Sirius headed toward North Haven, Maine, dodging a newly formed storm of towering purple cumulonimbus clouds. Static created by the highly charged air crackled through Anne's headphones, making radio communication difficult. About twenty minutes short of their destination the coastal sea mists fused into a blanket of thick fog, and Anne and Charles were forced to land and overnight in the small town of South Pond, Maine.

The next morning they arrived over the Morrow house at North Haven. As the plane circled to land, Anne looked down to see her mother and mother-in-law waving from the ground. Although she was reluctant to leave eleven-month-old Jon, knowing she wouldn't see him for months to come, her overnight visit with him and his grandparents reassured her. He would have the best of care, which gave her a "solid feeling," she wrote her mother after departing.[2]

On July 11 the Sirius winged to Halifax, Nova Scotia, but during the two-hour flight Anne had trouble working the radio. Her Morse code skills were still rusty from lack of practice. But by the following day, on the five-hour leg to St. John's, Newfoundland, she was sending and receiving messages

On July 9, 1933, Anne and Charles began their Atlantic survey flight—a 30,000-mile exploration to four continents that lasted over five months. Here they pose in front of the Lockheed Sirius in New York before departure. Lindbergh Picture Collection, Manuscripts and Archives, Yale University Library. Reproduced with permission.

with ease from KHCAL, the Sirius's call sign. The few hours of practice had refreshed her abilities.

Settled around the 1520s, St. John's is the oldest city in Canada and the easternmost city in North America. At nearby Signal Hill, Marchese Marconi, the inventor of the radio transmitting system, received the first transatlantic wireless message in 1901. Approaching the city, Anne saw green pastures, fields of daisies, myriad lakes, and sheer bluffs rising a thousand feet straight up from the water's edge. The Sirius swooped over the bluffs and touched down in Bay Bulls Big Pond, just south of the city. The waiting crowd cheered and shouted out Colonel Lindbergh's name. Locals held a special affinity for Lindbergh, who had dipped his wings over the narrows of St. John's harbor in May 1927, some twenty-two hours before reaching Paris. In commemoration of his flyover, fishermen had christened their schooners with names such as *Lone Flier, Charles Lindbergh,* and *Lucky Lindy.*

After spending the night in St. John's, the Lindberghs awoke to a dirty-white overcast morning. The weather thwarted their plan to fly to Cartwright, Labrador, where they had hoped to see General Italo Balbo's aerial armada on its way to the "A Century of Progress" World's Fair in Chicago. Twelve days earlier, on July 1, Balbo's fleet of twenty-five Savoia-Marchetti S-55X flying boats launched from Ortobello, Italy. The flamboyant Balbo and his pilots had flown hundreds of practice hours before departing, synchronizing their formation flights with orchestral perfection, though one of the planes had crashed while refueling in Amsterdam. After several stops, Cartwright included, the fleet would arrive in mid-July over Lake Michigan, where the huge flying boats would gracefully swoop down and stun onlookers with their show of Italy's air power. It was a phenomenal achievement, and when Balbo returned to Italy, Mussolini would promote him to air marshal.[3]

On July 14 the front pushed through and the gray clouds lifted, leaving a bright blue clear and cold day. Anne put on two wool blouses, a sweater, and a slicker, nearly everything she had brought. The Lindberghs set out for Botwood, Newfoundland, their only stop en route to Cartwright. After crossing Conception Bay, the Sirius passed over Harbour Grace, the launch site for many aviation pioneers crossing the Atlantic—and the last spit of land they saw until reaching Ireland. Anne's eyes swept the airport; she later described it as "one long runway and a big pile of rocks at the end."[4]

In Botwood's large sheltered bay, the Lindberghs stopped two hours to refuel while also assessing the location's potential for a Pan American landing site. (Later in the decade, thanks in part to their survey, Botwood would become a regular stopover for the flying boats of Pan Am and Imperial Airways winging their way across the Atlantic.) They then flew over iceberg-speckled seas, small fishing villages cupped in coves, and the stark wilderness of Labrador. Meanwhile, Anne was in radio contact with Pan Am's Miami station and began to pick up radio messages from the *Jelling*, the steamer chartered to support the Lindberghs' expedition in Greenland. Upon reaching Cartwright's harbor, Anne spotted its blue smokestack. Bobbing nearby was the gleaming white *Alicia*, Italo Balbo's support ship, still in port though the armada had taken off earlier.

The *Jelling*, provided by Pan Am, would play an important role in the Lindberghs' survey, meeting up with them at various ports; however, its propeller and rudder were not as well housed as those of other ships, and it could not travel to some areas, especially the northeast coast of Greenland, where icebergs abounded. Aboard the ship were fuel and supplies for the Sirius, as well as a repair shop and sleeping berths—if the Lindberghs chose to bunk there. Its chef laid out hearty Danish meals, including a variety of fish, meat, eggs, onions, cheeses, black bread, and beer. Its comfortable dining cabin featured a big table covered with a green cloth, atop which hung a swinging gas lamp, and a red plush sofa flanked by two marble-topped cupboards.

Indeed, Anne came to call the *Jelling* home. Charles was often preoccupied with the survey's technical aspects, and she sometimes craved companionship. Exacerbating her loneliness was her shyness, "a latent disease" she said, which would take an "uncontrollable virulent form" even after thinking she had conquered it. Although she cherished the hospitality and friendship that women extended to her on the survey, they were not of her world: Anne was a woman who crewed, whose technical training contributed to the success of the Lindberghs' flights. So when technicians, such as scientists and explorers, gave her a sense of belonging or appreciation for her work, she treasured the experience. One such kindred spirit was W. P. Jarbo, the *Jelling*'s radio operator, whom she described as "a pale, rather nervous, quick man in a navy serge suit like every radio operator." Anne and Jarbo would compare notes when they met in port. As radio operators, they had to share a balancing act: contacting stations along routes—part of their job duties—and appeasing Charles who feared publicity if people heard of the Sirius's position; he didn't want people to know of their schedules or whereabouts. She and Jarbo understood each other's problems. Another kindred spirit would be Danish officer Commander A. M. Dam, whom she would later meet in Godthaab, Greenland.[5]

On July 17 the *Jelling* steamed toward Greenland to await the Lindberghs, who were planning to fly north and scout potential landing sites. But after flying a few hours over snow-capped mountains to Carter Basin, they returned to Cartwright, where the weather closed in and stranded them. Despite Cartwright's bleak landscape dotted with scrubby pine trees, Anne eventually grew to like the settlement and its hard-working people. There two days, they worked on the Sirius between storms, as rain drenched the harbor amid a low overcast. They stayed in a two-story white frame house perched on a point, the only hotel between Newfoundland and Iceland. On Cartwright's boardwalk Anne observed fishermen at the "ice house, shaking out a net, or mending a boat . . . men on the dock in boots and so'westers, and those thick white cotton mittens . . . barrels and sawdust and the smell of fish."[6]

Overnight the deck of clouds rolled back, and the morning of July 20 dawned to a turquoise sky on the northeast horizon. Greenland beckoned, and the Lindberghs rushed to launch in Cartwright's harbor, but the Sirius floundered in the harbor's calm water. It was overloaded with fuel, with no headwind or ripples in the water to help its pontoons break free from the sea. It was neither the first nor the last time the plane would struggle to get airborne. Later, an insufficient headwind, calm water, and a heavy payload would almost spell the end of the successful survey flight at Bathurst, Gambia, on the west coast of Africa.

By the next morning, with a brisk wind churning the water and less gasoline in the tanks, they easily launched on a course straight to Frederikshaab, Greenland. Forty miles out from Cartwright, though, they hit a wall of fog, from which towering icebergs jutted. They once again gave up on Greenland, and they beat a hasty retreat toward Labrador's coast. Skirting the rocky coastline, they instead flew north to Hopedale, a small settlement of red-roofed white houses at the foot of a mountain and home to a Moravian mission, built in 1782. During the Lindberghs' three-hour layover, Hopedale's only missionary, a forty-two-year resident of the settlement, pleaded, "Tell them at Hebron that the boat left here several days ago."[7]

Hebron was another Moravian post located farther north in Labrador, and it was awaiting its yearly supply boat. As in Baker Lake, Canada, a stop on the Lindberghs' 1931 survey, a year's wait for news and provisions was typical—no fresh vegetables or meats, other than game hunted nearby, no mail, little if any contact with the "outside." That same day, the Sirius streaked north two hours to Hebron, where Charles landed in an open fjord and taxied in between icebergs. Soon a motorboat manned by Reverend George Harp, a weary missionary, and two Hudson's Bay men pulled up alongside the seaplane. On the dock were parka-wearing Eskimos flailing at swarms of mosquitoes. Anne and Charles patted their faces with citronella, pulled their helmets tight, and pushed up their collars. Running to meet them as they were led up a steep hill to the mission was a little blue-eyed, blonde girl dressed in calico and a white pinafore: Joan, the missionary's daughter. On her head she wore a blue straw hat draped with mosquito netting.

Inside the mission house, the missionary rubbed his hands together and said, "We are almost starving, literally." Charles told him that the supply boat was on the way, then went to retrieve sandwiches and one banana still on the Sirius. Remembering Cartwright, Anne thought it "impossible that we could have left such luxury only that morning."[8]

The supply boat held special significance for the Harps, all of whom would set sail to England on their year of leave so Joan could start school. There were no schools in Hebron, and the thought of leaving little Joan in

England was "almost breaking their hearts," Reverend Harp confessed to Anne.[9]

On a clear morning the following day, July 22, the Sirius departed for Godthaab, Greenland. Despite running into a low fog bank soon after take-off from Hebron, the seaplane punched through to a cloudless cobalt sky. Three hours into the flight over the Labrador Sea, Anne and Charles saw Greenland's ice-capped mountains forming a jagged wall high in the sky. Closer in, they saw the rocky coast, chiseled by fjords, spotted with white gleaming glaciers. About six hours after takeoff, they landed in Godthaab's harbor, which was framed by craggy hills and distant soaring peaks. A small armada of kayaks sliced through the water as they were towed in, while the town's cannons blasted three welcoming booms. In a sharp contrast to Labrador's monotony, Godthaab blazed with a cornucopia of colors. Steep-pitched houses of green, red, blue, and yellow, with white trim, lorded over the small settlement cupped near the harbor. "It looked like a toy village," recorded Anne in her diary, "so bright and clean and newly painted." Jamming the dock were Greenlanders wearing bright reds and blues, she noted, with women "dressed up in gala fashion, high bright embroidered boots, sealskin pants, bright blouses, and tall knitted caps, with pompoms on top." That evening, the *Jelling* chugged in from a nearby fishing bank, where it had awaited the Lindberghs' arrival.[10]

At the governor's house, they met Commander Dam, appointed by the Danish government to act as liaison officer in Greenland, supporting the Lindberghs and the Pan Am expedition. Tall, handsome, and cultured, he and Anne got along well. She appreciated his sensitive nature and sense of humor, later describing him as a "little like the Elizabethans—who all—as a matter of course could write poetry and sing and perhaps paint, but would rather be known as soldiers and adventurers."[11]

The next day damp, cold wind blew, and Anne and Charles tramped around Godthaab, sightseeing and snapping photos of the Greenlander belles decked out in their colorful costumes. They spent time with the locals the following day, too, when they went with the *Jelling's* crew to a dance held at the town's gymnasium. To Anne's surprise, the Greenlanders whirled around to old English and Irish rounds, Irish jigs, and Virginia reels, dances that had been taught to their ancestors by early Scottish whalers and traders. Anne became caught up in the fiddlers' music and the foot stamping, and she warmed to the rhythm, which she compared to both flying and "life itself, the beat of the heart." Still mourning her firstborn's death, she thought of "birth, and love, and death. I try to realize that it would not be complete without death, that death is part of the pattern, and so I must not be afraid of it." When the gaiety of the dance abruptly ended, the Greenlander women disappeared into the cold mist, hurrying to bed. Tomorrow they would rise at dawn to haul coal and work on the roads and docks. (The men, such work beneath them, would keep to their traditional jobs of hunting and fishing.)[12]

On July 25 Charles and Anne winged north to Holsteinsborg, the cockpit so cold that Anne transmitted while wearing mittens. On the way, they flew inland along a fjord to the polar ice cap's edge. Deeply furrowed with crevasses, the ice cap looked "dirty, like a week-old snow at home, and streaked as though snowplows had raked over it," Anne recalled. Upon reaching Holsteinsborg, the Lindberghs had again crossed the Arctic Circle, two years after their 1931 survey flight to Japan. In the little town of bright-colored houses, they boarded at the local governor's house. In the evening they looked out at small boats in the harbor and fog veiling the mountains, and the square where mothers walked with babies on their backs, rocking from foot to foot to put them to sleep. Snow squalls and fog blanketed the town during most of their stay, but Anne and Charles made time for diversions between exploratory flights. There were raucous parties aboard the *Jelling*, the red-faced Danish captain bantering with the governor's wife, and Victrola music on shore at the governor's house.[13]

They also paddled kayaks along the rocky coast. On Anne's first try, Charles pushed her boat far into the water, leaving her frightened and shaking so hard that the kayak rocked. Once she got the hang of it, she turned around and paddled in. He was also mischievous with the *Jelling's* crew and succeeded in having everyone, except the Danish captain, try kayaking, hoping someone would flip over. Charles still liked playing practical jokes as much as he had during his U.S. Army Air Service training. After four years of marriage, however, Anne had become less forgiving of his pranks.

In his downtime Charles also reviewed maps and climatic changes with the local governor and scientists, evaluating future landing sites. Meanwhile, Anne, shut out from the men's talk, became plagued with insecurity and retreated to the privacy of her diary to record her thoughts. In Holsteinsborg, the *Jelling's* Jarbo had paid his first compliment to Anne, saying that she was "obliging and therefore easy to work with," yet his remarks left Anne disappointed: he had not praised her work. "I must be as poor at sending as I think I am," she falsely concluded. Continually doubtful of her technical skills, she still worried that she didn't fit in with Charles and his male colleagues. She wanted to prove herself but felt she was the "weak link" in their world, sure she would be the first pulled out if anything went wrong. She ached to be more than a "rather pale and good shadow" to her husband, she later wrote, and her insecurity would continue to haunt her during the first part of the survey flight. She wanted to be recognized for her talents and wondered if she would ever find her own world. "And there is so little time left. I am almost thirty."[14]

Meantime, Anne struggled with another bout of insecurity when they flew to Canada's Baffin Island from Holsteinsborg, one of two exploration flights made during breaks in the foul weather. The four-hour flight back to North America over the Davis Strait took place on August 3. The *New York Times* later reported that it was a "perilous" flight with no place to make an emergency landing if their engine failed. Flying through fog, and then above a solid overcast, they were lost until Charles spotted an opening. He put the plane in a spiral, and the Sirius broke out over bare, treeless Baffin Island. Anne tried to work the radio and continued to change the coils, afraid she would miss transmissions from OYKC, the *Jelling*. The schedule had been prearranged and when she did not respond to OYKC, the ship sent frantic messages to KHCAL, the Sirius's call sign, trying to warn of bad weather nearby. When Anne still did not reply, the ship steamed toward open sea for better reception. Although Anne blamed herself for her problems working the radio, the malfunction was a dynamotor brush sticking, and Charles repaired it easily after they returned to Greenland. Overly sensitive to what she perceived as her failure with the equipment, Anne wrote in her diary, "If C. had had a regular operator, there would have been no failure. I feel very much a woman."[15]

On August 4 the Lindberghs awoke to cirrus clouds streaking high above and blue sky breaking through over Holsteinsborg. They could finally leave on their flight over the ice cap to Greenland's east coast. The governor's wife, rushing around her kitchen, packed them a lunch of black bread, smoked halibut, sardines, sausage, cheese, and vanilla cookies. (As Anne later said, when they traveled, lunches came to be more important than flowers given them by well-meaning locals.)

After takeoff, Anne and Charles skirted the coast north to Disko Bay, while continuing to climb to gain enough altitude to cross the ice cap. Along the way, they looked down at fjords and a mammoth glacier calving huge icebergs, some as high as mountains. With a great roar, ice floes broke apart, falling and crashing into water that churned and foamed with the impact. The Sirius then turned east and flew over the massive ice cap.

Two miles high at its center, the ice cap was an enormous mass of ice that covered Greenland like a blanket. Soon the drifting, brilliant white snow and ice created whiteout conditions. Whiteouts were—and still are—the bane of Arctic pilots: the glare blinded them and they lost a natural horizon with which to orient their planes. They could crash into the ground while thinking they were flying straight and level above Earth. No stranger to whiteout phenomena, Charles slid back the canopy hatch and put on amber-colored goggles to improve his vision. Though they flew at an altitude of 13,000 feet with an outside temperature of −13 degrees centigrade, Anne's upper body was warm, swaddled in layers of wool. She put on a second pair of mittens and would have added a third pair but the extra bulk would have made it impossible to use the radio key.[16]

During the seven-hour flight, Anne continually radioed OYKC, giving position and course. Midway across the ice cap, Charles handed back a note: "Every five minutes we save a day's walk!"[17] He was thrilled to be exploring the area by air, in contrast to the sled expeditions of an earlier era. Before long, Anne began receiving from Danish ships on the east coast. After seeing the shadows of mountains on the east horizon, Anne heard from the *Gustaf Holm,* one of two mother ships assigned to the renowned Danish explorer Dr. Lauge Koch and his aerial expedition of northeast Greenland. The ship advised KHCAL to land at Ella Island, one of Koch's bases.

In this expedition to Greenland, Koch commanded a party of 109 men, including 72 scientists and 37 sailors. His equipment consisted of fifteen motorboats and the *Gustav Holm* and the *Godthaab,* both of which carried seaplanes on their decks. The planes were used for aerial photography and map charting. By and large, it was a risky expedition, though Koch had seen worse in Greenland. That night on the *Godthaab,* he described for the Lindberghs a grueling journey he had taken across the ice cap as a young man, in which supplies were scarce and one man had died of starvation.

The following day, Anne and Charles flew to Koch's other base, Clavering Island. At seventy-four degrees latitude, it was the most northern point they would touch on the survey flight. Anne looked down at musk ox "herded together, their great manes shaking" and a polar bear that lumbered along a fjord's shore. The land of mountains, glaciers, and the mammoth ice cap seemed to be a "land hewn by giants," she observed. Aboard the *Gustaf Holm* off Clavering Island, the couple dined and slept overnight. There Koch invited them to see the midnight sun and his beloved scenery in Peary Land, a peninsula at the northernmost tip of Greenland, first explored by Robert E. Peary in his expedition of 1891–92. Koch explained to the Lindberghs how easy it was to damage the arctic environment: earlier explorers had decimated the game, and the vegetation was fragile and slow growing, with small plants taking decades or even centuries to grow.[18]

The next day, August 6, dawned bright and clear and cloudless. After leaving Koch's base, the Sirius turned south toward Angmagssalik, skirting the shore between ice pack and glaciers. After flying eight hours, they arrived in the late afternoon to see the town's harbor filled with floating icebergs. Not sure they could land, Anne pictured "spending the night on top of the sledge after a cold dinner of cold, canned baked beans." She had, however, underestimated her husband, who artfully threaded the Sirius through the floes, landing in the harbor.[19]

While in Angmagssalik, the Lindberghs spent time on the base ship of Dr. Knud Rasmussen, the Danish arctic explorer and ethnologist whose popular books had introduced Greenland to a worldwide audience. A small, friendly, affectionate man, he reminded Anne of her father. He put her completely at ease, and with him and his crew, she felt as much a part of a family as she did back in North Haven. Rasmussen, like some others meeting the Lindberghs, had assumed that they would travel in a large plane with a mechanic and a radio operator, a group of four. Toasting them at a dinner party, he praised their working together as a team, just the two of them.

Two days later, on August 8, Charles taxied the Sirius between towering chunks of ice at Angmagssalik, searching for a stretch long enough for a take-off. Because he wanted another flight across Greenland, they flew westward to the town of Godthaab. After refueling there, the couple set off at 6:00 P.M. for Julianehaab, Greenland's first, most prosperous, and largest settlement.[20] They followed the coast as they headed south, for now leaving behind the land of the midnight sun.

They stayed four nights in Julianehaab, where they boarded in an old Danish house and met up again with the *Jelling.* The layover gave Anne time to bring her radio log up to date and catch up on correspondence. Finally the weather cleared, and the Lindberghs prepared for a return to Angmagssalik. Residents gathered at the pier, waving farewell, and nature, too, orchestrated a send-off: six enormous whales outside the harbor blew hundred-foot plumes as the Sirius lifted off. Away from Angmagssalik only six days, they arrived to see its harbor free of ice and its cerulean seas speckled by sunshine. At this, their last stop in Greenland, they had the Sirius christened *Tingmissartoq,* or "one who flies like a big bird." Sitting on the plane's wing in the harbor, a Greenlander boy painted in bold letters the phrase that native children had shouted whenever they spotted the black and orange seaplane.

Three days later, on August 15, the Lindberghs reluctantly turned their backs on Greenland, completing a three-week aerial exploration that had crisscrossed the country. Of all their destinations on the Atlantic flight, Greenland became the Lindberghs' most-beloved stopover. There they had shed their celebrity status and replenished their spirits, easing painful memories of their firstborn's kidnapping and murder. There were no reporters to dog them at every turn, and the Greenlanders and Danes had treated them as they would ordinary people. In this "enchanted land," Anne wrote her mother, "you forget the rest of life, the rest of the world."[21] Regretfully, she turned her thoughts to the next stage of their journey—onward to Europe, rejoining the rest of the world.

10

Europe

Anne's first sight of Iceland, after the Sirius cut across the Denmark Strait from Greenland, was of flat-topped buttes crowned by a blue sky and green fields tucked beyond the fjords. She saw no peaked mountains, a sharp contrast with Greenland's black-colored, saw-toothed massifs. Ten minutes before landing, Charles's hand rose from the front cockpit, signaling Anne to sign off from KHCAL and reel in. The Sirius then dove over Reykjavik's harbor, where waves churned and whitecaps foamed—the water was so rough that they were forced to land in calmer seas near Videy Island.

The sun was setting, meanwhile, and hundreds of Icelanders crowded around the harbor, waiting to glimpse the Lindberghs. Anne and Charles's fears had come to pass—a return to cameras and crowds. After Reykjavik's mayor reached them by motorboat, he invited the couple to stay in a hotel, but Charles balked at the thought and said they often slept in the Sirius. Anne was livid, staring at her husband in disbelief. How could she possibly sleep cramped in the baggage compartment, after having pictured the comforts of the city? She wanted a haircut and hot baths, and needed to shop for toiletries. Charles caved in after seeing his wife's glare and suggested they stay at a nearby fishing village. And so it went—they spent two days there with an Icelandic family. The day after they arrived at Videy Island, Anne received letters from her mother-in-law and cables from Elisabeth and her mother. Of the correspondence, she most treasured news of Jon from Charles's mother, whose letters brought her up to date on the little boy's activities. By August 17 Charles had decided to completely give in to Anne's wishes, and they checked into the Hotel Borg in Reykjavik, a return to society and domestic comforts. Anne enjoyed a hot bath, then sent their laundry out, gushing about the hotel's amenities to her husband. Later on, she danced at a farewell reception for Crown Prince Frederick of Denmark, while Charles, who still turned up his nose at dancing, looked on.

The Lindberghs' five-day formal visit in Reykjavik was the official start of the European portion of the survey flight. From that point on, throughout Europe, they faced a packed agenda: sightseeing excursions, calls on diplomats and on airline officers, and presentations to royalty—to name just a few of their many commitments. Although in Iceland the press reported rumors of the Lindberghs' imminent return home, Anne and Charles had no intention of shortening the expedition. Frustrated by reporters hounding them and second-guessing their every step, they kept the media in the dark about their proposed itinerary. In late August, though, Anne explained to her mother-in-law a schedule they would possibly follow: a return home in late fall from Africa to South America, a shorter hop across water than the Azores route. One month later Hugo Leuteritz, Pan American's Chief Communication Engineer, sent the Lindberghs a list of direction-finding stations and a map illustrating the location, call letters, and frequencies of stations in South America. Anne would make good use of this for her radio work on the South Atlantic flight leg.[1]

On August 22 the *Jelling* pulled anchor and steamed away in becalmed seas from Iceland, heading westward. It had followed the Lindberghs from Greenland, but the time had come to end its support of the couple's northern expedition. In Anne's eyes, a lifeline was severed when the ship departed, and she regretted having to leave its radio operator Jarbo, her comrade who had understood the difficulties of her work. They had both walked a tightrope trying to do their jobs, alerting stations of their positions, yet appeasing Charles, who didn't want the Sirius's location known. Nonetheless, the next day she and Charles left Iceland and flew to the fog-shrouded Faroe Islands, landing under a 200-foot overcast at Tvera, where they laid over only one night. They next charted a course to Lerwick, in the Shetland Islands.

Unbeknownst to the couple, a horde of Danes had begun milling around Copenhagen's harbor on August 25. They awaited the Lindberghs, the press telling them they would arrive that day. The crestfallen crowd drifted away when they heard the Lindberghs remained in the Shetland Islands, but the confusion set the stage for a public relations fiasco that unfolded the following day. After flying five hours over the North Sea on August 26, the Sirius set down in Copenhagen's harbor. Suddenly hundreds of sailboats and kayaks swarmed close to the landing seaplane, ignoring its spinning propeller. Anne and Charles were stunned, having been promised a quiet welcome by the Danish authorities and Commander Dam, who had arrived earlier. Charles was infuriated by the turmoil and dangers the boats presented. He also wanted no part of the planned festivities—a short motorcade and a thirty-minute reception. While the Danish hosts stammered and paled, Anne tactfully tried to defuse the situation. Yet Charles insisted on avoiding the festivities, even after Commander Dam told him he would disappoint the people. Hard feelings would arise too, he added.

The Danes had no choice but to scuttle the festivities, leaving Anne caught between her husband's protests and Dam's entreaties. "I am intensely unhappy and wish we had never come."[2] Her husband conceded to one request, however, a brief welcoming ceremony at the town hall. There the brouhaha started up again when Anne and Charles had to shake the hundreds of hands thrust before them. It continued as they drove to the hotel, a mob of bodies pressing close and clawing at the car windows, and into the night, when they went to the United States Legation for an interview set up by Commander Dam—an olive leaf thrown to frustrated journalists to make up for the aborted festivities. Finally it ended, with Anne buckling under stress that left her sick all night and into the morning.

Later on, while returning from an afternoon excursion with Anne and Commander Dam—an audience with Sweden's Crown Prince—Charles had to dodge people snapping pictures of him. "I am not a Prince!" he complained to his wife and the commander. As they continued to talk, Dam considered Charles's situation, saying, "The only trouble is that people like you too much. If you had a scandal . . ." Charles replied, laughing, "Well, I'm perfectly willing, but my wife isn't."[3]

During the nine-day layover in Copenhagen, Anne stopped at the airport radio station, thanking radio operators who had given her bearings on the flight across the North Sea. Her husband visited Kastrup, the military base, where he inspected planes and later talked with airline officers. Both Lindberghs met dignitaries and attended dinners at the American and the British Legations.

Two days after they arrived, they called on Premier Stauning, who also served as the country's Minister to Greenland, and who urged Charles to consider using Copenhagen on Pan Am's transatlantic route. The same day, a Norwegian airline representative joined the fray and rushed to the city to meet Charles, hoping to persuade him that Norway provided an ideal stopover. "There is now keen competition among Scandinavian cities to obtain from Colonel Lindbergh sanction to establish bases," the *New York Times* reported.[4]

At various stops on the survey flight, Charles sent reports recapping his findings to Pan American. On September 15 he would write up his observations about both Iceland's and Greenland's capabilities to sustain operations on a transatlantic route. He reported to Juan Trippe that their survey during the summer indicated that Pan Am, even with its existing equipment, could well compete with the Atlantic steamship schedules. The harsh climate, however, undermined the route's main advantage—the shorter distances between land. Further, he stressed that until aircraft and radio equipment improved and meteorological stations were established along the course, the airline could fly this far north route only during the summer months.

The relentless pressures in Copenhagen dragged on, and Charles grumbled about the ritzy hotel, staffed with fawning employees serving besauced fish and other rich foods. One evening the chef sent up a fantastic, especially prepared ice cream castle to his table, but the well-intended, hospitable gesture left him pining for simple, hearty food. Wistfully, he told Anne that he wanted to return to Greenland. With her husband's unhappiness and the demands people made on Anne to get near him, she became stressed again. "Damn, damn, damn! I am sick of being this 'handmaid to the Lord,'" she confided to her diary.[5]

On September 3 the Lindberghs flew to Sweden, stopping for an extended visit to Stockholm and to Gårdlösa, the home of Charles's paternal ancestors. Fearful of repeating the chaotic Danish welcome, Sweden's Crown Prince Gustaf Adolf promised to make their visit as private as possible. With this in mind, afraid they would incur the Lindberghs' anger, some Swedes glanced away when they saw the couple, or looked down, pretending not to notice them. "We certainly have them scared to death," noted Anne.[6]

Both Lindberghs adored Stockholm, where they found they could pursue their own interests, aside from the usual Pan American business. Anne went on a shopping spree, buying Swedish toys for Jon and fabrics and glassware for family members. Her husband spent time with Sweden's Royal Air Force, test-flying a plane that officers had grounded because of several recent accidents. After wringing it through maneuvers, including spins, Charles declared it safe to fly.

Anne's long holiday in Stockholm, away from her radio equipment, came with a downside, however. Flying to southern Sweden on Sunday, September 17, she found she was "stiff and fuzzy at radio" and couldn't get good direction-finding loop signals, which could give her bearings to stations.[7] Sitting behind Charles, she felt her husband's unspoken criticism of her poor performance, which discouraged her further.

The Lindberghs had decided to fly to Russia from Sweden, but the last-minute change in their plans left them waiting for visas to enter the country. Still awaiting clearances to Russia on September 20, they flew to Finland, the Sirius swooping to land beneath low clouds and mists at Helsinki. Autumn was in full swing in northern Europe, and the warm sun would be a distant memory until Anne and Charles reached Lisbon in mid-November. In Helsinki the Russian minister telephoned to say that their documents were ready, and Anne conversed with him in French, confirming that they had been cleared for entry into Russia. On the way to Leningrad, Anne discovered that the Finns had a quaint sense of humor: in the Sirius's cockpit she found a teddy bear wearing a Finnish pilot's outfit.

In Russia one week—three days in Leningrad and four days in Moscow—the Lindberghs crammed in what Anne considered one month's worth of sightseeing. A government-appointed guide escorted them everywhere in Leningrad, and from early awakening to late evening, they dutifully followed her. Their activities included sitting in the opera house's royal box for a "sparkling" ballet, and visiting L'Hermitage, Peterhof, and the late Tsar's palace. Other stops included Lenin's former headquarters, and an antireligious museum at the gold-domed St. Isaac's Cathedral, which portrayed, through posters and photographs, the teachings of the Church "before the Revolution and what is true (or what the Soviet teaches now)," Anne observed. The usual "obnoxious press" was absent, she added. And in terms of accommodations, nothing was too good for the Lindberghs. In Leningrad they were put up in the grand suite of the Hotel Astoria, an elaborate old hotel that seemed like a step back in time with its old rugs, damask-covered chairs, and tables set with heavy china. Capping their stay in the city was an evening banquet held in their honor that, among other courses, consisted of caviar cupped in airplane and duck ice sculptures, fish, meat, salad, fruit, and rich desserts, accompanied with various wines.[8]

Flying to Moscow on September 25, the Sirius winged over miles of fields and woods, fertile flat land that reminded the Lindberghs of the American Midwest. As the sky cleared, patches of sun appeared, and three hours into the flight there appeared on the horizon Soviet planes sent to intercept the Sirius and guide it to a landing on the Moskva River. But where to land on this river section dotted with bridges? To the great delight of the thousands of Muscovites (including boisterous Russian aviators and a barricade of camera crews) who thronged the river's banks, Charles shoehorned a landing between two bridges. A thunderstorm of wild applause erupted.

The reception was quite different than in Leningrad. An "air of youth" suffused Moscow, as compared to Leningrad, which seemed "a city whose glories were in the past," Anne later wrote. In Moscow, escorts took the Lindberghs to the Kremlin, the opera, Lenin's Tomb, a prison commune, a foundry, and an aviation factory. They stopped off at an automobile factory too, whose work force was nearly half female. Anne noted that the Russians' views on women were progressive, as illustrated by the country's support of mothers and children, and her tours of government-sponsored children's homes in both Leningrad and Moscow. One nursery school in Moscow, for children of factory workers, ran around the clock and was staffed with cooks, maids, and one teacher and an assistant assigned to fifteen or twenty children. On streets and in factories, Anne saw posters for the Institute for the Protection of Motherhood and Childhood, a huge network throughout the country that educated women on abortion, birth control, and improvements in childcare. Anne reported that she found herself "enthusiastic" about the work being done on behalf of women and children. Her husband would express interest in the advances made by Russian aviators.[9]

Moscow's lavish welcome for the Lindberghs continued late in the evenings, when the country's civil aviators fêted them at banquets. Appearing at one banquet was a girl flyer just in from an eight-hour mail flight. Unlike America's civil aviation industry, which barred women career pilots, Russia welcomed women aviators in its industry. Rising to the occasion, Anne told the banquet's audience, "I am honored to sit at the same table with Soviet women aviators who are participating in the development of this science on equality with men."[10]

Overall, although Anne admired the single-mindedness Russians displayed, her diary and letters home complained of seedy, dirty cities, crowded by "dull, drab poor-looking people." Of the palaces and museums she saw, Anne wrote that they were "all shown from [a] social point of view rather than an aesthetic." And of the propaganda that guides presented to tourists, she wrote "one gets tired and feels like saying, 'Yes. I *get* that point now. People were in terrible condition before the revolution and things are now much, much better—I *get* it—*see?*—I *get* it!'"[11] Of course, statements such as these suggested that in fact

Anne didn't get it. Rather than offering a compelling glimpse into a country that fascinated many Americans, she seemed not to grasp the larger significance of the Russian Revolution, and in the process revealed her sheltered, affluent upbringing.

On September 29 the Sirius lifted into the air from the Moskva River, Charles dipping its wing in a farewell salute. The Lindberghs hopped to Estonia and Norway for brief visits before charting a direct course to England on October 4. Chased by British planes when they arrived over Southampton, Anne wondered, "What is this anyhow—an air race?" as she later described to her diary.[12] Soon an aircraft pointed to a canal, where after landing they were met by Aubrey Morgan, the husband of Anne's sister Elisabeth, and a few airline officials, but no crowds. Boarding overnight in a hotel with Aubrey before driving to Wales, they found the famous English reserve working in their favor, with hotel clerks keeping their whereabouts secret.

During what the press called their "mystery trip" in Great Britain, Anne and Charles visited Elisabeth and her husband at Tynewydd, their rented cottage near Cardiff, Wales. As Aubrey's car neared the white-fenced and gated cottage, Anne saw Elisabeth peeping from the rose garden. The Morgans' home abounded with Elisabeth's exquisite style and her attention to detail: a low dresser laid with beautiful china and vases of apricot and lemon dahlias, and a bedside table in the guest room arrayed with powder, pins, toiletries, and books chosen to suit Anne's tastes. For Anne, the reunion would be tinged with worry, however. Watching Elisabeth scamper about in her red shoes, squabbling with servants about menus, Anne realized that her sister's hospitable efforts came at great cost: her precarious health was worsening and her chest was constantly aching. Her doctors had ordered her to a warmer and drier climate, and within a month she and Aubrey would sail to America, then settle in Pasadena, California.

When Anne, Charles, and Aubrey left for a short trip to London on Wednesday, the eleventh, Elisabeth stayed behind, confined to bed rest. Even so, she had planned a party in Anne's honor to be held in London, with Aubrey as Anne's escort. It became the highlight of Anne's visit to the city, a party at the Berkeley Hotel that Charles hoped would last her a "long time"; not one for dancing, he had passed on the evening's entertainment. Decked out in a long, black velvet coat and a dressy frock, both borrowed from Elisabeth, and with her hair freshly done, Anne seemed to epitomize glamour and sophistication. In the hotel's formal dining room, as music played in the background, Anne and Aubrey enjoyed what Anne called a "perfect dinner" of smoked salmon, sole with lobster sauce, and crepes suzette. After seeing *Richard of Bordeaux*, they went back to the Berkeley and danced till 2:00 A.M. Still exuberant from the evening, she returned ready to console Charles. To her astonishment, he had been swept off to a nightclub to see the exotic dancer Josephine Baker. His escort had been the Lindberghs' London hostess Florence Grenfell, a society beauty and the wife of a partner of the firm Morgan Grenfell. If Anne felt anything other than surprise at this, she never mentioned it; most likely, she was only amused.[13]

While in London Charles met with George E. Woods Humphery, managing director of Great Britain's Imperial Airways, at Croydon Airdrome to talk shop. A primary player in developing transatlantic routes, Imperial had already established a close working relationship with Pan American. Charles and Woods Humphery discussed the airline's equipment and routes, especially the Azores/Bermuda course preferred by Imperial. After meeting with Imperial, Charles reported to Juan Trippe his belief that Pan Am's planes and engines were far superior to those of Imperial's. Poorly managed and flying antiquated biplanes on its far-flung line across the Empire, Imperial was ruled by a short-sighted British Air Ministry. Low morale affected operations, too, with its overworked pilots considered, at best, flying chauffeurs, near the bottom rung of the social hierarchy. Despite misgivings about Imperial's current equipment, Charles told Trippe that the airline had the best operation he had seen, with the exception of K.L.M. Royal Dutch Airlines, which he had yet to visit. (In the first week of November, he and Anne would meet K.L.M. officials.)[14]

In haze and fog, the Lindberghs departed Southampton on October 23, charting a course to Ireland, then Scotland. There they looked over potential bases for Pan American, after which they launched for Paris on October 26 in bitter cold with a north wind roaring at their backs as they crossed the English Channel's stormy seas. Just before dark the Sirius landed on the Seine at a French naval base, where in the fading light stood a small group of exuberant Frenchmen celebrating Charles's homecoming—his first return to Paris since his historic May 1927 flight to Le Bourget. That same night, at a small dinner party in Charles's honor, a surprise guest showed up: the French pioneer aviator Dieudonné Coste. Anne and Charles had met Coste earlier, at Roosevelt Field in September 1930, when he and his copilot Maurice Bellonte made history with their nonstop flight from Paris to New York. "*Mon brave!*" (my brave one) he cried to Charles before embracing him.[15]

At the welcoming soirée held by the aviators, Anne shone, wearing another stylish dress given her by Elisabeth, this one black with a flaring ruffle. The officers' wives were "perfectly dressed, in black, of course," she later wrote her sister. "But what is there about a Frenchwoman? She is always smartly dressed and yet never conspicuously so." The gathering marked the end of the Lindberghs' short-lived idyll, unfortunately. The press had caught wind of their arrival, the next morning's papers headlining "Lindbergh reported found in Paris hotel." Hordes of fans besieged Charles wherever he went. In a mad frenzy, women packed the streets to applaud him or chase his car, banging on the doors and shouting for his attention.[16]

All the fanfare directed at her husband left Anne feeling sidelined once again. The French did not connect her to him because, in her eyes, they thought of him as a "romantic young boy—the Fairy Prince." Typically, Charles felt as if he were a caged animal and was disgusted by the reporters following him and the hysteria in Paris. As the European survey entered its final stages, he remarked, "Sometimes the newspaper reporters and photographers make me feel like stopping flying and going into some work where it is possible never to see them." Anne was always sympathetic to his dislike of the press, and she also resented that fame had taken away their ability to live more normally. Moreover, as a pilot she well understood the dangers the public presented: crowds running near spinning propellers, among many other physical risks to their safety.[17]

After leaving France on November 2, the Lindberghs spent time in Amsterdam and Rotterdam with Albert Plesman, founder of K.L.M. Royal Dutch Airlines. They had hoped to leave for Geneva next, but a low-pressure system blanketed much of northern Europe. On November 7 Charles decided to risk a flight from Amsterdam to Geneva even though the weather was still marginal, but they never made Geneva that day, instead spending time in the air on another tense flight. They flew around Belgium and France nearly five hours—trying to get to Geneva, then attempting a return to their departure point. They ended up back at Rotterdam, normally a twenty-minute flight from Amsterdam.

During the hours-long flight to nowhere, they flew through fog and storms, barely above treetops and barreling through black clouds, in weather that had grounded other aviators and airlines. All during the flight, Anne sat white-knuckled. Charles flew like a demon, diving into fog and circling towns, while passing up potential landing areas at Ostend and Antwerp. (He wanted to look at castles, he later told Anne.) From the rear cockpit, Anne dashed off a note in red ink, "Where *are* you landing?" and shoved it forward. As the flight went on she moved between chastising herself for her lack of faith in Charles and thinking "wildly about going home, the train to Paris." This last thought was fleeting, though, for she realized she couldn't abandon her husband mid-trip—or face reporters' reactions to her doing so. When they finally landed in Rotterdam, Anne heaved a sigh of relief before climbing out. They heard Ostend was closed, with fog all the way down to the ground. Charles told his wife that they had never been in danger.[18]

Chilled and shaking, her nerves on edge, Anne warmed herself in the airport's clubhouse in Rotterdam. Seemingly out of nowhere, a grounded pilot appeared and sat beside her, drawing her into a conversation. He and his wife often flew together as partners, he told her, and had formed a very close bond from the flights they shared in good and in bad weather. Knowing the hardships of aviation, he expressed to Anne his admiration of both her courage and that she flew with her husband. Remorse overcame Anne, as she realized that Charles felt this way about their adventures together. In her diary that night she reconsidered the day's events: "And

I complain about it. . . . It may be the happiest time in my life and I am just wishing it away. We are young and happily married and having these experiences together. Then I think about saying before supper that I would have to give it up and Charles saying he liked to play with the clouds and he liked to get the best of them too. Then if he went to war, then how would I feel? I would wish I were back in the fog with him."[19]

Writing to her mother a week later from Lisbon, Anne described her panic at flying in fog and storms, but incredibly, she absolved Charles of any responsibility. "I do trust him perfectly and know that he is very careful and does not take chances."[20] She went on to recount the Amsterdam-Geneva-Rotterdam flight and her conversation with the clubhouse pilot, expressing the guilt she felt, as well as the admiration she had for her mother's staunch and unswerving support of Anne's father. The problem in Anne's analysis, of course, lay in the very different circumstances she and her mother faced. It's difficult to see how Anne thought Charles did not take chances flying, when he put them in danger countless times. Apparently, the supreme confidence he had in his piloting skills encouraged him to take on enormous risks. Throughout her flying career, Anne would continue to castigate herself for her fears, downplaying the dangers and exonerating Charles. In so many ways she cleaved to Charles, still considering him her "knight," as he had proven to be so often.

On November 8 the Lindberghs set off for Geneva, staying there until the eleventh while awaiting clearances to fly through Spain and into Lisbon. Charles warmed to Geneva, observing that it was a city of considerate people, in particular its newspaper men, who were "unusually decent fellows." The morning of their planned departure, they awoke to snow and overcast but managed a takeoff, flying over the new League of Nations palace as a farewell gesture. Dogged by worsening weather—rain and increasingly low ceilings—they landed five hours later, well short of Lisbon, at Santoña, Spain, in the Bay of Biscay. There they stayed as guests of a young English-speaking townsman, Señor Albo, and his family, who opened their home to them in all ways possible. Their unexpected visit set the town buzzing, with the mayor stopping by and a flurry of telephone calls coming in—the press looking for Charles. After a late supper, people began to stream into the Albos' home to peep at the guests, visits that included a return by the mayor, who asked Charles to write a letter of reference for the harbor. What Anne and Charles most wanted was sleep, but having dropped in uninvited, they appreciated the well-meant hospitality.[21]

Sleep would elude them for hours to come. Near midnight the guards who had been stationed at the Sirius burst into the Albos' home, saying that the plane had blown away. In sixty-mile-per-hour gale-force winds, Charles and the men ran to the waterfront, where they found the seaplane careening toward the stone sea wall. Aided by Basque fishermen, none of whom spoke English, Charles tied and anchored the plane. He later said that no storm came as close to damaging the Sirius, other than the 1931 gale at Ketoi in the Chishima, when he and Anne slept aboard the craft, rocked and buffeted all night long.

On November 13, a cold blustery day in Santoña, the ceiling lifted enough for a takeoff, but as they taxied out fishermen warned of storms ahead. As at Amsterdam, when he had decided to attempt a flight to Geneva in weather that would ground any mortal man, Charles decided to press on. "Oh, we'll go see what it looks like!" he shouted back.[22] The flight would become another battle in rain, fog, and low ceilings—lasting nearly four hours. After crossing mountains, they reached a high plateau, then found a river running west toward Portugal, which they followed into a steep, narrow canyon. Charles flew near the side of the canyon, so that he would have enough room to reverse course if necessary. Anne, meanwhile, desperately radioed for weather conditions.

Soon the river widened and valleys appeared, but a sea-breeze fog moved in from the ocean, decreasing visibility. They were squeezed lower to the ground, forced to fly just above the treetops. Suddenly Charles circled lower to land, and Anne pulled hard to crank in 150 feet of antenna. Not having time to reel in, Anne felt a tug with forty feet still left—the ball weight had struck water. "I've lost the antenna, Charles!" Anne yelled.[23] Without a weight the antenna was useless, but they always carried a spare and installed a new one when they landed. It was the first and last antenna she would lose during her flying career.

Not knowing where they had landed, and finding no one who spoke English or French, Charles took out his map. Gesticulating wildly, locals pointed to the Rio Minho, which bordered Spain and Portugal. The Lindberghs stayed two nights by the river, grounded by rain, sleeping in a cold Sirius whose interior was coated with dust and mud tracked in from the riverbank. During the night rain pelted down on the plane, and in the mornings they arose to a commotion of soldiers, police, peasants, and town officials. Anne particularly remembered the dismal first morning, wearing oil-splattered trousers, her finger aching from radio transmissions.

When the fog and rain cleared on November 15 they flew two hours down the coast to Lisbon. Nearing the city, they peered out at a brilliant sun beating down on softly-hued pink, blue, and yellow buildings, and a huge bay filled with boats. The steep-hilled city of narrow, winding streets, palms, and colorful flowers reminded Anne of Mexico, she wrote her mother upon arriving. She added that she was looking forward to the rest of the trip, when she could concentrate on flying and radio work in better weather. The day before their planned departure to the Azores, she studied radio schedules for KHCAL, translated from Portuguese.

Just after dawn on November 21 the Lindberghs set out toward a clearing sky, flying through rain squalls and low overcast toward the Azores, Europe's westernmost outpost, well out into the Atlantic. Anne radioed regularly, interrupting her calls for one hour only, when she flew while her husband took sights with a sextant. At 16:16 GMT she transmitted their imminent landing at the town of Horta, then reeled in. They had flown just over nine hours.

That night Anne slept fitfully and awoke before dawn "wildly impatient" at the thought of seeing her son, envisioning as quick a trip home as possible—a flight across the South Atlantic and a coastal route northward.[24] But ever restless and itching to cover new ground, Charles did not want to rush the return, as a disappointed Anne would soon find.

After resting and paying calls in Horta, a hilly town of cobblestone streets and red-roofed houses crowded amid palms, orange trees, and hedges of camellias, the Lindberghs took off on November 23 for a series of short stops in the Atlantic. For one night they stayed at Ponta Delgada, Azores, an unscheduled refueling stop. Originally, they had planned to fly straight to Madeira, but Horta's small harbor and rough seas prevented taking off with a full load of fuel. When they spotted more rough seas and a very small breakwater at Madeira, they continued to Las Palmas in the Canary Islands, a seven-hour flight. In this city of Moorish architecture, after meeting the American consul and calling on the governor, they tumbled into bed early in a lovely seaside hotel, sleeping beneath mosquito nets, resting for their next destination—the African coast.

11

Africa and Beyond: Into the Unknown

A few hours after leaving Las Palmas on November 26, the Lindberghs saw straight ahead Villa Cisneros, a small settlement in a sea of golden sand, in the Spanish colony of Rio de Oro, on the west coast of Africa. While the Sirius dove to land, Anne and Charles peered down on a Spanish fort, flat-topped white buildings, and a large hangar and landing field.

Just north of the fort lay a large band of brown tents, home to the blue-veiled nomadic tribesmen, the Moors. Until recent years rabidly anti-European, they had in the past held downed French pilots hostage or killed them outright. (Around 1928 hostilities with the Moors ceased, after the introduction of more reliable planes and the persuasive politicking of Antoine de Saint-Exupéry, the gifted pilot and writer who managed the airline's desert way station at Cape Juby on the Rio de Oro coast.)[1] The bold and adventurous French airmen flew for Lignes Aériennes Latécoère, then Aéropostale, until a bankruptcy scandal in 1931 all but shut it down. By 1933 all French carriers had been consolidated into Air France, a national airline. Villa

Cisneros was an Air France base, used by planes as they swung south to Dakar, Senegal, on the elbow of Africa, before hopping mail across the South Atlantic Ocean to South America.

On shore, the dark-eyed, turbaned Moors fascinated Charles, who knew of their battles with early French aviators. Lithe and graceful, swathed head to toe in blue robes, the Moors now seemed an oasis of calm, a timeless and eternal people impressing Anne with the "infinite dignity of their manner." Charles insisted that Anne ask the Spanish governor questions about how the Moors lived, traded, and traveled, which the settlement's doctor translated from Anne's French into Spanish. By mid-afternoon, Anne admitted that the battery of questions had taxed her, though she too was intrigued with their unusual customs, later recalling, "They shake hands languidly as though they thought it a dirty custom. If possible with the cloth between their hand and yours. No women come up but I see them in the background."[2]

After nightfall, the Lindberghs joined the Moors for a tea ceremony in a small stone house decorated as a tent, with cloth-draped walls and floor rugs. Sitting in a circle of people, on cushions in the candlelit room, Anne and Charles watched their hosts hack out sugar from a cone, drop chunks into a teapot, and pour tea into small glasses. While they sipped the hot, sweet tea, the Spanish governor told the Moors about Charles; after hearing "the first man . . ." Anne understood no more of the conversation, but it seemed to be a discussion of his 1927 flight. Then came a rustle of robes, and a majestic French-speaking Moor stood and looked directly at Anne. A spokesperson for all the tribes' chiefs, he welcomed Anne and Charles and wished them *bon voyage.* Suddenly, outside the door, the sounds of drums and odd cries rang out in celebration. In the center of a group of squatting boys and women, there was a woman dancing, her hands "like quick serpents—in flicking movements," noted Anne.[3]

With a tailwind roaring at their backs, the Lindberghs left Villa Cisneros in early morning, crossed the Tropic of Cancer, then took a southwest course to the Cape Verde Islands, situated about 320 miles west of Africa. The islands would be the Lindberghs' last stop before crossing the South Atlantic to Brazil—or so they thought at the time. Certain he could use them as a jumping-off point to South America, Charles had purchased fuel and oil to be cached there. The distance from Praia, Santiago, a small island in the group, was about 1,600 miles to Natal, on the bulge of Brazil—the shortest distance to Brazil, a route 200 miles nearer to South America than from the west coast of Africa. It was a crucial difference: the 200 miles allowed for an extra fuel reserve, a faster airspeed, and less time flown during night hours.

En route to Santiago, on an otherwise uneventful flight, Anne communicated with WSL at Sayville, Long Island, nearly 3,400 miles away. Her head down in the cockpit receiving and sending, she had sent a CQ (General Call) from KHCAL, then responded to WSL's CQ, established contact, and transmitted her position. When WSL acknowledged receipt, her heart began pounding. She had just set a radio communications record between an aircraft and a ground station of 3,388 statute miles.[4]

About four hours after takeoff from Villa Cisneros, there appeared on the horizon several gray and brown mounds: the Cape Verde Islands. Two hours later, bucking and bouncing in turbulence, the Sirius arrived over Praia. Circling round and round, looking for a suitable harbor, Charles saw only rough seas whose great waves crashed against the beach, conditions that forbade a landing there. A few miles west he spotted the Air France seaplane base, a haven of radio masts, a hangar, a derrick, and cottages perched on a rocky slope inside a small sheltered harbor. Landing in a strong northeast wind amid high waves, the Sirius bounced down hard, rose fifteen feet, and bounced again and again, until it finally settled. The pontoons thudded and groaned with each bounce. Even taxiing to shore was difficult, Charles found, as the seaplane teetered from one side to another, its wingtips almost touching water.

Help came in the form of a small rowboat manned by two young black boys and a sun-helmeted Frenchman, the Air France mechanic. His face was glistening and pale from tropical fever, possibly malaria. As the Sirius was towed in, Anne caught sight of two additional figures standing forlornly on the dock: a tall, emaciated black man and a thin mulatto girl wearing a flimsy cotton dress. Both wore white sun helmets. The man stepped forward and introduced himself as the airline's *chef* and the pretty black-haired girl as his wife. Bowing, he said to Charles that he had orders from France to offer all assistance. Shortly afterward, a chauffeured car arrived trailing a cloud of brown and red dust. From the back seat stepped a Portuguese official sent by the governor of the islands, who asked the Lindberghs for their passports and clearances. He invited them into Praia to meet the governor—the usual protocol—with the *chef* serving as a translator.

On the way the car rocked along a bumpy road, and Anne stared at the arid landscape of brown hills. Goats foraged nearby, nibbling at little blades of yellow grass. The wind blew relentlessly in Santiago, Anne and Charles soon learned; it droned day and night, whistling and moaning, pushing red sand into every nook and cranny. While going to Praia, the *chef* told Anne and Charles that Air France no longer operated from the islands—surprising news because they had understood that the airline used the seaplane base. That same evening another surprise awaited them when the French mechanic claimed the *chef* suffered with tuberculosis and lived in a contaminated bungalow. Whether this was true was not clear, but the Lindberghs chose to take the mechanic at his word. To the great chagrin of the *chef,* Anne and Charles turned down his offer to sleep in his bedroom. Although the *chef* and his wife warned them that bedbugs infested the other available room, they tried to stay in his home at least—until late at night they spotted a small army of the little creatures marching across the mattress, and so fled to sleep in the Sirius. Awakening in the morning, they again saw the *chef* and his wife standing on the dock, looking dejected and even more forlorn. Anne remained silent, knowing that anything she said would only worsen the humiliation they had suffered.

Nonetheless, the Lindberghs decided that they would take meals at the *chef*'s house. After breakfast, a car appeared in a blaze of dust. Out jumped two fuel agents, bubbling with enthusiasm as they handed Charles a list of his fuel and oil. But their appearance sounded the death knell for any hopes Charles harbored for a shorter trip to South America. One of the agents pointed out that the dry trade wind blew six months of the year. There was no escape from the wind and rough seas, making a takeoff with a full load of fuel impossible. They would have to fly to the seaplane base at Dakar, where they would launch the transatlantic flight, even though the distance would be 200 miles farther—yet even that plan was discarded when a wire from Dakar warned of a yellow fever epidemic and quarantine there. After trudging to the *chef*'s bungalow, Anne and Charles sat listlessly, questioning their next move. With an unexpected jolt the *chef* jumped from the table, shot a glance at his wife and told the Lindberghs they could not go. Yellow fever, he explained, attacked whites much worse than blacks: once they vomited blood, "*c'est fini!*"[5] His wife, of Italian heritage, had survived yellow fever, but her three sisters and a brother had perished from the mosquito-borne, quick-striking disease. Whether Charles believed the *chef*'s claims is unclear, but in any event, he decided to avoid Dakar, not wanting to risk the epidemic.

Once again, the Lindberghs slept in the Sirius's hot baggage compartment. In the morning Charles asked the *chef* to wire Bathurst, British Gambia, for landing permission. Though not a transatlantic seaplane base, Bathurst was just south of Dakar at the junction of the Gambia River and the ocean and could serve as a jumping-off point. During most of the day, the Lindberghs performed normal maintenance on the Sirius, which was made more difficult by the wear and tear of the tropics: corrosion from a salty sea and sun beating down on the wings' fabric and paint. Not only the plane suffered from the heat; Anne felt parched and withered, with her lips cracked and grit in her hair and trousers.

On November 30 the Sirius once again became airborne, after a long bouncing run through rough swells at Praia. And once again, the seaplane arrived in Africa, this time at Bathurst. Looking below, the Lindberghs eyed the muddy Gambia River winding through a lush green landscape. The Sirius swooped to a gentle landing on the wide river, the pontoons creating the barest of ripples over still water. "How different from the spanks off

Santiago!" Anne thought—but soon she and her husband would rue the lack of wind.[6]

With its British flag, well-paved streets, and helmeted policemen in white uniforms, Bathurst bustled with activity, and unlike Santiago, it evoked "peace, order, and security" for Anne. The Lindberghs were escorted to the luxurious Government House, where they would sleep on a bed draped with mosquito netting, be attended by the many servants gliding about, and refresh themselves with hot baths and lavender soap. That same night they were joined for dinner by British officers, fresh from a flight across Africa from the Sudan. The Brits and the Lindberghs both downplayed the perils of their flights with bravado, by regaling each other with flight stories. Anne later remembered: "We felt part of a large brotherhood of people who fly. They had just come from Egypt; we were going to Brazil. It was all very jolly—flying was easy."[7]

Traveling at an airspeed of 115 miles per hour, the Lockheed Sirius needed about sixteen hours to make the 1,875-mile flight from Bathurst to Natal, Brazil, unless it encountered headwinds. In any event, for an acceptable margin of error, the Sirius needed to carry a full load of fuel. Of the three options available—a takeoff at daybreak and a night landing, a night takeoff and a day landing, a takeoff at sunset and a landing at daybreak—Charles preferred the last. He needed light to land, and night flying offered many advantages, among them easier navigation and better radio communication. But flying at night in a single-engine aircraft across the South Atlantic? As nonchalantly as if she were making a trip to the corner store, Anne remarked that they "might, of course, have to make a night landing in the open Atlantic."[8] She reassured herself, thinking that modern engines were reliable, which cut down the chance of an engine failure. This was optimistic, to be sure: though a full moon at the time, shining bright overhead, would help a night crossing, Anne knew that some ocean flyers went in the drink, never to be seen alive again. Nonetheless, off went a cable to Pan American asking for daily weather forecasts over the Atlantic, including reports of storms, fog, and headwinds.

After Charles learned that an evening wind never blew that time of year in Bathurst, the Lindberghs were down to two options—a morning or a night departure. And so began countless attempts to take off on the Gambia River's calm water, starting the morning of December 3 and ending late that night. The Sirius continued to flounder in the water, straining to free itself from the river's grip. When finally the Lindberghs returned to Bathurst, an Englishman on the dock asked Charles the problem. Charles shrugged and made an attempt at cheerfulness, "It must be different down here in the tropics—maybe the density of the air."[9]

Given that he was unable to change the calm water, wind, and density of the air that reduced lift, Charles turned to his equipment. If he reduced his plane's payload, removing whatever weight he could, he knew that chances would improve for a successful launch. He gave meticulous attention to every detail to improve the odds. On December 4 he worked hours in stifling weather, using tin cutters to snip out, piece by piece, an empty gas tank inside the fuselage. He also took out oil not needed and in general discarded everything except absolute essentials. By day's end, he had achieved a 200-pound reduction in weight. Still, he knew their success depended on the winds. The moon had started to wane, and if they did not launch the next night, there would be no transatlantic flight from Bathurst; moonlight was needed for the takeoff run.

After resting the next day, December 5, Anne walked alone to the pier, where she found the early evening wind was rising. Panting, she ran back to Government House, telling Charles the good news. Without hesitation, he sprinted to the pier and confirmed what Anne had told him. He earmarked that night for a late launch. At midnight the Sirius finally soared into the air from Bathurst, the start of a grueling flight to Natal, Brazil. The overwater journey lasted nearly sixteen hours and saw them arriving at Natal at 3:00 P.M. local time on December 6. As was customary for long-distance aviators, the Lindberghs were whisked to a bungalow for rest. South Atlantic flyers needed sleep and good meals, and residents of Natal, used to welcoming them, allowed the couple a day's rest. Before falling into bed exhausted, Anne thought once more of getting home and seeing her son.

But home was not on Charles's mind. In his element exploring and charting new courses, he wanted to continue the expedition, and Anne soon realized that he would rather meander home at a leisurely pace. Besides, Juan Trippe had asked him to have a look at other routes in South America. No sooner had the Lindberghs recovered from the fatigue of the South Atlantic flight than Charles announced that he wanted to fly to Manaos on the way to Trinidad. It was a "punk idea," Anne countered, after considering the thousand-mile flight up the Amazon.[10] After he told her that he wanted to investigate the route, she admitted that she would like to see the area, too. With delight, he then sprang another bombshell. From Manaos, they would fly across jungle to Trinidad, rather than returning to the coast and taking the regular route north.

Anne took a dim view of the proposal. Her map showed a thousand miles of only wilderness between Manaos and Trinidad, she told him. Charles replied, "We could get down there anywhere—might smash the plane up, but we'd get out all right." And so on December 10, after a takeoff from Belem, Brazil, the survey flight continued, according to Charles's plan, over jungles and the muddy Amazon River to Manaos. Two days later they launched in early morning for Trinidad, flying over more jungles and over mountains in a witches' brew of rain and thunderstorms a good part of the time. One of the flight's more harrowing episodes took place between the South American mainland and Trinidad: as rain pummeled the Sirius, the sky turned pitch-black and the forward visibility lowered to less than half a mile. The Sirius skimmed the water, flying less than a hundred feet from its surface, and even Charles agreed with Anne that the weather was "bad stuff." The Lindberghs landed at Port of Spain, Trinidad, after having flown nearly ten hours non-stop. They were back on familiar ground, having come through the area some four years earlier with the Trippes while inaugurating Pan American airmail routes. Upon landing, Anne reported feeling "extremely happy, as though at home again."[11]

After stops in Puerto Rico, Santo Domingo, Florida, and South Carolina, the Lindberghs headed to New York on December 19. On this final flight leg, her radio work complete and call sign KHCAL retired, Anne's thoughts turned to the responsibilities awaiting her at home: family demands, finishing the Orient survey book, endless invitations, scores of people wanting to

In the rear cockpit of the Sirius, Anne smiles while taking a break from her crew duties as radio operator, copilot, and navigator. Lindbergh Picture Collection, Manuscripts and Archives, Yale University Library. Reproduced with permission.

see her and Charles, and her radio report to Pan Am's Hugo Leuteritz. Though she desperately wanted to get home, the trip had at least one advantage over home: "You only have to look to the day you're in. Your work is finished at the end of that, results are quick, and when the job is done well, Charles is pleased."[12]

The Lindberghs' Lockheed Sirius came upon New York during the afternoon. Shortly thereafter, on the ramp at Flushing Bay, close to their point of departure five months and ten days earlier, Charles pulled the throttle, cut the switches, and watched the propeller revolving one last time. The plane that the Greenlander children had named *Tingmarssatoq* would be retired to a museum, its mission complete. Since leaving on July 9, the Sirius had been airborne about 261 hours.[13] Anne had become the first woman ever to fly in an airplane across the South Atlantic (and only two women pilots had preceded her in crossing the North Atlantic: Amelia Earhart and Amy Johnson, with her husband Jim Mollison). She had also become the first woman to fly either Atlantic in an open-cockpit plane. But the trip report to Pan Am would wait. By 6:00 P.M. Anne and Charles had arrived at Next Day Hill's gate, where family anxiously awaited.

For years to come, Pan American Airways's attempts to fly the North Atlantic would be hamstrung by Britain's refusal to grant it landing rights, primarily because Imperial's older equipment lacked the ability to make such flights. Thus, there could be no reciprocal rights. In early 1939, however, preoccupied with the threat of war, Britain would finally allow Pan Am entry into England. On May 20, 1939, Pan American's *Yankee Clipper*, a huge Boeing 314 flying boat, would lumber into the air from New York, dip its wings over a crowd at the New York World's Fair, and cross the North Atlantic to Europe. A little more than a month later, Pan Am would fly the first transatlantic passenger service on another B-314, the *Dixie Clipper*, all thanks in no small part to the information the Lindberghs had gathered on their flights.[14]

12

Acclaim

On the Saturday afternoon of March 31, 1934, in Explorers' Hall of the National Geographic Society, all eyes were riveted on the petite figure of Anne Morrow Lindbergh, smartly attired in a two-tone dress and a black beret, with a broad smile creasing her face. Behind her hung the society's historic flag, its colors of green, brown, and blue representing the sea, the earth, and the sky. The society's president, Dr. Gilbert H. Grosvenor, handed Anne a small case lined with blue velvet. Inside lay a solid gold medal commemorating "her part in helping blaze 40,000 miles of new sky trails," airways charted on survey flights she flew in 1931 and 1933. In the small audience—the ceremony was modest at her request—Charles leaned against a pillar, listening to his wife's brief words of acceptance. His casual stance belied his pride at her achievement, the first woman, and only the tenth person, to be awarded the Hubbard Medal in the half century of its existence. Lauded for the "critical role" she played in the success of the flights, acting as her husband's copilot, radio operator, and navigator, the society also noted that she was the first woman ever to fly those routes.[1]

When the twenty-seven-year-old Anne Lindbergh returned home in December from the 1933 Atlantic survey flight, she was showered with awards honoring her role on the nearly six-month-long journey. Even before the year 1933 ended, the United States Flag Association gave her the Cross of Honor in recognition of her skills, aeronautical knowledge, and courage. In short order, she received more distinctions. She became the first woman to earn the Veteran Wireless Operators Association's gold medal, and the third woman pilot to be awarded an honorary membership in the National Aeronautic Association of the United States of America. Yet more recognition would come her way from Paris in late April, when the International League of Aviators awarded her the Harmon National Trophy as America's champion aviatrix for 1933, because she had "done most to advance aviation during the year." Her prestige was further enhanced by aviation magazines such as *U.S. Air Services,* which splashed her photo on the cover. In January the National Broadcasting Company asked her to join a panel on the future of aviation.[2] Soon Anne's influence and prominence carried over to her alma mater, Smith College, when in November 1934 its young women students started a flying club.[3]

It seemed that all America considered her a beloved public figure whose popularity was "altogether comparable to that of her husband," read the *Mobile Press Register.*[4] Yet throughout her flying career and even later in life, her diaries and letters would neglect to mention the honors she received. Indeed, she would expurgate almost all honors from her published collections of diaries and letters. She turned down requests to speak on aviation and publicly accept aeronautical awards, other than the ceremony at the National Geographic Society. Humble to a fault, she disliked pomp, ceremony, and accolades, and when forced to acknowledge an award, she would say that neither her work nor her experience qualified her for the recognition, a standard response that she would repeat for years to come.

Though modest, Anne must have relished these awards and acclaim. In any event, she touched on the rigorous flights occasionally, describing segments of the Atlantic flight in her diary. In her sixties, she was much less guarded and wrote in 1974: "The feminist in me longed passionately to prove that I could hold my own and take the place of a man. And in the radio operation, I succeeded to a large degree." Her work had been "indispensable" to the success of the flights, she added. In 1934 she admitted missing the

Lockheed Sirius, too. After seeing *Tingmissartoq* hanging against a painting of a tropical sky in the American Museum of Natural History in New York, she thought it "so dreadful never to be able to fly in it again."[5] (The plane is now at the National Air and Space Museum in Washington, D.C.)

In February 1934 the Lindberghs changed residences yet again, moving into a Manhattan apartment on East 86th Street, a penthouse with two terraces, one for each bedroom, and a river view. They wanted their own place again and reasoned that a doorman-screened apartment in the city would provide safety and security to Jon. Despite wondering why she "ever left that beautiful clean home in Englewood" within weeks of the move, the apartment offered a respite of sorts for Anne.[6] She enrolled eighteen-month-old Jon in a neighborhood nursery school, trying to give him a taste of normal life with children his age. With the family's dogs on a leash, she and Jon would set out on weekday mornings, walking the short distance to the school.

Charles, meanwhile, was caught up in a furor created by President Roosevelt, who had issued a decree on February 9, 1934, canceling domestic airline airmail contracts, effective on February 19. With only ten days to prepare and train, U.S. Army pilots would fly all airmail. The drastic measure stemmed from a Senatorial investigation, chaired by Hugo L. Black of Alabama. The committee claimed that the Republican postmaster general had shown favoritism when he awarded airmail contracts in 1930, at what some would later dub the "Spoils Conference." Suddenly without airmail revenue, commercial airlines faced dire financial straits, shutting down routes, delaying equipment purchases, and furloughing pilots. As Anne wrote to Elisabeth, Charles felt that the carriers had suffered a "terrible setback" and indeed, several years would elapse before America's domestic airlines financially recovered from Roosevelt's rash decree. Even worse, the president's decision would leave twelve Army airmen dead and numerous planes crashed. The Army pilots not only flew unsuitable planes, they did not possess the skills needed to maneuver through foul weather—fog, icing, rain, and snow.[7]

Charles jumped into the fray right away. He fired off a telegram to the White House, denouncing the decree and its damage to American aviation. By late March the tide of public opinion turned against Roosevelt's stance; by May commercial carriers, some under slightly changed names, were back to flying the mail. Complying with the postmaster's order that only new carriers apply for contracts, some big operators took on a name change when they submitted new bids. Consequently, American Airways became American Airlines; Eastern Air Transport became Eastern Airlines, and Transcontinental and Western Air turned up as TWA, Inc.

With the approach of summer, Anne began work on a new writing project, an article for the *National Geographic Magazine* about the Atlantic survey flight, slated for the September 1934 issue. About 10,000 words, it would include eighty-two photographs taken by the Lindberghs. It had to cover the entire journey, however, and Anne struggled to keep it under its allotted number of words. She also felt pressured to meet the deadline and put aside her book to concentrate on the article. Although it was written in a more prosaic style than her later works, it was well received—the magazine's editors called the piece a "literary gem"—and helped launch her writing career.[8]

The Lindberghs spent July at Deacon Brown's Point in Maine, the Morrows' summer retreat, where Anne luxuriated in the peace, playing with Jon, and sailing, swimming, and cruising on the *Mouette,* the family's motorboat. Charles flitted back and forth from Maine to New York on airline business in a borrowed Monocoupe—the type of plane he had on order to replace the retired Sirius. With Pan Am's pilots, including the airline's Edwin Musick, he test-flew the S-42, a Sikorsky flying boat he had helped design and that soon saw service on Pan Am's South American routes as the *Brazilian Clipper.*

While vacationing in Maine, the Lindberghs agreed to let their penthouse lease go, telling friends that the landlord raised the rent because of their celebrity status. It was a flimsy excuse on their part; they could easily afford the increase in rent, which might very well have come about because their dogs tramped dirt in and out. Ever restless and feeling confined by the city, Charles rebelled at the thought of a winter in New York. Anne wrote to Elisabeth, "The only place we can agree on is California. Still that is just an idea."[9]

As August rolled to a close, the Lindberghs turned up in St. Louis at the Lambert Aircraft Corporation to pick up the NX-211, their specially designed Monocoupe plane built to Charles's specifications. Among other innovations, the wing's ailerons—which raised or lowered the wings—were interconnected with the flap controls, whereas they usually worked independently of one another. Thus, flap action would affect the entire trailing edge of the wing. While waiting in St. Louis, touring the factory, Anne expressed concerns about her husband's experimental plane. She wrote to Elisabeth that "with a new plane—never flown—there is a chance of its falling to pieces in the air!"[10] Several weeks later, the couple climbed into the 145-horsepower, two-seat plane and took up a course for California, where they planned to visit Elisabeth and Aubrey Morgan and look at prospective properties.

On September 11, while landing in Wichita, Charles ground looped the plane, and he and Anne heard the sound of screeching metal. The Monocoupe's left landing gear had folded up; its left wing struck ground, cracking a wing spar. Though Anne later said that a faulty wheel brake caused the accident, Charles claimed that other factors also contributed to the accident: full flaps and down aileron in high winds gusting to thirty to thirty-five miles per hour, the fully swiveling tail wheel, high wing construction, and the narrow wheel spread. After repairs, another pilot flew the plane back to New York.[11]

Even so, their adventures in Monocoupes continued when the Lambert factory provided them with another plane in Wichita. They started out again, but less than two hours after takeoff from Wichita the engine banged and shook, then stopped suddenly. "What is it, Charles?" Anne asked, while "thinking a wing had come off at least." Calmly, he replied, "Just engine," then glided to a perfect landing in a plowed field near Woodward, Oklahoma. They stayed with a farm family for about three days, enjoying the visit until the *third* Monocoupe arrived from St. Louis. Thankfully, the remainder of the cross-country flight proved uneventful.[12]

During this time, the press praised Anne's recently published *National Geographic* article. On August 30 the *New York Times* printed selections from her article and called it "a fast and friendly narrative," written in a "gay humor." That same day, the publisher Harcourt, Brace and Company, prompted by the *Times* story, wrote to Anne: they wanted her to write a narrative of book length. She made no mention of the letter at the time and most likely did not receive it, possibly because it was addressed to her care of the Lindberghs' attorney, Colonel Henry Breckinridge.[13]

On the evening of September 19, 1934, only three days after joining Elisabeth and Aubrey Morgan at Will Rogers's Pacific Palisades ranch, Charles was called to the telephone. From New Jersey, Colonel Norman Schwarzkopf told him that the kidnapping case had been cracked and announced the arrest of Bruno Richard Hauptmann, a thirty-six-year-old German-born carpenter. The Lindberghs flew back to New Jersey, arriving within a week and returning to the refuge of Next Day Hill. Although the turn of events energized Charles, Anne looked upon the arrest as bringing more turmoil and unneeded publicity. She told her mother-in-law that Hauptmann was "beyond doubt one of the right people," but added, "what may develop we don't know."[14]

A blue-eyed man with a pointed chin and athletic build, Hauptmann had recently bought 98 cents' worth of gas at a Lexington Avenue service station in New York, paying for the purchase with a $10 gold certificate from the Lindbergh ransom. (Though ransom bills had begun appearing by May of 1932, shortly after the ransom money changed hands, they became easier to spot after May 1, 1933, when a presidential order went into effect, directing persons holding gold certificates worth more than $100 to deposit or exchange them at a Federal Reserve Bank.) The Lexington Avenue attendant, alerted to be on the look-out for gold certificates, wrote down Hauptmann's license number, 4U-13-14 N.Y., on the bill's face. When it was deposited at a Bronx bank, a sharp-eyed teller found a match against the ransom money list and notified authorities, who looked at the bill and saw the license number. They tracked Hauptmann down, staking out his Bronx apartment at 1279 East 222nd Street the next morning, September 19.

The circumstantial evidence would mount quickly. Police found another listed gold certificate in his wallet, more than $15,000 of ransom money stashed in his adjacent garage, and a five-room flat filled with expensive, new furniture. Searching his apartment, police also discovered a sketch of a ladder similar to that used in the kidnapping, along with Dr. John Condon's address and former phone number written on a closet's door trim. Even a plank in the flooring of his attic had been matched with a rung in the kidnap ladder. Shortly afterward, an analysis of Hauptmann's handwriting samples matched the peculiar writing of the ransom demand notes. Furthermore, soon Hauptmann would be identified by Dr. Condon, the cab driver Joseph Perrone, and Charles Lindbergh, who had heard him shout "Hey Doctor!" at St. Raymond's Cemetery on the night the ransom was paid. Yet even with all this, Hauptmann proclaimed his innocence. After being confronted with the ransom money and other evidence, his wife Anna Schoeffler Hauptmann, a German-born bakery clerk, remained convinced that her husband could not have committed the crime.

In October Hauptmann was indicted for murder in the first degree and was extradited to Flemington, New Jersey. At his arraignment he pled not guilty. While waiting for his trial, set to start January 2, 1935, he paced his jail cell smoking one cigarette after another, when he wasn't reading biographies—or sometimes weeping. An overhead bulb burned day and night above his cot.

✈

After returning east in the fall of 1934, the Lindberghs found another man ensconced in what Anne called the "harem" at Next Day Hill.[15] On the recommendation of Anne and Elisabeth, Mrs. Morrow had hired Harold Nicolson—author, diplomat, and husband of novelist Vita Sackville-West— as the official biographer of her late husband. The Lindberghs had first become acquainted with the English couple at a Waldorf Astoria dinner party in January 1933. Harold was a skilled raconteur and a brilliant conversationalist, though Anne was slightly intimidated by Vita: a tall, dark-eyed beauty who wore masculine clothing set off with pearls, lace, and frilly blouses, she had had an affair with Virginia Woolf, the Bloomsbury writer Anne so admired.

While a houseguest at Next Day Hill, Nicolson came to be a great fan of Charles Lindbergh's. The two men got on well, with Charles regaling him with tales of his travels around the States and his impressions of all classes of Americans, but what Nicolson most remembered were his unassuming manner, decency, and integrity. His high opinion of Charles bordered on veneration. Writing his wife, he declared that Lindbergh "really is a hero in this continent and he never cheapens himself." Nicolson was impressed with Anne, too, and as an early champion of her writing career, his effect on her was profound and long lasting. After he praised Anne's "excellent" *National Geographic* article, she was thrilled that he had treated her as a serious writer and had encouraged her efforts, but when a month later he reported that his wife liked the article, Anne chided herself about taking writing too seriously, saying she put too much "sacredness" around it. She was determined never to let anyone know that she cared about writing "more than anything else," though she would flinch at any criticism throughout her literary career.[16]

On the Friday morning of November 23, Aubrey Morgan called Betty Morrow with alarming news: Elisabeth was critically ill with pneumonia, a complication that arose after her recent appendectomy. Desperate to see her daughter immediately, and without regard for her safety—the commercial carriers had been grounded because of storms—Betty boarded a chartered plane in Newark late on that cold, rainy evening. Charles had reluctantly arranged the charter, and authorities telephoned him as the plane exited each region of stormy weather.

That same night Anne wrote in her diary a premonition of Elisabeth's death. Despite a desire to see her sister, she and Charles felt that the publicity attending such a visit would prove distracting to the Morgans. Elisabeth's health rallied, but soon declined. In the predawn hours of December 3, a deep chill coursed through Anne, prompting her to get out of bed, take an aspirin, and put a warm wrapper on. When Charles asked her what was wrong, she replied, shivering, after she returned to bed, "I'm so cold—still so cold."[17] A half hour later, they heard a knock on their bedroom door. It was a call from Pasadena, the night watchman announced. Charles took the call; Elisabeth Morrow Morgan had died at age thirty, her husband and her mother at her bedside.

Despite Charles's attempts to comfort her, Anne felt defeated thinking of her mother's pain and a future without her sister. Her chief consolation came from her diary. As in the past, it gave her an outlet for her sorrow and an alternative to her husband's typical suppression of emotion. As the year concluded, her thoughts turned to her family and she resolved "not to disappoint C. at the Trial, to finish the book for him." Although devastated by another death, she also wanted to give Charles "a home and a sense of freedom and power and fulfillment."[18]

The trial of Bruno Richard Hauptmann for the kidnapping and murder of Charles Augustus Lindbergh, Jr., started on January 2, 1935, in Flemington, New Jersey, normally a sleepy town of less than 3,000 people. Outside the century-old Hunterdon County Courthouse in Flemington, thousands of newcomers—the press, tourists, and hawkers selling souvenirs—scrambled to witness what the press called "the trial of the century." Considered in some circles the social event of the season, it drew celebrities who turned out in droves, wearing chic outfits. Actress Lynn Fontanne sported a leopard skin coat, and the veteran Hearst reporter Adela Rogers St. Johns came every day bedecked in a different Hattie Carnegie ensemble, charged to her expense account. Other notables included the novelist Edna Ferber, comedian Jack Benny, mafia kingpins, and a twenty-one-year-old rookie Hearst reporter named Dorothy Kilgallen.

In the small, packed courtroom on January 3, a composed and very pale Anne Morrow Lindbergh took the stand for forty minutes of questioning by the lead prosecutor, Attorney General David T. Wilentz. Spectators had stood to get a look at her when she appeared, until remanded to their seats by a gavel tap from Judge Thomas W. Trenchard. She concentrated on keeping her

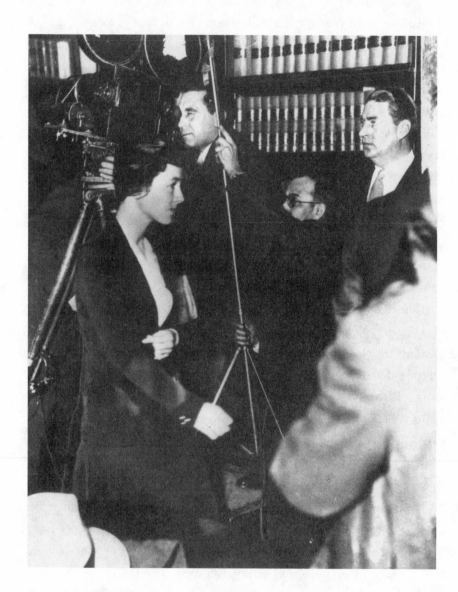

Anne entering the courtroom to testify at the Hauptmann trial in January 1935. Lindbergh Picture Collection, Manuscripts and Archives, Yale University Library. Reproduced with permission.

emotions in check. Speaking in a faint but clear voice, Anne presented her brief testimony, while occasionally looking out a courthouse window at a patch of blue sky to maintain her composure. The chief attorney for the defense, Edward J. Reilly, then declined to question her, saying "that the grief of Mrs. Lindbergh requires no cross examination."[19] After stepping down from the stand, Anne immediately left the courthouse.

She went back to the courthouse only once, on February 9, to provide moral support to her mother, who testified as a character witness on behalf of Violet Sharpe, the Morrow servant who had killed herself. Having unshackled the restraints she had relied on during her testimony, Anne observed carefully the proceedings and people: Hauptmann's "pale profile" and the "pathetically bedraggled thin face" of his wife.[20]

Within a week of her January court appearance, Anne wrote in her diary of her joy in resuming work on *North to the Orient,* but between short bursts of writing she fought feelings of despair and crying jags, alone. "I must control my mind—I must control my body—I must control my emotions—I must finish the book—I must put up an appearance, at least, of calm for C." Whimpering in bed at night, trying not to wake Charles, she kept herself rigid. She continued the battle to control her emotions well into February. "Making masks and keeping them smooth and perfect—that takes more time and strength than anything else," she wrote a friend. Meanwhile, her husband and her mother continued to hide their grief. Decades later, with the healing of time, Anne would tell an interviewer that she considered this sort of stoical behavior to be "dishonest."[21]

During the night of February 13, a raucous crowd outside the courthouse began chanting, "Kill Hauptmann! Kill Hauptmann!" Later that night jurors found the defendant guilty of murder in the first degree. After Attorney General Wilentz moved for immediate sentencing, Judge Trenchard pronounced that Hauptmann "suffer death at the time and place, and in the manner provided by law." His face blanched, Hauptmann returned to his cell, while in the courtroom his wife Anna started to sob. In the drawing room at Next Day Hill family members and houseguests, including Harold Nicolson, gathered around the wireless, listening to what

Anne called "that howling mob" over the radio. She begged Charles to turn it off. "How incredibly horrible and bitter to realize that this has to do with us," she wrote in her diary that night.[22]

The New Jersey Court of Appeals voted to uphold Bruno Richard Hauptmann's conviction in October 1935, and he died in the electric chair at the state penitentiary in Trenton on April 3, 1936. Charles Lindbergh never wavered in his conviction of Hauptmann's guilt; he also did not talk with his other children about his first child. Anne preferred not to discuss the case publicly, but her daughter Reeve said that she occasionally spoke of her first-born and his death. One striking instance occurred when Reeve's own son Jonathan, who at about the same age as little Charlie, died in his crib during the night. Her mother, who was with her at the time, stressed how important it was for her to sit with her dead son. As Anne pointed out, she had never seen her child's body after he died. "I never sat with my son this way."[23]

Speculating about the kidnapping in her memoir, *Under a Wing*, Reeve wrote: "I have heard scores of theories and speculations that have grown up around the story of this tragedy. . . . Yet I have never doubted the truth of what must have happened. It was very simple, very brutal, and very fast."[24]

After the trial Anne's strength and concentration returned, day by day. In April, with *North to the Orient* complete, she mustered up the courage to make an appointment at Harcourt, Brace and Company. Although she had not received the letter they had sent her in 1934, Harold Nicolson had recommended her to Harcourt, which would soon release his biography of Dwight Morrow. Assailed by doubts, Anne jotted down questions before hailing a taxi to the publisher's offices on Madison Avenue. Was the book too short, at 42,000 words, or too late, having been completed several years after the 1931 flight? Still, she reminded herself that she was only soliciting their opinion, not a contract.

Once seated with Alfred Harcourt, Anne began to talk, somewhat apologetically, while her stomach turned over nervously. Harcourt, meanwhile, rolled a cigarette, digging up tobacco from a white bag and twirling the brown shreds into the thin paper. He wanted to read the manuscript and assured Anne that he would not publish the book "just because Anne Lindbergh wrote it." Anne handed it over one week later, after a frenzied week of editing with her husband's assistance. Later that same day, Alfred Harcourt called and praised the book lavishly, saying, "It's a good story, it's moving, it's well constructed, and parts of it border on poetry." He wanted to close the deal the next day.[25]

As she paced the gardens at Next Day Hill, waiting for Charles, Anne brimmed with happiness. Harcourt's news was a moment of "personal triumph," one she compared to winning the Jordan Prize at Smith, the birth of her children, and soloing a plane for the first time. Charles shared her joy. "C. is so beaming and so happy I feel as if I had borne him another child," Anne wrote to a friend about his response to her news. Her hard work had paid off, and she put aside her resentment of his earlier criticism. In the past Charles had told her she was wasting her energies and literary talent crafting diary entries and long letters; he wanted her to write books, "something worthwhile." Decades later, however, she became a popular diarist when her collections of diaries and letters were published.[26]

Anne signed a contract with Harcourt on May 13, and the next day news of her forthcoming book hit the papers. The reaction was mostly positive, though the Lindbergh fame did provoke a backlash: some reporters claimed the book had been ghost-written until such speculation was stopped in its tracks by a press release from Anne's publisher. Advance notice of the book sparked renewed interest in Anne's flying career. In June *Town and Country* asked her to write on women flyers, a request she turned down, along with another she received later that fall—a chance to chair an Amelia Earhart lecture, "Skyways of the Future," at Temple University.[27]

After the book's August 15 release, glowing reviews propelled it to the top of bestseller lists, making it the number-one nonfiction bestseller of 1935. One after another, the critical reviews echoed that of Sinclair Lewis's, who called it "one of the most beautiful and great-hearted books that have ever been written." It remains in print today, having fascinated generation after generation with its portrayal of aerial travel in 1931. While reminiscing about *North to the Orient* years later, Anne wrote that it was a "somewhat glazed account of our adventures." She had "politely smoothed out" the trip's stresses to guard her and her husband's privacy. Nonetheless, its success gave her an impetus to begin work on another book—an account of the Atlantic survey flight.[28]

On June 17, 1935, Anne was awarded an honorary degree of Master of Arts at the Smith College commencement ceremony. Despite being one of the college's most celebrated graduates, Anne balked at the honor. Again denying her achievements, she said she did not deserve the degree, not having earned it in her own right. Charles and her mother, a Smith trustee who would confer a summa cum laude degree upon her daughter Constance that day, had to convince Anne to attend the ceremony.

That July the Lindberghs flew their Monocoupe to Minnesota, a "surprise visit" to Little Falls, reported the town's newspaper. It was Charles's first trip there since August 1927, on his goodwill tour in the *Spirit of St. Louis*. It was also Anne's first visit to his hometown, six years after her marriage. In the air again, Anne relished flying, finding it "soothing." At the same time, as Anne looked down at the Lindbergh farm while the plane circled above, she asked herself, "How did I stand up against that background—that stood for independence and hard work and endurance." After another flight to Minnesota in late August, she wrote to a friend that the trips "taught me a great deal." (It was unclear exactly what she had learned, but it seemed to involve a better understanding of her husband.)[29]

Between trips to the Midwest, the Lindberghs idled away their time at North Haven, although Charles broke away for his usual business commitments in New York. Living at Deacon Brown's Point—or for that matter, Next Day Hill, too—surrounded by many Morrow friends and Anne's family, would try almost any son-in-law's patience, Anne believed. Mrs. Morrow, a charitable, well-meaning woman, could not tolerate being alone after her husband's death; even as a young woman, she had wanted people around her at all times. Her boundless energies spilled over not only into her humanitarian causes but also into maintaining a revolving group of houseguests. "C. is sick of people and silly talk and useless dinner conversation," Anne wrote.[30]

On a Saturday afternoon in mid-October, only a few days before the Lindberghs departed North Haven for Next Day Hill, Charles took Anne for a casual drive around the island. As he steered the car he began to talk of a trip he had his heart set on, a months-long survey flight around the Pacific Ocean, departing from San Francisco and going on to Hawaii, Midway, Guam, the Philippines, and China, among other stops. It would be the culmination of their transoceanic survey work, finally linking all the continents. One by one Charles laid out his reasons for making the trip, but his primary arguments were similar to those of their earlier Pan Am survey flights. He wanted constructive work, an opportunity to contribute to aviation, and time together with Anne away from sensational publicity. (Hauptmann's execution was coming up.) Jon would stay in Englewood, well guarded and with his grandmothers, he added.[31]

Suddenly, Anne burst out crying. She felt overwhelmed by his news, the "Pan Am Pacific trip bombshell," as she called it. Even though she recognized that his arguments were sound, she considered it a "terrible blow," she later wrote in her diary. But trying to analyze why she did not want to accompany Charles proved difficult for Anne. Summing up her feelings that night, she wrote down myriad reasons: a reluctance to leave Jon, an interruption in her writing, a fear of long overwater flights in a single-engine aircraft, and the sheer fatigue such a big trip entails. There would be the "terrific uphill pull of preparation, the terrific plunge, the complete submersion in it, the long recovery afterwards."[32]

Another obstacle crossed her mind—going back, she wrote, to a "world I can never excel in, competing unhappily where I never was anything but 'good for a woman' and where I minded." Crewing on another survey flight, a woman in a man's world, she would again be forced to "compete and worship at the shrine of those gods in a world of pure action." Even though she could become very absorbed in her work as a radio operator, she realized that on such a long flight "only 'their' standards count. It is a matter of life and death."[33]

Still, she asked herself if her response to Charles's proposal was nothing more than an impulsive reaction, part of her "natural inertia" to take on no new projects. She took pride in her marriage and her husband, and she did not want to stand in the way of his dreams and his work. She conceded, "I cannot *bear* to have anyone else in it and I want, somehow, to go with him."[34]

The next morning the Lindberghs avoided further discussion of the trip until Charles returned from an hours-long walk. He told his wife that he had decided against the trip, not because of her contrary reaction but rather, because it would involve more organization than pioneering. And what would be gained? he asked. Relief swept over Anne. Whether Charles's decision to abort the trip was due to an actual change of heart or to Anne's unhappiness at his news is open to speculation. For better or worse, Charles had given up his dream of linking all the continents. Perhaps she felt guilt over her reaction: she expurgated any mention of the Pacific survey flight, and her reaction, from her published diaries. Although she would later accompany Charles on flights from England to Germany, Russia, and India, her role as crew on arduous survey flights had ended after the Atlantic expedition.[35]

That November Anne rented a studio apartment in Manhattan, a sanctuary from the hectic pace of Next Day Hill and family interruptions, the endless stream of her mother's visitors, and a husband who actually whistled when he wanted her attention. Writing of her "physical relief" in getting away from her mother's estate, she realized that "this is the way C. feels *all the time* here." She called the studio "my own room," a label lifted from Virginia Woolf's popular essay, *A Room of One's Own*. She decorated it with furniture and art she chose, including a large Orozco reproduction over the fireplace and books reflecting her newfound interests in Greek civilization and European history.[36]

The first of many writing refuges she sought throughout her life, the studio would provide her solitude and serenity, a haven to continue work on her new book about the Atlantic flight. Decades later, her philosophy about solitude would evolve and crystallize in her book of essays, *Gift from the Sea*. Although being alone in a room of one's own helped surmount the "revolving wheel of relationships, obligations, and activities" facing women, Anne would write, women must also "feed the soul" by laying aside distractions and replenishing the spirit with "those pursuits which oppose the centrifugal forces of today."[37]

Writing a new travel book posed special challenges, Anne discovered during the fall of 1935. She wanted a different presentation from that of her earlier aerial travelogue, which had covered a shorter trip. After carefully considering the new book and looking over her notes and radio logs, she settled upon highlighting only a portion of the nearly six-month-long survey flight. Published as *Listen! the Wind* in 1938, the book consisted of three parts—Santiago, Bathurst, and Natal—only a ten-day period of the Atlantic survey flight. Rather than the more outward focus of people and events depicted in *North to the Orient,* it portrayed a more mature and philosophical writer whose journey battling the rough seas and strong winds—or no wind—led to introspection. The book would become a bestseller and so move the celebrated pilot and writer Antoine de Saint-Exupéry that he wrote a nine-page introduction to the French edition. "It is an extraordinary revelation," he noted, "to see this kind of inner anxiety in a couple whom the whole world has applauded."[38]

However, Anne's aspirations for her writing studio evaporated on Saturday, December 7, 1935, when Charles abruptly announced his decision to move the family to England or Sweden for the winter, if not longer. "Be ready to go by the end of the week—at twenty-four hours notice," he told his wife.[39] What had pushed Charles over the edge were his fears for his family's safety. In late fall cameramen had ambushed a car taking Jon home from the Little School, the nursery school founded by his late aunt. Mrs. Morrow's chauffeured Cadillac was forced onto the curb by a press van and a camera pushed near the little boy's face. Added to this were ongoing threats against his family's safety, including crank letters and relentless pursuit by fanatics.

After further discussion, Charles and Anne agreed to seek shelter in England, convinced that the English respected law and order more than the citizens of any other country. Charles's announcement brought a period of turmoil to the family, a rush of making lists and preparing for the move, but the suddenness of his decision wasn't unusual, Anne wrote in her diary. "All my life seems to be trying to 'get settled' and C. shaking me out of it." She then added, somewhat oddly, "But you like it? Yes."[40] Whether she really wanted to move abroad is unclear, but the pressures of life in America left no alternative.

At 10:30 P.M. on the Saturday of December 21, 1935, a chauffeured limousine inched through the gate at Next Day Hill. Inside the limousine traveling to a nearly deserted dock in lower Manhattan sat Charles, Anne, Jon, and Margaret "Monte" Bartlett Millar, Anne's part-time secretary. An hour later they climbed the gangplank of the *American Importer* and settled in their rooms, the only passengers on the freighter bound for England. Monte wistfully bid farewell, and Jon opened one of his many Christmas presents before Anne tucked him into bed. Ten days later, the Lindbergh family disembarked in Liverpool.

13

The Artist Survives

The Lindberghs' self-imposed exile in Europe heralded a new and welcome era in their lives, joyful years when they lived out of the public eye. Once news broke of their sudden departure, editorials blamed their leaving on the nation's moral decline and lawlessness: Americans had forced them out. Essentially homeless when they arrived abroad, they relied on the hospitality of Aubrey Morgan's family in Wales. At first Anne found it difficult to adjust and admitted feeling bewildered in a letter to Charles's mother. On the other hand, any doubts she may have had about the move vanished when she looked at three-and-a-half-year-old Jon playing unguarded in the Morgans' gardens.

After several frustrating weeks of house hunting in England, Anne and Charles heard about Long Barn, a property owned by Harold Nicolson and Vita Sackville-West in Kent, not far from London. The couple had moved into an Elizabethan castle near Sissinghurst, Kent, but wanted to lease Long Barn rather than sell it: it had been their first home as a married couple. Harold downplayed the property's rustic charms, but the Lindberghs fell in love with it as soon as they laid eyes on its cottages and landscaping: gardens of fruit trees, roses, tulips, crocuses, and hyacinths, designed by Harold and planted by his wife. The fifty-foot long hall had originally been built in 1380, out of oak beams from salvaged ships, and it, along with an attached newer wing, formed a court outside. True, its floors sloped, its walls slanted, and the hall's roof sagged and leaked, but the seven bedrooms, pool, and tennis courts enchanted the Lindberghs, and they would live there from the spring of 1936 until 1938, when they relocated to France.

The Lindberghs found many benefits to living at Long Barn. No longer shadowed by an armed guard, Jon flourished there, running about outside and digging in the gardens. Walking with his mother one day, he announced that he wanted a baby and that if he couldn't find one, he would buy one. Patiently, Anne explained that things did not work that way, though he would soon get what he most wanted when she became pregnant again.

The Lindberghs' marriage also grew stronger during this time. The couple held hands as they walked the grounds, relishing their sense of security and the chance to rebuild their lives. The property also provided a convenient base for their travels. Footloose as ever, Charles ordered a new airplane, a Miles Mohawk, which he would take delivery of in August. Meantime, in late April Anne and Charles went on a short driving trip to France, leaving Jon with his nurse and their two servants. Seeing Mont-Saint-Michel on a moon-lit night and looking for inns in the countryside revived the couple's taste for adventure: they could now travel about like ordinary people. Charles first flew the Mohawk in August at Woodley Aerodrome. His August 22, 1936 logbook entry noted that the plane "was specially designed, according to our specifications, to give the maximum flexibility for any flights Anne and I may wish to make."[1] They would fly hundreds of hours in the Mohawk, a British-built, tandem-cockpit airplane that sported a 250-horsepower engine and cruised at 170 miles per hour. Its orange wings and black fuselage—the same colors as the now-retired Lockheed Sirius—would carry the couple through-out Europe, North Africa, the Middle East, and Asia.

Although flying with her husband enabled Anne to stay a "part of the big things in C.'s life," as she wrote her mother, the trips left her grappling with the upheaval they created. The previous year she had refused to make the

Pacific survey flight, but now she wanted to travel in Europe with her husband. At the same time, she wanted to work on her new book, saying, "I can't give up writing because that contributes to the 'flow' in marriage too, at least for me." It was the same dilemma she had struggled with for years: the conflict between sharing her husband's adventures while also carving out time for writing and her children. Yet aviation had provided the backbone of her writing thus far. *North to the Orient* had sold some 166,000 copies within six months of its publication, according to her publisher, and would soon see foreign releases. She was also continuing to write the account of the South Atlantic flight, *Listen! the Wind.* Indeed, another of the Lindberghs' flights, in February 1937, would serve as a literary vehicle for Anne and become her third travel narrative, *The Steep Ascent.*[2]

Aside from sightseeing, other pressing reasons compelled Charles to travel while living abroad. He reported on Europe's aviation industry to Juan Trippe, even though the airline had discontinued his retainer, at his request. Furthermore, the U. S. government urged him to make several trips to Germany. Under Hitler's leadership, Germany was building up its economic resources, and Hitler was taking steps to prepare the workforce for mobilization. In 1935 he declared German rearmament, and in March 1936 German forces reoccupied the Rhineland zone between France and Germany. Major Truman Smith, the military attaché with the American Embassy in Berlin, was alarmed in particular by the rapid development of the Luftwaffe, Germany's air force. In need of an aviation expert to inspect its air factories, he suggested to the German Air Ministry that Charles Lindbergh visit, an idea wholeheartedly embraced by General Hermann Goering, head of the Luftwaffe. Though Smith's invitation came as a surprise to Charles, he was enthusiastic about the chance to assess Germany's aviation industry and its progress since the First World War. On July 22, 1936, the Lindberghs flew to Berlin, where over ten days Charles evaluated the Luftwaffe. Welcomed by the German aviation community, he visited factories, piloted military planes, and talked with scientists.

Anne recapped details of the trip in her diary, writing of Berlin's sense of festivity as it prepared for the Olympic Games. She also described a lunch conversation with General Goering, who asked about her role during the survey flights: While Goering eased into questions about Charles, she watched as his pet lion urinated onto his gold-braided uniform pant leg; his wife, a statuesque blonde wearing a floor-length gown and a diamond-and-emerald swastika pin, looked on and giggled. Regardless, both Lindberghs were seduced by German propaganda during their visit. The Germans impressed Anne with their vitality, and Charles praised the country's spirit and its advanced aircraft technology. The seeds had been planted for a political controversy that would eventually embroil them both.

Back in England, Anne and Charles became less reclusive, their social calendar filled with engagements that included dinners at the American Embassy and visits with Lady Astor, a celebrated society hostess. They dined with Edward VIII and his married mistress, Mrs. Wallis Warfield Simpson, whose poise and sense of style imbued her with a vital spark, Anne felt. After Edward VIII abdicated, the Lindberghs attended a ball at Buckingham Palace at the invitation of the new monarch, George VI, and his wife, Queen Elizabeth. Waltzing around the dance floor until 3:00 A.M. in a tiara and blue taffeta dress, Anne lost herself in a sort of "intoxication," as she put it. Her husband sat out the dances, watching her "drunk with happiness," and later said he had never seen her happier. Anne and Charles also frequented Paris and Brittany, spending time with Dr. Alexis Carrel—who continued to mentor Charles in his biological research—and his wife at their summer residence on Ile Saint-Gildas. (Although Dr. Carrel still worked at the Rockefeller Institute in New York, his wife had refused to move to the United States and spent her time in France.) Interspersed with the Lindberghs' travels were visits from their families, including the Morrows, Mrs. Lindbergh, and other relatives.[3]

✈

By the beginning of November 1936, Anne was overjoyed to find that she was expecting. Even so, she wanted to accompany her husband after he announced a trip in the works—a flight to India planned for early 1937. The first of the Lindberghs' long flights while they resided abroad, its ultimate destination would be Calcutta, in time for a conference of the World Fellowship of Religions. By now, Charles counted among his newfound diversions a fascination with mysticism and yogic meditation—interests encouraged by Dr. Carrel and his wife, both of whom dabbled in the occult.

Charles also wanted to investigate air routes during the trip. The long journey in the Mohawk saw him and Anne flying over the Alps, Tunis, Tripoli, Cairo, Jerusalem, the deserts of Arabia, and the Persian Gulf. From Cairo, they followed the established air routes of Imperial Airways and K.L.M. Royal Dutch Airlines. What most impressed Anne as she looked beneath her were the remains of old civilizations—Egyptian pyramids, Roman ruins, and Greek temples. Although engine problems in Nagpur, India, scuttled their hopes of flying to Kashmir and the Himalayas, they did reach Calcutta by train in time for the conference. Charles threw himself into the proceedings there, taking part in prayer meetings. Meantime, Anne felt it all slightly ludicrous, and laughed at the sight of the swamis, barefoot Indian monks, and hangers-on.

Flying the repaired Mohawk, the Lindberghs returned to England in early April. Regrettably, Anne turned down an offer from the *National Geographic* to write an article about the journey, for what surely would have been another engaging travel piece.[4] It is possible that pressure to finish *Listen! the Wind* prompted her decision: work on her earlier *Geographic* article had delayed the completion of her first book. In any event, she included no details of the offer in her published diaries.

An incident on the journey did become the basis for her third and final travel narrative, however. On the first day of February 1937, flying over the Alps, the Lindberghs had been caught in overcast and fog, losing all visual contact with the ground. Charles put the Mohawk in a gradually descending spiral. Looking out, Anne watched the low wing turn on a "slow, strange descent into the underworld," not knowing if it would bring "death or escape and life for us both." They circled until they broke out of the clouds over the Mediterranean Sea, close to a volcanic island, and just off the coast of Genoa. Anne turned the frightening event into a short fictional account, *The Steep Ascent.* The novella described more a spiritual flight than a geographical one and became a "woman's story, the story of a woman's life and ordeal—any woman and any ordeal," as she wrote in its preface. Published in 1944, this philosophical and meditative book pointed toward the type of work she would do later in her career.[5]

In a London clinic in May 1937 Anne gave birth to her third son; Anne and Charles named him Land, which was also Evangeline Lindbergh's maiden name. Despite the new baby, the Lindberghs traveled constantly during the remainder of 1937. They made two trips to visit the Carrels at their home off the Brittany coast, and in mid-October they returned to Germany, where Charles again inspected bases and factories and tested fighter planes. In early December the couple sailed to the United States for a three-month trip that combined Charles's aviation business with family visits. He also wanted to confer with Dr. Carrel about the medical book that he and the doctor would publish in 1938, *The Culture of Organs,* which detailed their collaborative research and work on the development of the perfusion pump. The children stayed behind at Long Barn with a governess, thereby avoiding what Anne considered the "excitement and nervous tension" of Englewood.[6]

Shortly before leaving New York, Charles told Anne that he wanted to live on a four-acre rocky island named Illiec, off the Brittany coast, a kilometer away from the Carrels' summer home on Ile Saint-Gildas. Initially Anne did not share his enthusiasm at leaving Long Barn, a property she loved, and relocating the family. Nonetheless, she went along with his decision, and in the spring of 1938 they purchased the island. Life at Illiec revolved around the tides. To reach the mainland, the Lindberghs motor-boated during high tide, or walked across the tidal flats when the sea receded. They lived in a Breton stone house that had been built around 1865 by French composer Ambroise Thomas, who wrote the opera *Mignon* there. The house lacked heat, plumbing, and electricity and sorely needed renovation—new walls and furniture, not to mention indoor toilets. As if Anne did not have enough on her hands already, she had to finish the book she had promised to Harcourt, translate the locals' French for her husband, and deal with the Carrels' constant criticism of her child-rearing practices. Autocratic and opinionated, Dr. Carrel had firm ideas about how children should be reared and expected the Lindberghs to follow his advice. Although Anne seemed to take his nit-picking in stride, he often drove the children's nurse to tears.

Charles, however, loved Illiec. In the mornings, he and Anne awoke to the soothing sound of breakers crashing against boulders, which they both came to cherish. With quick-forming gales painting the sky with unusual cloud patterns, and quieter weather draping the island with different hues of color, it's not surprising that the island appealed to Charles. In many ways, it reminded him of his boyhood in Little Falls, Minnesota, sleeping on a porch overlooking the Mississippi River.

It was also Illiec's proximity to the Carrels that led to Charles's desire to relocate there. As a mentor and friend, Dr. Carrel continued to profoundly influence him. "In Carrel, spiritual and material values were met and blended as in no other man I knew," Charles would write years later. Sitting before a fireplace in the doctor's ivy-covered stone house, the two men talked nightly on topics such as mystic visions, clairvoyance, and prayer. (Madame Carrel, a nurse, shared her husband's beliefs in telepathy and psychic phenomena, and on one occasion, described auras emanating from Charles and Anne—deep violet and pale blue, respectively.) They also discussed methods for improving the hereditary qualities of the human species. At the time, it was not so unusual to advocate for eugenics, and many people embraced sweeping social prescriptions for curing society's ills. Carrel's book, *Man, the Unknown,* addressed the topic and became a best-seller in 1935. Despite being vehemently anti-Nazi, Carrel proposed euthanasia for hardened criminals and lamented the decline of the white race, and many readers were put off by his advocacy of what seemed a mild form of fascism. For her part, Anne wondered if Carrel's proposals would "breed a race of tall soft-headed athletes." She was awed by the Carrels, but found their discussions of "the strong and the weak" irritating. Characteristically, rather than say anything, she criticized herself in her diary for not meeting their standards.[7]

In August 1938, a few months after the Lindberghs moved to the island, the military attaché with the American Embassy in London asked Charles to fly to Russia and survey its aviation industry. Charles wanted his wife to come along, but Anne was beset with doubts about leaving the two children. She also struggled with what she called "womanly fears," anxiety perhaps triggered by the memory of the horrible flight over the Alps the previous year. In the end, she agreed to accompany Charles, writing in her diary, "I must go even though I am afraid to go." If nothing else, she thought that her children—and all children—might benefit from seeing their parents take on adventures that proved they weren't frightened of life.[8]

On August 16 they took to the air in the Mohawk and landed in Moscow the following evening. Once again, five years after their 1933 flying tour, the country welcomed them lavishly. They saw an air show attended by 800,000 spectators, dined with aviators and officials, and toured the museum of the Red Army and Moscow's subway. Charles went to aviation factories, later remarking to the U.S. military on the inferior workmanship and low productivity he witnessed there. Despite their warm welcome, within two days of arriving Anne observed a noticeable change in Muscovites as compared to 1933. They lacked their earlier enthusiasm and spirit, and she attributed the change to Stalin's purges: the espionage, executions, and exiles. On the hot, hazy morning of August 26, 1938, the Mohawk left Moscow. Under Soviet escort, the Lindberghs flew to Rostov, Kiev, and Odessa during the next days. Leaving Russia on August 31, they set course for Romania, then Poland, Czechoslovakia, Stuttgart, and Paris, arriving back on Illiec on September 10.

An era in the Lindberghs' marriage ended with this Russian odyssey, the last extended flight they made together in a small plane. (It also terminated Charles's practice of marking their flights on a globe of the world.) The famous couple, who had so captured the essence of aviation's first decades and whose marriage had symbolized universal themes—adventure, romance, and loyalty—for countless people, no longer flew as a team on expeditions. Anne later remarked on the flights' hardships, but wrote that their "flying life had compensated C. and me, too, for the 'life' fame had taken away from us."[9]

After their visit to the USSR, Charles felt that even Hitler's Germany offered greater freedom, and his concerns mounted about a westward expansion of communism. Just nine days after the Lindberghs' return home, Ambassador

Joseph Kennedy wired Charles, asking him to come to London right away to discuss military aviation in Europe. He and Anne departed Illiec the next day. Both Lindbergh and Kennedy believed that England and France could not win a war against Germany, given their current state of unpreparedness. At Kennedy's request, Charles put together a report offering his opinions on military aviation in Europe, which was transmitted to both the White House and Whitehall. Anne shared her husband's pessimism. In a letter to her mother written during this visit, Anne doubted if the dictators could "now be stopped," adding, "practically, I think the only way to stop them is to let them come up against Russia." [10]

Meanwhile, tension grew between Germany and other European countries. Germany had annexed Austria in March 1938 and was now preparing to invade Czechoslovakia. Because both France and the USSR had alliances with the Czechs and war seemed imminent, on September 15 the British prime minister, Neville Chamberlain, rushed to confer with Hitler at his mountain retreat in the Bavarian Alps. On September 29 and 30, 1938, Benito Mussolini, Chamberlain, Hitler, and Edouard Daladier, the French prime minister, gathered for a conference in Munich. There the four parties signed a pact that let Germany take over the Sudetenland region in October, though the agreement would be abandoned in March 1939, when most of the area became a German protectorate.

The Lindberghs made a third trip to Germany in October 1938, one that lasted eighteen days. They had been invited by the American ambassador, Hugh Wilson, and the Germans, and as on his previous trip there, Charles attended an aeronautical congress of the Lilienthal Society, an organization that had been established by the Third Reich. He was also toying with the idea of living in Berlin during the winter while he gathered more information about the country's aviation industry. As a result, much of Anne's time in Berlin went toward looking at house rentals. Meanwhile, at a men's-only dinner at the American Embassy, General Goering, without forewarning, presented Charles the Service Cross of the German Eagle in recognition of his 1927 flight. Like other men at the dinner, Charles gave little thought to the medal, but later that night, when he showed Anne the white cross decorated with four small swastikas, she suggested that it might become an "albatross" around his neck. Major Truman Smith's wife, Kay, also looked on; she, too, felt the medal would bring Charles bad fortune.[11]

Several weeks after this third visit to Germany, Charles abandoned his plans to move to Berlin, for on November 9, 1938, there occurred the worst pogrom yet seen under the Third Reich: *Kristallnacht,* the Night of Broken Glass. During this night of looting and burning, ninety-one Jews were murdered throughout Germany. Step by step, the Third Reich was implementing solutions to what it called its "Jewish Question." The first steps were expulsion and emigration that would be followed in time by ghettoization, local killing squads, and ultimately, the "Final Solution": forced labor and extermination camps. The Lindberghs were stunned by the brutality of *Kristallnacht* and realized they couldn't possibly live in Germany. In his journal Charles admitted that he did not understand the anti-Semitic riots, writing: "My admiration for the Germans is constantly being dashed against some rock such as this."[12]

Instead, the Lindberghs decided to winter in Paris. In late fall of 1938, Anne arranged to lease an apartment in the city, across from the Bois de Boulogne. The French capital offered a school for Jon and cultural events that were lacking on Illiec. While in Paris, they dined with French aviators, the Duke and Duchess of Windsor, and Gertrude Stein and Alice B. Toklas, among others. Anne splurged on clothes and wedding gifts for her family— recently, Constance had married Aubrey Morgan, Elisabeth's widower, and Dwight had wed Margot Loines, a friend of Constance's. Anne and Charles did not confine themselves to Paris either. In February of 1939 the couple visited England, spending a week at Clivenden, the Astors' opulent country estate, where they talked with Neville Chamberlain and Joseph Kennedy, both of whom had favored avoiding war and appeasing Hitler.

The move to Paris hardly stanched the criticism that was increasingly befalling Charles in the United States. Newspapers decried his earlier decision to live in Berlin, Americans hissed when he appeared in movie theater newsreels, and TWA dropped the "Lindbergh Line" from its advertisements. While Anne was in Germany, Harcourt released *Listen! the Wind,* and despite its critical success, not everyone received it with open arms. In particular, many Jewish booksellers boycotted the new book. All the controversy disturbed Anne, who considered it unfair treatment of her husband, but she realized that the "ball of rumor and criticism, once it starts rolling, is difficult to stop."[13]

The Lindberghs lived in Paris until April 1939, when they headed back to America. Before leaving Europe Charles hangared the Miles Mohawk in England; he would eventually donate it to the British government at the start of the war. Despite his concerns about crime and publicity, he felt he should return home. "If there was to be war, then my place was back in my own country," he wrote many years later.[14] Nonetheless, he was convinced another European war would topple Western civilization and crusaded against America's entry into the Second World War, following in the footsteps of his father, who, decades earlier, had argued for nonintervention in the First World War.

Before Anne departed Europe, she pondered how her life had changed since her youth, with its "*too* literary outlook." She described her marriage by writing, "I was plunged into life—active life—loving and living and having children and those terrific trips and the suffering too." She had "tossed aside" her previous life before marrying, but now her roles as a wife and as her own person had "fused," she wrote. At age thirty-two, she was beginning to see how to overcome one of the conflicts in her life, her "old self, suppressed, passionate, insisting to come out—pushed down by that other new self, practical, active, outward, and comparatively efficient."[15]

She had let her pilot's license lapse while she lived in Europe, though upon her return home she occasionally flew in small planes with Charles, and on commercial carriers, of course. On April 19, 1937, her license expired and was canceled, according to documentation in her file at the Federal Aviation Administration.[16] She chose not to renew the license, having decided to close that chapter in her life. She seemed unable to reconcile the dual roles of author and aviator. Certainly, she did not think the two were very compatible, a fact driven home after she talked with Antoine de Saint-Exupéry in New York, in August 1939.

While in the city to promote his book, *Wind, Sand and Stars,* Saint-Exupéry asked to meet Anne, whose *Listen! the Wind* he had admired so greatly. The Lindberghs invited him to visit on the weekend of August 5 at their Long Island home, a white clapboard rental in Lloyd Neck, overlooking the Sound. As it happened, Charles was unexpectedly delayed elsewhere, and he telephoned Anne to drive to New York and meet the French aviator. In the bar of the Ritz she found Saint-Exupéry, a "not at all good looking" man who spoke no English. They left the hotel together, but after driving one block the De Soto's engine stalled out, and they hopped on a train from Pennsylvania Station to Long Island. Meanwhile, they talked excitedly in French. Anne found herself developing a schoolgirl infatuation with the author, and by the time Charles arrived home late at night, she was certain that no one understood or appreciated her as well as Saint-Exupéry. During his weekend visit, the author held the couple spellbound, recounting his aerial adventures in Africa and South America. He described in detail the desert, whose beauty blossomed when danger was present, and his many brushes with death, particularly one accident in which he had nearly drowned. Anne was amazed at his "*incredible* number of crashes." She did not "see how a man who is that much of an artist can fly *at all.* . . . I am convinced he is going to be killed if he goes on flying."[17]

Obviously, her perspective on Saint-Exupéry's life reflected the themes in her own life. She had retired from aviation, putting aside her husband's world and committing herself to her artistic development. But Saint-Exupéry continued flying until July 31, 1944. On that date, he failed to return from a P-38 reconnaissance flight over southern France and was reported missing in action, never to be seen again. He was not the only one of her flying contemporaries to meet an early end: Amelia Earhart, Jean Mermoz, Wiley Post, and countless other long-distance flyers died while blazing trails across the world. The legendary Amy Johnson perished in January 1941, when she bailed out over the Thames estuary while ferrying a twin-engine Oxford for Britain's Air

Transport Auxiliary. Marga von Etzdorf, whose celebrated flight from Berlin to Tokyo in 1931 catapulted her to fame, killed herself after what she considered a humiliating accident in Syria in 1933.

On the other hand, the artist Anne Morrow Lindbergh survived. Aviation had laid the foundation for Anne's adult life and it was the lens through which she perceived the world, but her art is what ultimately sustained her. In addition to her three travel narratives, Anne would go on to write ten other books. Many were bestsellers, though one was a controversial work she regretted ever having published: *The Wave of the Future: A Confession of Faith*. A hastily written, forty-one page essay expressing her opposition to the war, it tarnished her literary reputation upon its release in October 1940 and diminished her confidence in her writing skills for some time thereafter. The book promoted her husband's political views in eloquent language, but it was widely misquoted, and critics labeled Anne a coward and fifth columnist. Attempting to clarify her noninterventionist arguments, in June 1941 Anne published a piece titled "Reaffirmation" in the *Atlantic Monthly*, but the article failed to sway public opinion. Many years later, she would regret her naiveté in politics then, remarking that there were worse things than war.

About a year before *The Wave of the Future*'s release, and less than two weeks after the outbreak of war in Europe, Charles had delivered his first speech opposing the United States entering the war. Like his father before him, he was not a natural politician, and managed to antagonize even those close to him. In November 1939 *Readers' Digest* published his article, "Aviation, Geography, and Race," a piece with racist overtones that characterized the war as a threat to the white race. In the fall of 1940, he became a key spokesperson for the America First movement, an organization dedicated to keeping the country neutral; its 800,000 eventual members included politicians, educators, and business leaders. He crisscrossed the country giving numerous speeches, but it was one in Des Moines, Iowa, on September 11, 1941, that loosened an avalanche of criticism. The British, the Roosevelt administration, and Jewish activists were the three groups agitating for the United States' entry into the war, Charles claimed. Anne listened to the radio broadcast at her home, having decided not to accompany him. Despite her pleas for him to tone down the speech, he had stubbornly refused and considered his comments not at all racist. But he was denounced nationwide and called a Nazi and an anti-Semite. Most people wanted nothing to do with him and, by association, his wife, and the Lindberghs were effectively ostracized by many of their friends. Fortunately, their families remained close to them, though Anne's mother Betty actively crusaded for aid to the Allies, and Mrs. Lindbergh disagreed with her own son's political views.

When the United States finally entered the war after the attack at Pearl Harbor, Charles worked briefly as a consultant at Willow Run, Henry Ford's B-24 Liberator bomber plant in Detroit, and later, as a test pilot with United Aircraft's fighter, the F4U Corsair. He served out the war as a civilian, but after being given the opportunity to contribute, he flew fifty combat missions in the Pacific. There he piloted Corsairs and the Lockheed P-38 Lightning, while earning the praise and appreciation of General Douglas MacArthur and fellow airmen.

During most of the war years, Anne and the children lived near Detroit. Charles was frequently away during the war, and as she adjusted to her first extended absence from him, she came to like her newfound independence and growing confidence. Certainly, she missed her husband, and he spent time with the family as often as possible. Still, Anne was now the head of the household, a spot many "war widows" then shared, and she had her hands full, even with hired help: her first daughter, Anne, was born in October 1940, and a fourth son, Scott, in August 1942. The Lindberghs' last child, Reeve, would be born in 1945 on her sister's birthday. In her free time, Anne found a new circle of friends at the Cranbrook Academy of Art, where she took up sculpting.

After seventeen years of living in rented homes and staying with family members, other than the brief time at their Hopewell house, the Lindberghs settled in a permanent residence. In 1946 Anne and Charles purchased a large house at Scott's Cove on the shores of Long Island Sound, near Darien, Connecticut. A year later, Anne spent nine weeks traveling alone in Europe, gathering material for a series of articles she would write on its postwar situation for leading American magazines. Upon returning, she refocused her energies on her family, while continuing to write. From the mid-1950s through 1962, Anne published three books. The first, in 1955, became her most-loved work: *Gift from the Sea,* a slender book of essays on women's evolving roles in society. An immediate bestseller, it found an audience among women of all ages and went on to sell millions of copies. Following this book, in 1956 she published the collection, *The Unicorn and Other Poems,* and six years later, *Dearly Beloved,* a novel about marriage.

The world traveler Charles, meanwhile, was free to pursue his own interests and roam the globe. No longer shunned because of his antiwar sentiments, he again became active in aviation: helping to reorganize the Strategic Air Command, serving as a consultant to the U. S. Air Force, and working on top secret military projects and the space program. In 1954 President Dwight D. Eisenhower restored his commission in the military and promoted him to the rank of brigadier general in the U. S. Air Force Reserve. Commercial aviation drew his attention also, and he was persuaded by Juan Trippe to accept a position on Pan American's Board of Directors in 1965. He advised on new air routes and the development of the Boeing 747, but would oppose the United States granting landing rights to the supersonic transports (SSTs), commercial carriers that he considered an environmental menace.

Eventually, Charles's continued absences created a deep rift in the marriage. With the purchase of the Scott's Cove house, Anne had envisioned settling down with her husband, yet he considered it a base from which to launch his travels. He kept Anne in the dark about his whereabouts, often not calling or writing for long stretches of time, then suddenly appearing at home. Little Anne once greeted him at the door by instructing him to take off his coat and asking if he would be staying. At home he expected his family to follow the myriad rules he established, lectured against dangers to society such as white bread and television, and nit-picked at their smallest faults. True, he was an affectionate father, teaching his children sports and guiding them in their careers and friendships. But the stress his presence engendered wore on Anne, who took a gentler approach to parenting, and at times she welcomed his absences. As the marriage became more strained, she even considered leaving Charles but decided that she did not want to live without him. Her continued love for him and the strong bonds of the marriage, cemented by their history together, sustained her and she remained devoted to him.[18]

The 1960s ushered in great changes for the Lindberghs. They sold their house at Scott's Cove and built a smaller one there, and added new homes: a chalet near Vevey, Switzerland, and a cottage at Maui, Hawaii. Their social horizons broadened, too. They were guests of President Kennedy and his wife at the White House, where they attended a state dinner. There Anne became friends with the vice president's wife, Lady Bird Johnson, who admired her writings. The Lindberghs continued to travel together, and in the mid-1960s Anne joined her husband on several African safaris.

The safaris came out of the Lindberghs' interest in the environment and the natural world, which had first been sparked in their early years, when they flew in small planes above the Earth. Over time they had witnessed the encroachment of civilization on the lands they so loved: smog in California and urban sprawl on the East Coast and elsewhere. Frustrated by destructive technological advances and the endangerment of species, in 1969 Anne published *Earth Shine,* a book of two essays about the environment, one describing African wildlife and the other the December 1968 Apollo 8 launch, which she and Charles had attended. (During the pre-launch lunch with mission astronauts Frank Borman, James Lovell, and William Anders, Charles had entertained the group with anecdotes about rocket pioneer Robert Goddard, whose rocket experiments he had found funding for decades earlier, when financiers said that airplanes provided sufficient fantasy.) As his work on ecological matters intensified, Charles emerged as a prominent advocate for conservation and served on the board of the World Wildlife Fund. Both he and Anne gave generous donations to the fund. They also contributed to The Nature Conservancy, and Anne deeded the group Big Garden Island, off the coast of Maine—a wedding present from her parents in 1929.

In 1974 Charles died from cancer at the house on Maui, with Anne by his side. During the next five years Anne worked on preparing her final volumes of diaries and letters for publication, bringing the total number to five: *Bring Me a Unicorn* (1972), *Hour of Gold, Hour of Lead* (1973), *Locked Rooms and Open Doors* (1974), *The Flower and the Nettle* (1976), and *War Within and Without* (1980). Beyond these, Anne did not publish any new books after her husband's death, although she did give serious consideration to writing a sequel to *Gift from the Sea*. She continued to write, but she became less concerned with seeing her works published, and increasingly, her time was absorbed in working with her husband's estate and spending time with her family.

The advent of World War II had brought the golden age of aviation to a close, but flying would always play an important part in Anne's legacy. She and Charles, among other pioneer aviators, had explored future air routes and made reality out of dreams. Anne had chosen to be an active partner in her husband's adventures, serving as copilot, navigator, and radio operator on survey flights in an era when many women were discouraged from pursuing a career at all. In addition to the honors she earned while she was actively flying, in later years she received several awards recognizing her contributions to aviation. These included induction into the National Aviation Hall of Fame (1979); the Katherine B. Wright Memorial Award (1982); the Aerospace Explorer Award from Women in Aerospace (1993); the New Jersey Aviation Hall of Fame (1997); and induction into the Women in Aviation, International Pioneer Hall of Fame (1999). Smith College, Amherst College, the University of Rochester, and Gustavus Adolphus College all conferred upon her honorary degrees. Even after all of this, she continued to shun recognition for her achievements. She had treasured her life in the air, however. "I learned a great deal from this active period of living in a so-called masculine world," she said in 1978, adding, "It was perhaps my most feminist period."[19]

After suffering a series of strokes in her later years, Anne moved to her daughter Reeve's farm in Vermont, where she lived in a small house built to replicate her chalet in Switzerland. On February 7, 2001, at age 94, she lay frail and ill, surrounded by caretakers and family. Outside, snow blanketed the ground, muffling all sound except that of bare tree limbs creaking in a light breeze; according to those who were there, the birds had been quiet for days beforehand. Anne died peacefully at 10:00 A.M., and as chickadees and blue jays came to perch on the tree branches outside, she departed for one last journey—as pilots say, her final flight.

NOTES AND SOURCES

The backbone of this book is the compilation of the books listed below, newspapers, magazines, and documents housed in Manuscripts and Archives in Sterling Memorial Library at Yale University, New Haven, Connecticut, which include the Anne Morrow Lindbergh Collection (#829) and the Charles A. Lindbergh Collection (#325). Other documents cited below are housed in the Charles Augustus Lindbergh Papers in the Missouri Historical Society at St. Louis, Missouri, and the Charles A. Lindbergh and Family Papers in the Minnesota Historical Society at St. Paul, Minnesota. The flight logbooks are housed in the above collections at Yale University, the Missouri Historical Society, and the Minnesota Historical Society.

ABBREVIATIONS INCLUDE:

AML: Anne Morrow Lindbergh

CAL: Charles Augustus Lindbergh (husband of AML)

DWM: Dwight Whitney Morrow (father of AML)

ECM: Elizabeth Cutter Morrow (mother of AML)

CMM: Constance Morrow Morgan (sister of AML)

ERMM: Elisabeth Reeve Morrow Morgan (sister of AML)

BMAU: AML, *Bring Me a Unicorn, Diaries and Letters, 1922–1928* (New York: Harcourt Brace Jovanovich, Inc., 1972; New York: reprint, first Harvest edition, 1993).

HGHL: AML, *Hour of Gold, Hour of Lead, Diaries and Letters, 1929–1932* (New York: Harcourt Brace Jovanovich, Inc., 1973; New York: reprint, first Harvest edition, 1993).

LROD: AML, *Locked Rooms and Open Doors, Diaries and Letters, 1933–1935* (New York: Harcourt Brace Jovanovich, Inc., 1974; New York: reprint, first Harvest edition, 1993).

F&N: AML, *The Flower and the Nettle, Diaries and Letters, 1936–1939* (New York: Harcourt Brace Jovanovich, Inc., 1976; New York: reprint, first Harvest edition, 1994).

WWW: AML, *War Within and Without, Diaries and Letters, 1939–1944* (New York: Harcourt Brace Jovanovich, Inc., 1980; New York: reprint, first Harvest edition, 1995).

LTW: AML, *Listen! the Wind* (New York: Harcourt, Brace and Company, 1938).

NO: AML, *North to the Orient* (New York: Harcourt, Brace and Company, 1935; New York: reprint, first Harvest edition, 1967).

FLB: Flight Logbook

MOHS: Missouri Historical Society

MNHS: Minnesota Historical Society

NGM: AML, "Flying Around the North Atlantic," *National Geographic Magazine,* September 1934.

NYT: New York Times.

NOTES

PROLOGUE: THE MAGIC OF FLIGHT

1. Anne Morrow Lindbergh, *Listen! the Wind* (New York: Harcourt, Brace and Company, 1938), p. 210.
2. Ibid., p. 229.
3. Ibid., p. 235.
4. Anne Morrow Lindbergh Papers at Yale University Library, radio logs.
5. Library of Congress, Prints and Photographs Division, *New York World-Telegraph* and the Sun Newspaper Photograph Collection, 1929 photo caption, LC, USZ62-114901.
6. Anne Morrow Lindbergh, *North to the Orient* (New York: Harcourt, Brace and Company, 1935; New York: first Harvest edition, 1967), p. 31.
7. Ibid., p. 138.

CHAPTER 1: A WALLED GARDEN

1. Anne Morrow Lindbergh, *Bring Me a Unicorn: Diaries and Letters of Anne Morrow Lindbergh, 1922–1928* (New York: Harcourt Brace Jovanovich, 1972; New York: first Harvest edition, 1993), p. xxii.

2. Ibid., p. xix.
3. Quoted in Harold Nicolson, *Dwight Morrow* (New York: Harcourt Brace Jovanovich, Inc., 1935; London: Constable & Co. Ltd, 1935), p. 6.
4. Ibid., p. 36.
5. Constance Morrow Morgan, *A Distant Moment* (Northampton, MA: Smith College, 1978), p. 10.
6. Ibid., pp. 139, 145.
7. Nicolson, *Dwight Morrow*, p. 118.
8. Mary Margaret McBride, *The Story of Dwight W. Morrow* (New York: Farrar and Rinehart, Inc., 1930), p. 63.
9. Anne Morrow Lindbergh Papers at Yale University Library, Diary, 1923; Author interview with Reeve Lindbergh, February 3, 2003 (telephone).
10. Missouri Historical Society, Anne Morrow Lindbergh Diary, September 5, 1926.
11. Nicolson, *Dwight Morrow*, p. 109.
12. Ibid., p. 131.
13. Quoted in A. Scott Berg, *Lindbergh* (New York: G. P. Putnam's Sons, 1998; New York: Berkley Books, 1999), p. 181.
14. *BMAU*, p. 65; Quoted in Dorothy Herrmann, *Anne Morrow Lindbergh: A Gift for Life* (New York: Ticknor & Fields, 1992), p. 8; *BMAU*, p. xxii.
15. Ibid., pp. 5, xxiv, xxi.
16. Ibid., p. xxii.
17. Corliss Lamont, *Yes to Life: Memoirs of Corliss Lamont* (New York: Horizon Press, 1981), p. 17.
18. Anne Morrow Lindbergh, *The Journey Not the Arrival* (New York: Harcourt Brace Jovanovich, 1978), p. 3. From a transcript of a speech AML gave at Smith College.
19. Yale, AML Diary 1923.
20. *BMAU*, pp. 6–7; Yale, AML Diary 1923, pp. 24–25; Author's note: Although the *BMAU* entry indicated that AML wanted to attend Vassar, the AML papers at Yale University and other sources clearly show Bryn Mawr.
21. Yale, AML Diary 1923.
22. Julie Nixon Eisenhower, *Special People* (New York: Simon & Schuster, 1977), p. 127.
23. *BMAU*, p. 19; MOHS, AML letter to Elizabeth Cutter Morrow, March 4, 1925; *BMAU*, p. 19.
24. MOHS, AML letter to ECM.
25. Eisenhower, *Special People*, p. 145; *BMAU*, pp. 34, 36; Robin A. Thrush, "A Hero's Wife Remembers," *Good Housekeeping*, June 1977, p. 74.

26. *BMAU*, p. 131; AML, *The Journey Not the Arrival*, p. 2; Interview with Anne Morrow Lindbergh, "Crossing the Distance," David McCullough, host, PBS, 1984.

27. *BMAU*, p. xviii; Yale, AML Diary 1923.

28. Quoted in Nicolson, *Dwight Morrow*, p. 296.

29. Ibid., p. 301.

30. Alvin M. Josephy, Jr., ed., *The American Heritage History of Flight* (New York: American Heritage Publishing Co., 1962), p.203.

31. Nicolson, *Dwight Morrow*, pp. 307, 304.

32. *BMAU*, pp. 77, 81.

CHAPTER 2: A DIFFERENT DRUMMER

1. A. Scott Berg, *Lindbergh* (New York: G. P. Putnam's Sons, 1998; New York: Berkley Books, 1999). See this definitive biography for additional details.

2. Dee Brown, *The Gentle Tamers: Women of the Old Wild West* (New York: Putnam, 1958; University of Nebraska Press, Bison Books, reissued 1981), p. 208.

3. Booklet, Little Falls, Minnesota, 2001: Little Falls Convention and Visitors Bureau, p. 3.

4. Quoted in Berg, *Lindbergh*, p. 33; Reeve Lindbergh, *Under a Wing: A Memoir* (New York: Simon & Schuster, 1998; New York: reprint, Dell, 1999), p. 167; "Lindbergh," in the "American Experience" documentary, produced by Stephen Ives and Ken Burns, written by Geoffrey Ward. PBS, October 1990.

5. Charles A. Lindbergh, *The Spirit of St. Louis* (New York: Charles Scribner's Sons, 1953; St. Paul: reprint, Minnesota Historical Society Press, 1993), p. 377.

6. Ibid., p. 311.

7. Quoted in Berg, *Lindbergh*, p. 42.

8. Ibid., p. 40.

9. "Home Town Bets Lindbergh Will Hop Across Atlantic," *Little Falls Daily Transcript*, May 14, 1927.

10. Charles A. Lindbergh, *Autobiography of Values* (New York: Harcourt, Inc., 1978; New York: first Harvest edition, 1992), p. 117.

11. Charles A. Lindbergh, *"WE"* (New York: Grosset & Dunlap Publishers, 1928; published by arrangement with G. P. Putnam's Sons, 1927), p. 23; CAL, *The Spirit of St. Louis*, p. 403; CAL, *Autobiography of Values*, p. 64.

12. CAL, *The Spirit of St. Louis*, p. 263.

13. "Famous Sons of Famous Fathers," *Post-Bulletin,* Rochester, MN, March 3, 1934.
14. CAL, *"WE",* p. 77.
15. Ibid., p. 81. Quoted in Berg, *Lindbergh,* p. 74.
16. Missouri Historical Society archives, Certificate of the Oath of Air Mail Messengers, issued to CAL, April 13, 1926.
17. CAL, *The Spirit of St. Louis,* p. 15.
18. CAL, *Autobiography of Values,* p. 71; CAL, *The Spirit of St. Louis,* p. 18; Barry Schiff, "The Spirit Flies On," *AOPA Pilot,* May 2002, pp. 93–97: Anne Morrow Lindbergh once flew this replica, according to Mr. Schiff's article.
19. CAL, *The Spirit of St. Louis,* p. 390.
20. Morrison County Historical Society, Little Falls, MN, Associated Press Clipping, May 24, 1927.

CHAPTER 3: A WHIRLWIND

1. Anne Morrow Lindbergh, *Bring Me a Unicorn: Diaries and Letters of Anne Morrow Lindbergh, 1922–1928* (New York: Harcourt Brace Jovanovich; New York: first Harvest edition, 1993), p. 89.
2. Ibid., p. 98.
3. Charles A. Lindbergh, *Autobiography of Values* (New York: Harcourt Inc., 1978; first Harvest edition, 1992), p. 123; *BMAU,* p. 103.
4. Ibid., pp. 100, 109; Robin A. Thrush, "A Hero's Wife Remembers," *Good Housekeeping,* June 1977.
5. *BMAU,* p. 116.
6. Ibid., p. 127.
7. Ibid., pp. 124, 129, 171.
8. Ibid., p. 135.
9. Valerie Moolman and the editors of Time-Life Books, *Women Aloft* (Alexandria, VA: Time-Life Books, 1981), p. 54.
10. CAL, *Autobiography of Values,* p. 122.
11. Ibid., p. 119; *BMAU,* p. 194.
12. Ibid., pp. 196, 198, 214.
13. Ibid., p. 205; Charles A. Lindbergh and Family Papers, Minnesota Historical Society, St. Paul, MN, logbook entry; *BMAU,* pp. 211, 212.
14. CAL and Family Papers, MNHS, logbook entry; *BMAU,* p. 221.
15. Quoted in A. Scott Berg, *Lindbergh* (New York: G. P. Putnam's Sons, 1998; New York: Berkley Books, 1999), p. 196; Author interview with Reeve Lindbergh, February 3, 2003 (telephone).

16. *New York Times,* February 13, 1929, p.1; CAL and Family Papers, MNHS Papers, logbook entry.
17. James Newton, *Uncommon Friends: Life with Thomas Edison, Henry Ford, Harvey Firestone, Alexis Carrel, and Charles Lindbergh* (New York: Harcourt, Inc., 1987), pp. 256–59.
18. *NYT,* February 13, 1929, p.1; CAL, *Autobiography of Values,* p. 125.
19. Anne Morrow Lindbergh, *Hour of Gold, Hour of Lead: Diaries and Letters of Anne Morrow Lindbergh, 1929–1932* (New York: Harcourt Brace Jovanovich, 1973; New York: first Harvest edition, 1993), p. 3.
20. CAL and Family Papers, MNHS, logbook entry.
21. *HGHL,* p. 18.
22. Ruth Nichols, "Aviation for You and Me," *Ladies Home Journal,* May 1929; Alvin M. Josephy, Jr., ed., *The American Heritage History of Flight* (New York: American Heritage Publishing Co., 1962), p. 284.
23. CAL and Family Papers, MNHS, logbook entry.
24. *The New Republic,* June 12, 1929, p. 90.
25. *HGHL,* p. 43.

CHAPTER 4: THE GOOD SHIP ANNE

1. *New York Times,* June 19, 1929, p.33; Author's note: the Bird biplane did not win the contest but many pilots then considered it the best all-around light airplane built. Instead, the Curtiss Tanager later won.
2. Anne Morrow Lindbergh, *Hour of Gold, Hour of Lead: Diaries and Letters of Anne Morrow Lindbergh, 1929–1932* (New York: Harcourt Brace Jovanovich, 1973; New York: first Harvest edition, 1993), p. 47; "Test Pilot," *AOPA Pilot,* December 2004.
3. *HGHL,* p. 49; Anne Morrow Lindbergh, *Bring Me a Unicorn: Diaries and Letters of Anne Morrow Lindbergh, 1922–1928* (New York: Harcourt Brace Jovanovich, 1972; New York: first Harvest edition, 1993), p. xxiii; See also *HGHL,* introduction; *HGHL,* p. 59.
4. Ibid., pp. 4, 6, 49.
5. Minnesota Historical Society, Charles A. Lindbergh and Family Papers, flight logbooks.
6. *HGHL,* p. 62.
7. MNHS, FLB.
8. Missouri Historical Society, Charles A. Lindbergh Papers, Falcon logbook.
9. Ibid., written in the logbook.
10. *New York Times,* August 1, 1929.

11. *HGHL,* pp. 70–71.

12. Yale University Library, flight logbook.

13. *St. Paul Pioneer Press,* St. Paul, MN, August 24, 1929; Yale, FLB; *Post Dispatch,* St. Louis, MO, March 16, 1930.

14. Robin A. Thrush, "A Hero's Wife Remembers," *Good Housekeeping,* June 1977, p. 76.

15. *NYT,* August 27, 1929, p. 1.

16. Richard Sanders Allen, *Revolution in the Sky: The Lockheeds of Aviation's Golden Age* (Atglen, PA: Schiffer, 1993, revised edition), p. 35.

17. *HGHL,* p.73.

18. Marilyn Bender and Selig Altschul, *The Chosen Instrument: Pan Am, Juan Trippe, the Rise and Fall of an American Entrepreneur* (New York: Simon & Schuster, 1982). See this book for additional information.

19. *HGHL,* p. 97.

20. Ibid., p. 95.

21. MNHS, FLB.

22. MOHS, letter dated November 4, 1929.

23. Author interview with Donald H. Westfall, Site Manager, CAL house, Little Falls, MN, September 21, 2001.

24. Anne Morrow Lindbergh, *War Within and Without: Diaries and Letters of Anne Morrow Lindbergh, 1939–1944* (New York: Harcourt Brace Jovanovich, Inc., 1980; New York: first Harvest edition, 1995), p. xv.

25. *HGHL,* p. 109; Yale, FLB.

26. *HGHL,* p. 114; Reeve Lindbergh, *Under a Wing: A Memoir* (New York: Simon & Schuster, 1998; New York: reprint, Dell, 1999), p. 41; *NYT,* January 4, 1930.

27. Yale, FLB; *HGHL,* p. 120.

28. René J. Francillon, *Lockheed Aircraft Since 1913* (New York: Putnam, 1982), pp. 93–100.

29. *HGHL,* pp. 64, 120.

30. Doris L. Rich, *Amelia Earhart: A Biography* (Washington, D.C.: The Smithsonian Institution Press, 1989), p. 101; Amelia Earhart, "Mrs. Lindbergh," *Hearst's International-Cosmopolitan,* July 1930; *HGHL,* p. 121.

31. MOHS, letter from Amelia Earhart to Anne Morrow Lindbergh, dated January 30, 1930; MOHS, handwritten memo from Amelia Earhart to AML; Amelia Earhart, "Mrs. Lindbergh"; Valerie Moolman and the editors of Time-Life Books, *Women Aloft* (Alexandria, VA: Time-Life Books, 1981), p. 64.

32. Quoted in Bender and Altschul, *The Chosen Instrument,* p. 109.

33. Yale, FLB; Gary Fogel, *Wind and Wings: The History of Soaring in San Diego* (San Diego: Rock Reef Publishing House, 2000), various pages.

34. *HGHL*, p. 126.

35. Ibid., pp. 126–27.

36. "Anne 'Lindy' Qualifies as Glider Pilot," *San Francisco Chronicle*, January 30, 1930.

37. Gary Fogel, *Wind and Wings*.

38. Helen Van Dusen, "Anne Flies a Home Product," *The Modern Clubwoman*, May 1930.

39. "Making America 'Glider Conscious,'" *The Literary Digest*, February 22, 1930, p. 40.

40. MOHS, letter dated April 3, 1930.

41. *HGHL*, pp. 133–34.

42. Yale, FLB; *NYT,* April 21, 1930, p. 1.

43. Interview with AML, "Crossing the Distance," David McCullough, host, PBS, 1984.

44. Edna K. Wooley, "Flying Colonel's Wife Shows Rare Courage," *The Cleveland Plain Dealer,* April 25, 1930.

CHAPTER 5: A CHALLENGE MET

1. Anne Morrow Lindbergh, *Hour of Gold, Hour of Lead: Diaries and Letters of Anne Morrow Lindbergh, 1929–1932* (New York: Harcourt Brace Jovanovich, 1973; first Harvest edition, 1993), p. 134; Yale, flight logbook.

2. *HGHL*, p. 138.

3. Quoted in Dorothy Herrmann, *Anne Morrow Lindbergh: A Gift for Life* (New York: Tickor & Fields, 1992), p. 70.

4. Missouri Historical Society, July 20, 1930, letter to Constance Morrow Morgan.

5. *HGHL*, p. 142; Yale, FLB.

6. MOHS, letter from Amy Johnson to the Lindberghs.

7. Yale, FLB.

8. Quoted in A. Scott Berg, *Lindbergh* (New York: G. P. Putnam's Sons, 1998; New York: Berkley Books, 1999), p. 219; *HGHL*, p. 144.

9. Ibid., p. 145; Donald E. Keyhoe, "Lindbergh Four Years After," *The Saturday Evening Post*, May 30, 1931.

10. *HGHL*, p. 9.

11. *New York Times*, October 26, 1930.

12. *HGHL*, p. 156.

13. Yale, FLB; *HGHL*, p. 11; Federal Aviation Administration, Airman Certification Branch, AML file.

14. *HGHL,* p. 11; Interview with AML, "Crossing the Distance," David McCullough, host, PBS, 1984; Whether Anne flew solo after 1933 is unknown because the author did not find AML solo log entries recorded after this date.

15. Anne Morrow Lindbergh, *North to the Orient* (New York: Harcourt, Brace and Company, 1935; New York: first Harvest edition, 1967) p. 14.

16. *Scientific American,* October 1931; *NO,* p. 9.

CHAPTER 6: THE LAND OF THE MIDNIGHT SUN

1. Sources used for this chapter include: *New York Times;* Anne Morrow Lindbergh, *North to the Orient* (New York: Harcourt, Brace and Company, 1935; first Harvest edition, 1967) and letters in *Hour of Gold, Hour of Lead* (New York: Harcourt Brace Jovanovich, 1973; New York: first Harvest edition, 1993); aeronautical charts and travel brochures. Anne Morrow Lindbergh did not keep a diary during this time.

2. *NO,* p. 18.
3. Ibid., p. 21.
4. Ibid., p. 29.
5. Ibid., p. 31.
6. Ibid., p. 35.
7. Ibid., p. 44.
8. Ibid., p. 43.
9. Ibid., p. 52.
10. Ibid., p. 63.
11. Ibid., p. 63.
12. Ibid., p. 64.
13. Ibid., p. 66.
14. Ibid., p. 69.

CHAPTER 7: INTO THE RAGING YANGTZE

1. See chapter 6, endnote number 1 for sources.
2. Anne Morrow Lindbergh, *North to the Orient* (New York: Harcourt Brace, and Company, 1935; first Harvest edition, 1967), p. 77; Interview with Anne Morrow Lindbergh, "Crossing the Distance," David McCullough, host, PBS, 1984.
3. *NO,* pp. 80–82.

4. Ibid., pp. 84–85.
5. Ibid., p. 87.
6. Ibid., p. 88.
7. *New York Times*, August 22, 1931.
8. *The Japan Advertiser*, Tokyo, September 1931; Anne Morrow Lindbergh, *Hour of Gold, Hour of Lead: Diaries and Letters of Anne Morrow Lindbergh, 1929–1932* (New York: Harcourt Brace Jovanovich, 1973; first Harvest edition, 1993), p. 191.
9. *NYT,* August 26, 1931.
10. "Lindberghs Guest at Official Dinner," *The Trans-Pacific,* Tokyo, September 3, 1931, p. 6.
11. *NO,* pp. 103–105; Anne Morrow Lindbergh Papers at Yale University, letter dated September 20, 1931; *HGHL*, p. 193.
12. Missouri Historical Society, maps folder; *HGHL,* p. 197.
13. Ibid., p. 196.
14. Ibid., p. 201.
15. *NO,* p. 130.
16. *NO,* pp. viii, ix, x.

CHAPTER 8: A TIME OF MOURNING

1. Anne Morrow Lindbergh, *Hour of Gold, Hour of Lead: Diaries and Letters of Anne Morrow Lindbergh, 1929–1932* (New York: Harcourt Brace Jovanovich, 1973; New York: first Harvest edition, 1993), p. 203.
2. Anne Morrow Lindbergh Papers at Yale University Library, AML letter to Sue Vaillant, January 14, 1932; *HGHL,* p. 204.
3. Missouri Historical Society, Charles Augustus Lindbergh Papers; Federal Aviation Administration, Aircraft Registration branch, File on AML's Bird airplane.
4. Yale, letter from Mrs. Clark D. Stearns to AML, November 14, 1931; Author's note: In October 1931 the Department of Commerce listed 474 licensed women pilots, as compared to 16,798 licensed male pilots.
5. MOHS, letter from Amelia Earhart to AML, January 9, 1932; MOHS, letter from AML to Amelia Earhart, January 14, 1932.
6. Yale, AML letter to Sue Vaillant, January 14, 1932.
7. Yale, AML Papers; *New York Times,* February 22, 1932.
8. Anne Morrow Lindbergh, *Locked Rooms and Open Doors: Diaries and Letters of Anne Morrow Lindbergh, 1933–1935* (New York: Harcourt Brace Jovanovich, 1974; first Harvest edition, 1993), p. xvi.

9. Quoted in Berg, *Lindbergh* (New York: G. P. Putnam's Sons, 1998; New York: Berkley Books, 1999), p. 242.

10. *HGHL*, pp. 229, 231.

11. Quoted in Berg, *Lindbergh*, p. 255.

12. *HGHL*, p. 248; Frederick Lewis Allen, *Since Yesterday: The 1930s in America* (New York: Harper Row, 1939; Perennial reprint, 1972), p. 55; *HGHL*, p. 250.

13. Ibid., p. 252.

14. *New York Times*, June 24, 1933.

15. MOHS, AML Diary, June 10, 1932.

16. MOHS, AML letter to Elisabeth Reeve Morrow Morgan, July 27, 1932.

17. *HGHL*, p. 302.

18. MOHS, AML Diary, September 29, 1932.

19. *LROD*, p. 6.

20. MOHS, AML letter to Amelia Earhart, January 26, 1933.

21. *LROD*, pp. 13, 17.

22. Ibid., p. 22.

23. MOHS, AML Diary, March 30, 1933.

24. John T. Greenwood, ed., *Milestones of Aviation: Smithsonian Institution National Air and Space Museum* (Westport, CT: Hugh Lauter Levin Associates, 1989; revised edition, 1995), p. 253; Oliver E. Allen and the editors of Time-Life Books, *The Airline Builders* (Alexandria, VA: Time-Life Books, 1981), pp. 133–35.

25. Ninety-Nines Museum of Women Pilots, Archives, Oklahoma City, OK; MOHS, AML Diary, April 19, 1933.

26. *NYT*, May 7, 1933.

27. Foreword by Charles A. Lindbergh in Anne Morrow Lindbergh, *Listen! the Wind* (New York: Harcourt, Brace and Company, 1938), p. v.

28. Marilyn Bender and Selig Altschul, *The Chosen Instrument: Pan Am, Juan Trippe, the Rise and Fall of an American Entrepreneur* (New York: Simon & Schuster, 1982), p. 198.

29. *NYT*, June 26, 1933; *LROD*, p. xvii.

30. Ibid., p. 41.

CHAPTER 9: AN ENCHANTED LAND

1. Anne Morrow Lindbergh, "Flying Around the North Atlantic," *National Geographic Magazine*, September 1934, p. 263.

2. Anne Morrow Lindbergh, *Locked Rooms and Open Doors: Diaries and Letters of Anne Morrow Lindbergh, 1933–1935* (New York: Harcourt Brace Jovanovich, 1974; New York: first Harvest edition, 1993), p. 48.

3. John T. Greenwood, ed, *Milestones of Aviation: Smithsonian Institution National Air and Space Museum* (Westport, CT: Hugh Lauter Levin Associates, 1989; revised edition, 1995), p. 62.

4. *LROD*, pp. 50–51.

5. Missouri Historical Society, Anne Morrow Lindbergh Diary, July 28, 1933; *LROD*, p. 52.

6. MOHS, AML Diary, July 19, 1933.

7. Frederikshaab is now known as Paamiut, Greenland; *NGM*, p. 269.

8. Ibid.

9. MOHS, AML Diary, July 21, 1933.

10. Godthaab is now known as Nuuk, Greenland; MOHS, AML Diary, July 22, 1933.

11. MOHS, AML Diary, Aug. 9, 1933.

12. *LROD*, p. 63.

13. Holsteinsborg is now known as Sisimiut; *LROD*, p. 64.

14. MOHS, AML Diary, July 27, 1933; *LROD*, pp. 69, 107.

15. *New York Times*, August 4, 1933, p. 1; *LROD*, p. 72.

16. *NGM*, pp. 280–81.

17. *LROD*, p. 74.

18. *LROD*, p. 75; *NGM*, p. 282.

19. Angmagssalik is now known as Tasiilaq; MOHS, AML Diary, August 6, 1933.

20. Julianehaab is now known as Qaqortoq.

21. *LROD*, pp. 79–80.

CHAPTER 10: EUROPE

1. Anne Morrow Lindbergh Papers at Yale University, radio logs.

2. Anne Morrow Lindbergh, *Locked Rooms and Open Doors: Diaries and Letters of Anne Morrow Lindbergh, 1933–1935* (New York: Harcourt Brace Jovanovich, 1974; New York: first Harvest edition, 1993), p. 102.

3. Missouri Historical Society, Anne Morrow Lindbergh Diary, August 31, 1933.

4. *New York Times*, August 30, 1933.

5. *LROD*, p. 107.

6. Ibid., p. 108.

7. Ibid., p. 113.

8. MOHS, AML Diary, September 25–29, 1933.

9. Anne Morrow Lindbergh, "Flying Around the North Atlantic," *National Geographic Magazine*, September 1934, p. 293; MOHS, AML Diary, September 27, 1933.

10. *New York Times,* September 29, 1933.

11. MOHS, AML Diary, September 29, 1933.

12. MOHS, AML Diary, October 4, 1933.

13. MOHS, AML letter to Aubrey Morgan, October 21, 1933; MOHS, AML Diary, October 12, 1933.

14. Charles A. Lindbergh Collection at Yale University, CAL letter to Juan Trippe, October 16, 1933; Marilyn Bender and Selig Altschul, *The Chosen Instrument: Pan Am, Juan Trippe, The Rise and Fall of an American Entrepreneur* (New York: Simon & Schuster, 1982) p. 224.

15. *LROD,* p. 135.

16. Ibid., pp. 135–136.

17. Ibid., p. 136; MOHS, Charles A. Lindbergh notes in AML diary, November 12, 1933.

18. Anne Morrow Lindbergh papers, Yale University, radio logs; *LROD,* p. 141.

19. MOHS, AML Diary, November 7, 1933.

20. *LROD,* p. 148.

21. MOHS, CAL notes in AML diary, November 10–12, 1933.

22. *LROD,* p. 143.

23. Ibid., p. 144.

24. Ibid., p. 153.

CHAPTER 11: AFRICA AND BEYOND

1. Curtis Cate, *Antoine de Saint-Exupéry* (New York: G. P. Putnam's Sons, 1970), p. 130.

2. Anne Morrow Lindbergh, "Flying Around the North Atlantic," *National Geographic Magazine,* September 1934, p. 303; Missouri Historical Society, Anne Morrow Lindbergh Diary, November 26, 1933.

3. Ibid.

4. *NGM,* p. 307; Anne Morrow Lindbergh Papers at Yale University, radio logs.

5. Anne Morrow Lindbergh, *Listen! the Wind* (New York: Harcourt, Brace and Company, 1938), p. 97.

6. Ibid., p.122.

7. *NGM,* p. 314; *LTW,* p. 128.

8. Ibid., p. 137.

9. Ibid., p. 193.

10. *NGM,* p. 333.

11. Ibid., p. 335; Anne Morrow Lindbergh, *Locked Rooms and Open Doors: Diaries and Letters of Anne Morrow Lindbergh, 1933–1935* (New York: Harcourt Brace

Jovanovich, 1974; New York: first Harvest edition, 1993), p. 179; *NGM*, p. 336.

12. *LROD*, p. 182.

13. Yale, AML Radio Logs. Pan Am's final report of the survey flight stated: "The excellent communication service on this trip is in no small measure due to Mrs. Lindbergh's manipulation of the equipment and the ease with which she changed frequencies."

14. John T. Greenwood, ed., *Milestones of Aviation: Smithsonian Institution National Air and Space Museum* (Westport, CT: Hugh Lauter Levin Associates, 1989; revised edition, 1995), p. 75; Oliver E. Allen and the editors of Time-Life Books, *The Airline Builders* (Alexandria, VA: Time-Life Books, 1981), p. 166.

CHAPTER 12: ACCLAIM

1. "The Society Awards Hubbard Medal to Anne Morrow Lindbergh," *National Geographic Magazine,* June 1934, pp. 791–94.

2. Anne Morrow Lindbergh Papers at Yale University Library, various folders.

3. The Ninety-Nines Museum of Women Pilots, Archives, Oklahoma City, OK.

4. *The Mobile Press Register,* Mobile, AL, February 4, 1934.

5. Anne Morrow Lindbergh, *Locked Rooms and Open Doors: Diaries and Letters of Anne Morrow Lindbergh, 1933–1935* (New York: Harcourt Brace Jovanovich, 1974; New York: first Harvest edition, 1993), pp. xviii, 187–8.

6. Ibid., p. 190.

7. Alvin M. Josephy, Jr., ed., *The American Heritage History of Flight* (New York: American Heritage Publishing Co., 1962), p. 244; *LROD*, p. 189.

8. *National Geographic* letter to Anne Morrow Lindbergh, July 7, 1934.

9. Missouri Historical Society, Anne Morrow Lindbergh letter to Elisabeth Reeve Morrow Morgan, July 29, 1934.

10. *LROD*, p. 196.

11. Yale University Library, flight logbook.

12. *LROD*, p. 201.

13. *New York Times,* August 30, 1934; AML Papers at Yale, letter from Harcourt to AML, August 30, 1934.

14. *LROD*, p. 202.

15. Ibid., p. 209.

16. Quoted in A. Scott Berg, *Lindbergh* (New York: G. P. Putnam's Sons, 1988; New York: Berkley Books, 1999); *LROD*, pp. 209, 216.

17. Ibid., p. 223.
18. Ibid., p. 232.
19. Quoted in Berg, *Lindbergh,* p. 314.
20. *LROD,* p. 247.
21. Ibid., pp. 240–41; Yale, AML letter to Monte Barlett Millar, February 23, 1935; Julie Nixon Eisenhower, "Anne Lindbergh—Then and Now," *Modern Maturity,* December-January 1977–1978, p. 10.
22. Quoted in Berg, *Lindbergh,* p. 333; *LROD,* p. 249.
23. Reeve Lindbergh, *Under a Wing: A Memoir* (New York: Simon & Schuster, 1998; New York: reprint, Dell, 1999) p. 84.
24. Ibid., p. 90.
25. MOHS, AML Diary, April 30, 1935; *LROD,* pp. 269–70.
26. Ibid., p. 271; Yale, AML letter dated May 1935 to Monte Bartlett Millar; *LROD,* p. 206.
27. Yale, AML Papers.
28. *LROD,* p. xxv.
29. MOHS, AML Diary, July 26, 1935; Yale, AML letter to Monte Bartlett Millar, September 13, 1935.
30. *LROD,* p. 287.
31. MOHS, AML Diary, October 12, 1935.
32. Ibid.
33. Ibid.
34. Ibid.
35. Ibid.
36. *LROD,* pp. 323, 331.
37. Anne Morrow Lindbergh, *Gift from the Sea* (New York: Pantheon Books, 1955; reprint 1997), pp. 51, 56.
38. Antoine de Saint-Exupéry, *A Sense of Life* (New York: Funk & Wagnalls, 1965), p. 174. This quote was first published as part of the introduction to the French version of *Listen! the Wind.*
39. *LROD,* p. 331.
40. Ibid.

CHAPTER 13: THE ARTIST SURVIVES

1. Missouri Historical Society, flight logbook.
2. Anne Morrow Lindbergh, *The Flower and the Nettle: Diaries and Letters of Anne Morrow Lindbergh, 1936–1939* (New York: Harcourt Brace Jovanovich, 1976; New York: first Harvest edition, 1994), p. 74.

3. *F&N*, pp. 289, 292.
4. Anne Morrow Lindbergh Papers at Yale University Library.
5. *F&N*, p. 136; Anne Morrow Lindbergh, *The Steep Ascent* (New York: Harcourt, Brace & World, 1944), p. vi.
6. *F&N*, p. 203.
7. Charles A. Lindbergh, *Autobiography of Values* (New York: Harcourt, Inc., 1978; first Harvest edition, 1992), p. 17; *F&N*, p. 90.
8. Ibid., pp. 336–37.
9. Anne Morrow Lindbergh, *War Within and Without: Diaries and Letters of Anne Morrow Lindbergh, 1939–1944* (New York: Harcourt Brace Jovanovich, Inc., 1980; New York: first Harvest edition, 1995), p. 443.
10. *F&N*, p. 412.
11. *F&N*, p. 437.
12. Charles A. Lindbergh, *The Wartime Journals of Charles A. Lindbergh* (New York: Harcourt Brace Jovanovich, 1970), p. 115.
13. *F&N*, p. 471.
14. Lindbergh, *Autobiography of Values*, p. 187.
15. *F&N*, p. 518.
16. Federal Aviation Administration, Airman Certification Branch, file for AML.
17. *WWW*, pp. 22, 29.
18. Author interview with Reeve Lindbergh, February 3, 2003 (telephone).
19. Anne Morrow Lindbergh, *The Journey Not the Arrival* (New York: Harcourt Brace Jovanovich, 1978), p. 6.

SELECTED BIBLIOGRAPHY

Allen, Frederick Lewis. *Only Yesterday: An Informal History of the 1920s.* New York: Harper & Row, 1931; New York: Bantam, 1946.

———. *Since Yesterday: The 1930s in America.* New York: Harper & Row, 1939; New York: Perennial reprint, 1972.

Allen, Oliver E., and the editors of Time-Life Books. *The Airline Builders.* Alexandria, VA: Time-Life Books, 1981.

Allen, Richard Sanders. *Revolution in the Sky: The Lockheeds of Aviation's Golden Age.* Atglen, PA: Schiffer, 1993 revised edition.

Bell, Elizabeth S. *Sisters of the Wind: Voices of Early Women Aviators.* Pasadena, CA: Trilogy Books, 1994.

Bender, Marilyn and Selig Altschul. *The Chosen Instrument: Pan Am, Juan Trippe, the Rise and Fall of an American Entrepreneur.* New York: Simon & Schuster, 1982.

Berg, A. Scott. *Lindbergh.* New York: G. P. Putnam's Sons, 1998; New York: Berkley Books, 1999.

Boyne, Walter J. *The Smithsonian Book of Flight.* Washington, D.C.: Smithsonian Books, 1987.

Brooks-Pazmany, Kathleen. *United States Women in Aviation 1919–1929.* Washington, D.C.: Smithsonian Institution Press, 1991.

Brown, Dee. *The Gentle Tamers: Women of the Old Wild West.* New York: Putnam, 1958; University of Nebraska Press, Bison Books, 1981.

Brown, Dorothy M. *Setting a Course: American Women in the 1920s.* Boston: Twayne, 1987.

Cassagneres, Ev. *The Untold Story of the Spirit of St. Louis: From the Drawing Board to the Smithsonian.* New Brighton, MN: Flying Books International, 2002.

Cate, Curtis. *Antoine de Saint-Exupéry.* New York: G. P. Putnam's Sons, 1970.

Christy, Joe. *High Adventure: The First 75 Years of Civil Aviation.* Blue Ridge Summit, PA: Tab Books, Inc., 1985.

Dear, I. C. B., general editor, and M. R. D. Foot, consultant editor. *The Oxford Companion to World War II*. New York: Oxford University Press, 1995; New York, Oxford University Press, reissued 2005.

Donovan, Frank. *The Early Eagles*. New York: Dodd, Mead & Company, 1962.

Earhart, Amelia. "Mrs. Lindbergh." *Hearst's International-Cosmopolitan,* July 1930.

———. *The Fun of It: Random Records of My Own Flying and of Women in Aviation*. New York: The Junior Literary Guild and Brewer, Warren & Putnam, 1932.

Eisenhower, Julie Nixon. *Special People*. New York: Simon & Schuster, 1977.

———. "Anne Lindbergh—Then and Now." *Modern Maturity,* December– January 1977–1978.

"Famous Sons of Famous Fathers." *Post-Bulletin,* Rochester, MN, March 3, 1934.

Fleischmann, John. "High Society." *Air and Space Magazine.* February/March 1999.

Fogel, Gary. *Wind and Wings: The History of Soaring in San Diego*. San Diego: Rock Reef Publishing House, 2000.

Francillon, René J. *Lockheed Aircraft Since 1913*. New York: Putnam, 1982.

Gill, Brendan. *Lindbergh Alone*. New York: Harcourt Brace Jovanovich, 1977.

Greenwood, John T., ed. *Milestones of Aviation: Smithsonian Institution National Air and Space Museum*. Westport, CT: Hugh Lauter Levin Associates, 1989; revised edition, 1995.

Harris, Sherwood. *The First to Fly: Aviation's Pioneer Days*. New York: Simon & Schuster, 1970.

Herrmann, Dorothy. *Anne Morrow Lindbergh: A Gift for Life*. New York: Ticknor & Fields, 1992.

Hertog, Susan. *Anne Morrow Lindbergh: Her Life*. New York: Doubleday, 1999.

Josephy, Alvin M., Jr., and the editors of *American Heritage*. *The American Heritage History of Flight*. New York: American Heritage Publishing Co., 1962.

Keyhoe, Donald E. "Lindbergh Four Years After." *The Saturday Evening Post,* May 30, 1931.

Lamont, Corliss. *Yes to Life: Memoirs of Corliss Lamont*. New York: Horizon Press, 1981.

Leary, William M., ed. *Aviation's Golden Age: Portraits from the 1920s and 1930s.* Iowa City: University of Iowa Press, 1989.

Levine, Isaac Don. *Mitchell: Pioneer of Air Power.* New York: Duell, Sloan and Pearce, 1943.

Lindbergh, Anne Morrow. "Flying Around the North Atlantic." *National Geographic Magazine,* September 1934.

———. *Bring Me a Unicorn: Diaries and Letters of Anne Morrow Lindbergh, 1922–1928.* New York: Harcourt Brace Jovanovich, 1972; New York: first Harvest edition, 1993.

———. *Dearly Beloved.* New York: Harcourt Brace, 1962.

———. *Earth Shine.* New York: Harcourt Brace, 1969.

———. *The Flower and the Nettle: Diaries and Letters of Anne Morrow Lindbergh, 1936–1939.* New York: Harcourt Brace Jovanovich, 1976; New York: first Harvest edition, 1994.

———. *Gift from the Sea.* New York: Pantheon Books, 1955; reprint 1997.

———. *Hour of Gold, Hour of Lead: Diaries and Letters of Anne Morrow Lindbergh, 1929–1932.* New York: Harcourt Brace Jovanovich, 1973; New York: first Harvest edition, 1993.

———. *The Journey Not the Arrival.* New York: Harcourt Brace Jovanovich, 1978. (A speech AML gave at Smith College on April 12, 1978.)

———. *Listen! the Wind.* New York: Harcourt, Brace and Company, 1938.

———. *Locked Rooms and Open Doors: Diaries and Letters of Anne Morrow Lindbergh, 1933–1935.* New York: Harcourt Brace Jovanovich, 1974; New York: first Harvest edition, 1993.

———. *North to the Orient.* New York: Harcourt, Brace and Company, 1935; New York: first Harvest edition, 1967.

———. *The Steep Ascent.* New York: Harcourt, Brace & World, 1944.

———. *The Unicorn and Other Poems, 1935–1955.* New York: Pantheon Books, 1956.

———. *War Within and Without: Diaries and Letters of Anne Morrow Lindbergh, 1939–1944.* New York: Harcourt Brace Jovanovich, Inc., 1980; New York: first Harvest edition, 1995.

———. *The Wave of the Future: A Confession of Faith.* New York: Harcourt, Brace and Company, 1940.

Lindbergh, Charles A. *Autobiography of Values*. New York: Harcourt, Inc., 1978; first Harvest edition, 1992.

———. *Boyhood on the Upper Mississippi: A Reminiscent Letter*. St. Paul, MN: Minnesota Historical Society Press, 1972; first paperback printing, 1987.

———. *The Spirit of St. Louis*. New York: Charles Scribner's Sons, 1953; St. Paul, MN: Minnesota Historical Society Press, 1993.

———. *The Wartime Journals of Charles A. Lindbergh*. New York: Harcourt Brace Jovanovich, 1970.

———. *"WE."* New York: Grosset & Dunlap Publishers, 1928; published by arrangement with G. P. Putnam's Sons, 1927.

Lindbergh, Reeve. *No More Words: A Journal of My Mother, Anne Morrow Lindbergh*. New York: Simon & Schuster, 2001.

———. *Under a Wing: A Memoir*. New York: Simon & Schuster, 1998; New York: reprint, Dell, 1999.

"Lindberghs Guest at Official Dinner." *The Trans-Pacific,* Tokyo, September 3, 1931.

Lukacs, John. *Five Days in London: May 1940*. Yale Nota Bene, 2001; New Haven, CT: Yale University Press, 2001.

Mackaye, Milton. "The Lindberghs—First Romancers of the Air." *Vanity Fair,* October 1935.

"Making America 'Glider' Conscious." *Literary Digest,* February 22, 1930.

Mayer, Elsie F. *My Window on the World: The Works of Anne Morrow Lindbergh*. Hamden, CT: Archon Books/The Shoe String Press, 1988.

McBride, Mary Margaret. *The Story of Dwight W. Morrow*. New York: Farrar and Rinehart, Inc., 1930.

Milton, Joyce. *Loss of Eden: A Biography of Charles and Anne Morrow Lindbergh*. New York: Harper Collins Publishers, 1993.

Moolman, Valerie, and the editors of Time-Life Books. *Women Aloft*. Alexandria, VA: Time-Life Books, 1981.

Morgan, Constance Morrow. *A Distant Moment*. Northampton, MA: Smith College, 1978.

Newton, James. *Uncommon Friends: Life with Thomas Edison, Henry Ford, Harvey Firestone, Alexis Carrel, and Charles Lindbergh*. New York: Harcourt, 1987.

Nichols, Ruth. "Aviation for You and for Me." *Ladies Home Journal,* May 1929.

The New Republic, June 12, 1929.

Nicolson, Harold. *Dwight Morrow.* New York: Harcourt Brace Jovanovich, Inc., 1935; London: Constable & Co. Ltd, 1935.

Nicolson, Nigel. *Portrait of a Marriage.* New York: Atheneum, 1973.

Rich, Doris L. *Amelia Earhart: A Biography.* Washington, D.C.: Smithsonian Institution Press, 1989.

Saint-Exupéry, Antoine de. *A Sense of Life.* New York: Funk & Wagnalls, 1965.

Schiff, Barry. "The Spirit Flies On." *AOPA Pilot,* May 2002.

Scientific American. October 1931.

Smith, Elinor. *Aviatrix.* New York: Harcourt Brace Jovanovich, 1981.

"The Society Awards Hubbard Medal to Anne Morrow Lindbergh." *National Geographic Magazine,* June 1934.

"Test Pilot." *AOPA Pilot.* December 2004.

Thrush, Robin A. "A Hero's Wife Remembers." *Good Housekeeping,* June 1977.

Van Dusen, Helen. "Anne Flies a Home Product." *The Modern Clubwoman,* May 1930.

Vaughan, David Kirk. *Anne Morrow Lindbergh.* Boston: Twayne, 1988.

Winters, Nancy. *Man Flies: The Story of Alberto Santos-Dumont.* Hopewell, NJ: The Ecco Press, 1998.

Wooley, Edna K. "Flying Colonel's Wife Shows Rare Courage." *The Cleveland Plain Dealer,* April 25, 1930.

Woolf, Virginia. *A Room of One's Own.* New York: Harcourt, Brace and Company, 1929.

Wurz, Trude. *Anne Morrow Lindbergh: The Literary Reputation.* New York: Garland Publishing, 1988.

Television Interview with Anne Morrow Lindbergh: "Crossing the Distance." David McCullough, host, PBS, 1984.

INDEX

Abbreviations: AML—Anne Morrow Lindbergh; CAL—Charles Augustus Lindbergh